MONEY MAGIC

MONEY MAGIC

MAGIC

AN ECONOMIST'S SECRETS
TO MORE MONEY, LESS RISK,
AND A BETTER LIFE

LAURENCE J. KOTLIKOFF

LITTLE, BROWN SPARK

New York Boston London

Little, Brown Spark
Hachette Book Group
1290 Avenue of the Americas, New York, NY 10104
littlebrownspark.com

First Edition: January 2022

Little, Brown Spark is an imprint of Little, Brown and Company, a division of Hachette Book Group, Inc. The Little, Brown Spark name and logo are trademarks of Hachette Book Group, Inc.

The publisher is not responsible for websites (or their content) that are not owned by the publisher.

The Hachette Speakers Bureau provides a wide range of authors for speaking events. To find out more, go to hachettespeakersbureau.com or call (866) 376-6591.

ISBN 9780316541954 (hardcover) / 9780316435994 (international edition)
LCCN 2021939624

Printing 1, 2021

LSC-C

Printed in the United States of America

For Bridget, my love and joy

Contents

Contents

MONEY MAGIC

Preface

When I started college, I hoped to become a doctor. But a frog derailed my plans. The frog and I came eye to eye in a biology lab as I injected it with death serum, sliced open its chest, checked its pulse, declared it dead, and proceeded to rub its tiny heart back to life. My instructor walked over and said, "Excellent. Now do it again and record the results." For the next two hours, it was kill-resurrect-record, over and over again. By the end of the lab, I was majoring in economics.

I got hooked on economics. There was no torture of slimy amphibians. Plus, I liked the math, the curves, the statistics, the theory. But what really grabbed me was economics' potential to help people.

In grad school, I focused on public finance, particularly how tax and benefit policies affect the macro (overall) economy. This was the mid-1970s, and economists were just starting to use apartment-sized machines called computers. We'd type up our code on seven-by-three-inch punch cards in an ancient language called FORTRAN, run them through a noisy card reader, and wait hours for yard-wide printouts. Mostly, the program would fail because of a typo on card 7,239 of a 10,000-card deck. But if the program ran and the results made sense, we'd write up our earth-shattering findings and pray someone would read them.

Studying the macro economy requires understanding the micro economy—the financial actions and reactions of individual companies and households. For households, this includes coding personal financial behavior. Hence, public finance led me to personal finance and the work of a long list of prominent economists. The list starts in the 1920s with Yale economist Irving Fisher.

Fisher was, hands down, the top economist of his day, and his most important achievement was a simple but powerful mathematical description of optimal saving behavior. Fisher's model looked for the saving sweet spot that keeps us from starving when young and splurging when old (or doing the opposite). Finding that spot, he argued, entails saving precisely what's needed to ensure a smooth living standard over time. Thus was born the principle of "life-cycle consumption smoothing."

Fisher is the father of economics-based financial planning. But he left lots of issues unexplored, including how to manage one's investments. The answer is certainly not to put all your eggs in one basket, especially a basket as fickle as the stock market. Yet this is precisely what Fisher did. Being the smartest economist on the planet, Fisher assumed he knew how the market would behave. Except he didn't. On the eve of the Crash of 1929, Fisher publicly pronounced that "stock prices have reached what looks like a permanently high plateau...I expect to see the stock market a good deal higher within a few months."[1]

As the market dropped 86 percent by 1933, Fisher went from rich to poor to bankrupt. Had Yale not interceded, Fisher would have ended up living on the street. He died in 1947, disgraced in the public's eye by his infamous prognostication yet still revered by economists for his amazing theoretical insights. Over the next two decades, Milton Friedman, Franco Modigliani, Paul Samuelson, Robert C. Merton, and Peter Diamond—all future economics

Nobel laureates—and a host of other prominent economists began extending Fisher's life-cycle model.

Hence, by the time I reached grad school, economists had formed a clear theory of how people should save, insure, and invest. They also understood why no one—not even an Irving Fisher—could predict the stock market. Of course, developing a theory and expecting people to adhere to its tenets are two different things. Were real-world households doing as economic theory prescribed? Were they saving enough? Were they buying enough insurance? Were they choosing the right careers? Were they taking on too much debt? Were they investing appropriately? Were they making the right Social Security and tax moves?

These and similar questions took up residence in my brain and those of other econ eggheads. Many of us started to compare actual personal financial behavior, as reported in nationwide household surveys, with theoretically appropriate behavior. Within two decades, the picture was both clear and ugly. Essentially everyone was making big financial mistakes: saving far too little or far too much, buying the wrong amount of life insurance, borrowing irresponsibly, leaving great sums of lifetime Social Security benefits on the table, paying significantly more taxes than required, becoming house poor. The list goes on.

The economics profession took this news poorly. "What? People aren't adhering to our beautiful theory? How dare they? They must be financially sick. They lack self-control! They are myopic, financially illiterate, or both!" People's greedy present selves were ripping off defenseless future selves by overspending and undersaving. Overnight, a new field of economics arose, "behavioral finance," devoted to studying the precise pathologies underlying individuals' awful financial decisions.

Economists don't always agree. Indeed, they don't always agree with themselves. President Truman said he needed a one-handed economist to stop hearing "On the other hand." I'm a two-handed economist, but my take on behavioral finance is unequivocal. I strongly dispute the premise that people screw up their finances because they are badly behaved, financially lost, shortsighted, or mentally ill. Even the most responsible, prudent, financially well-educated, and psychologically balanced people make major mistakes. The reason is simple: the financial problems we face are unbelievably complex—far beyond the capacity of our brains to solve without some clear direction.

Why do I think this? Three reasons.

The first reason is self-reflection. I recognize that even my own economically pretty well-trained brain isn't remotely up to the task. If, for example, you tell me all about your personal finances and ask me the annual amount you can permanently spend this year and every year through the rest of your life—in other words, if you ask me to smooth your consumption off the top of my head, with no paper and pencil—my answer will surely be off by 30 percent or more.

Other economists are no better at what is essentially a guessing game. I once asked a roomful of economists—all of whom were gathered to discuss household personal finance—to answer, on the fly, the consumption-smoothing question for a hypothetical forty-year-old. I gave them the pertinent information and watched their faces. They weren't happy. They all knew they were about to produce a very wrong answer. Right then and there, they seemed to realize that even financially literate people like themselves couldn't make proper financial decisions via introspection.

The precisely calculated, i.e., computer-calculated, answer to the problem was $75,589 per year. None of the assembled experts got within $15,000. Their answers ranged from $30,000 to $135,000.

Here's the second reason making financial decisions is so tough:

doing so requires getting government benefit and tax programs right. In the US, that's a heavy lift. Take the Social Security system. It has *2,728* rules governing its thirteen benefits. As if that's not enough, its Program Operations Manual System has hundreds of thousands of rules governing those 2,728 rules. Add the complexities of federal and state income tax, and, well, things get craaaazy. How can we possibly maximize our lifetime benefits and minimize our lifetime taxes without having a handle on these provisions?

My third reason why decisions concerning finances can be so difficult? Back to what I originally stated: financial problems are complex. We have to decide how much to spend, save, insure, and invest in different assets over time. And we have to do so in the face of cash-flow constraints, those craaaazy tax and benefit rules, and the nasty chicken-or-egg questions.

The nasty chicken-or-egg questions?

Yes. Here's an example: What comes first, the spending or the taxes? Each depends on the other. How much we can spend over time depends on what taxes we pay over time. But what taxes we pay over time depends on how much we spend over time.*

When I first sat down, twenty-eight years ago, to design a computer algorithm to do consumption smoothing while handling cash-flow constraints and our complex tax and benefit systems, I had no idea where to start. The problem seemed completely overwhelming. But then, as we say in Boston, "Dawn rose on Marblehead." (Marblehead is a town on Boston's North Shore.) My insight was to solve the problem one task at a time, with the results of each task providing inputs to the other tasks. I dubbed my algorithm "iterative dynamic programming." It garnered a patent. (Dynamic programming, by the way, is a technique used by engineers to adjust

---

* If we spend more, we save less, and have less asset income and, consequently, pay lower taxes in the future.

the flight paths of missiles and space vehicles. Thus, making perfectly correct personal financial decisions literally requires rocket science.)

I've now spent decades designing computer programs that correctly make economics-based personal financial decisions.[*] I do this for my research and to produce personal financial planning tools for my software company, Economic Security Planning, Inc. Our main product, MaxiFi Planner, is the behind-the-scenes star of this book. Were I to print out the program's highly efficient code, it would take seven reams—3,500 pages—of paper, reinforcing what we already know: financial problems are complex.

MaxiFi Planner is my primary guide for safely finding you more money, lowering your risk, and raising your quality of life. But rest assured, this book is *not* a long-winded software sales pitch. The book is self-contained. There is no need to run software. I'm going to tell you what economics generally prescribes as well as what MaxiFi specifically prescribes. As for the examples I present, they'll be based on MaxiFi and, therefore, right on the money.

Having this economics-based financial planning machinery to help me help you is, well, magical. That's why I chose the book's title and why I'm delighted to present my money magic show. I'm also keen to demonstrate that economists can do more than study people's financial "mistakes." We can also prescribe financial penicillin—all the things you can and should do to ensure a steady, secure, and higher lifetime living standard. That's exactly what I'll prescribe in the pages ahead.

---

[*] Note, I used one of these programs to calculate the answer I posed to my fellow economists.

Introduction

We all want money—some of us dangerously so. King Midas begged Dionysus for the golden touch and got his wish, starving to death as even the food he touched turned to gold. Imelda Marcos, the infamous First Lady of the Philippines, had very little as she was growing up. When her husband took power and started plundering the country, shoes topped her shopping list. Twenty-one years and almost three thousand pairs of footwear later, the people revolted. The couple escaped with their lives, but not with Imelda's shoes. Hundreds of them are still tastefully displayed at the Marikina Shoe Museum near Manila.

Midas and the Marcoses are outliers. They were addicted to wealth. The vast majority of us aren't money hungry out of sheer greed. We want money for a good reason: we need it. Many US workers haven't seen a real pay raise in years, and most retirees will run out of money before they run out of breath.

Thankfully, there are simple and powerful ways to get more money without gambling your hard-earned savings. There are also ways to lower your risk. And there are ways to buy more happiness with a given amount of money.

THE MAGIC OF ECONOMICS-BASED FINANCIAL PLANNING

Every profession makes magic. Biologists cure plagues. Engineers build skyscrapers. Physicists split atoms. Geologists date rocks. Astronomers discover planets. Chemists decompose matter.

And economists like myself? You know, the folks who can't predict the stock market, who missed both the Great Depression and the Great Recession, and who begin most sentences with "If you assume..." Despite the challenges of the field, economists make marvelous magic. Adam Smith, our first grand wizard, conjured up the "invisible hand," which transforms individual greed into collective good. David Ricardo used "four mystical numbers" to explain why, what, and when countries trade. Alfred Marshall produced the numinous supply-and-demand curves that rule all markets. And our belated great sorcerer Paul Samuelson transposed ancient economic laws into mathematical runes.

Smith, Ricardo, Marshall, and Samuelson are the top economic magicians of all time. But every economist is trained to solve mysteries using the tricks of our trade. This is why economics is so fascinating, surprising, important, and useful, whether applied to understanding global markets, taxing our emissions, or saving our jobs.

Though the common conception of economics is that it's focused on big, world-spanning issues, economists have, in fact, spent what is now a century studying personal finance. But historically they've worked out of the public's eye—writing research papers, presenting seminars, and publishing in academic journals. To be sure, economists have periodically emerged from their scholastic cloisters to espouse some general, commonsense principles: "Save for retirement!" "Diversify your assets." "Buy insurance." But when asked seemingly simple questions at the neighborhood Christmas party—"Does getting an MA make sense?" "Can I afford to retire?" "Should I prioritize paying off student debt or funding my IRA?"—economists traditionally blush and change the subject.

I used to be one of those blushing, subject-changing economists. Like others cornered at the punch bowl, I knew how to think about people's money problems. I could list all the relevant factors and formulate a mathematical model to provide an answer. What I didn't know was how to solve the model. There were simply too many interdependent, ultra-complex, nasty-looking equations at play. And even if we could figure out a software procedure to fit the myriad pieces, using early computers to find the answers took forever.

In recent years, amazing algorithmic and computational advances plus access to cloud computing, with its essentially unlimited computer-processing power, have changed everything. Meet me at a cocktail party today and I'll go full nerd about iterative dynamic programming, adaptive sparse grids, non-convexities, interpolation bias, certainty equivalence, parallel processing, and so on.

Thanks to these advances, no practical money question remains beyond economists' ken. Indeed, economics-based financial planning is poised to revolutionize personal finance. Conventional financial "advice"—a collection of crude rules of thumb that lure households into buying expensive and dangerous financial products—will surely be replaced by financial planning that calculates, rather than guesses, what to do. Your reading this book is testimony to that process.

MY BOTTOM LINE — YOUR LIVING STANDARD

All of our financial decisions—whether about our education, career, job, lifestyle, marriage, retirement age, taxes, Social Security, or investments—involve our living standard, a general term for the spending per household member we can afford over our lifetime. Yet most of us make financial decisions with no clear idea of their living-standard impact, let alone the economic dangers they entail. Instead, we rely on either the financial industry's self-interested heuristics or questionable advice from friends and family. In so doing, we forgo boatloads of money, are far less happy, and put ourselves at risk.

Here are ten queries, pertaining to different stages of your life, that illustrate how your financial decisions help to define your living standard:

1. If I quit work and go back to school will I be able to pay for lunch let alone rent?
2. Would I have more to spend in a low-paying job in a low-cost city than in a high-paying job in a high-cost city?
3. How much will choosing a higher-paying but harder job matter to my discretionary spending?
4. We just had another baby. Do I need more life insurance to ensure my family's living standard?
5. How much should we save in our working years to maintain our living standard in retirement?
6. Does a Roth IRA beat a regular IRA in lowering my lifetime taxes and thus give me more money to spend over the long term?
7. Will prepaying my mortgage raise my living standard?
8. How would it hurt my sustainable living standard if I retired early?
9. The kids have moved out. How much spending power can we gain by downsizing?
10. What's the risk to my living standard if I invest primarily in stocks?

These questions may be yours. Or they may be your relatives', colleagues', or friends' questions. You're here to get answers for yourself. But helping others, particularly your parents and children, now or later, may be just as rewarding. We all are our brother's financial keeper, particularly when push comes to shove. This is why everything in this book applies to you. Yes, you're retired and aren't choosing a career. But your grandson is. And yes, you're thirty years from collecting Social Security. But your parents are about to take their benefits way too early. Are you going to sit back and say, "Not my problem"? Not when you realize that the less they receive from Social Security the more you'll need to help them out if they run out of money before they run out of time.

A LIVING-STANDARD MACHINE

Imagine a machine that could answer your full range of living-standard questions, making you richer, safer, and happier. Such a machine actually exists! As mentioned in the preface, I spent years building it through my personal financial planning software company. The machine incorporates breakthrough technologies and overcomes what used to be unmanageable technical hurdles. It's also jam-packed with the fine details of our income, payroll, and state tax systems as well as the provisions of our most complex fiscal system: Social Security.

My living-standard machine does four things. First, it figures out what you should spend—in other words, your sustainable living standard. Economists call this consumption smoothing—maintaining your living standard on an even keel, or as close as possible given your cash-flow constraints. Second, the machine figures out safe ways to raise your living standard. Third, it calculates risks to your living standard and finds ways to make it safer, including the best ways to invest. Fourth, it helps you buy more happiness with your money by measuring what lifestyle decisions really cost before you make them.

While our brains are no match for computers, years of studying economics as well as building and running my software have taught me all manner of financial lessons I'll convey in the following pages. Each chapter of this book will examine an aspect of your personal finance through the lens of economics principles and the findings of my living-standard machine, helping you gradually build a full picture of all the different ways you can create your own money magic. Along the way, I'll focus on three of the same priorities my software does: making you more money, reducing your risk, and enhancing the amount of happiness you derive from the money you spend.

MAKING YOU MORE MONEY

My top priority is simple: to get you more money. Here's an example to whet your appetite. It involves the Smiths, a Boston couple who share the same birthday and turned sixty-two last week. (The Smiths are members of a hypothetical household, the first of many in this book. You'll also meet actual household members but with altered names to protect their privacy.)

The Smiths have worked in demanding jobs since they were twenty-five. Like others their age, they burned out. This is why last week's terrific birthday party was also a terrific retirement party. Today, though, the Smiths are heartbroken. They finally sat down to look at their finances and realized that they've saved far too little to pay for a retirement that could last longer than they worked. Their dreams of annual European vacations, a summer home, a luxury car, and season tickets to the Celtics all evaporated in an hour.

Why didn't the Smiths examine their finances years ago? They figured that Social Security and maxing out their 401(k) contributions would be enough. They assumed, like most of us, that Uncle Sam and their employers, the parent figures guiding our financial behavior, would get things right and set them on a secure financial path. On top of this wishful thinking, the Smiths were simply too scared to look.

Fortunately, there are five safe and simple ways by which the Smiths can rescue their retirement. First, they should wait to begin taking their Social Security benefits till age seventy, rather than immediately at sixty-two. Next, they should start to withdraw from their 401(k) accounts now, rather than wait till seventy. They also should take their 401(k) withdrawals in the form of joint survivor annuities. Next, they should downsize their four-bedroom house by half. And finally, they should move to New Hampshire, which has no state income tax.

This retirement makeover will make an amazing difference. In fact, it will more than double the Smith's sustainable retirement spending! Under their original plan, the Smiths could afford to spend $5,337 per month in addition to covering their housing costs and taxes. Under the new plan, they can spend $11,819 per month in addition. That's a ginormous increase and adds up to a $1,578,374 increase in lifetime spending measured in present value.

In other words, the new plan amounts to handing the Smiths a bag filled with around $1.5 million in cash. This is money magic, pure and simple.

REDUCING YOUR RISK

My second priority is helping you limit your risk. Risk is defined as how far your living standard can range both above and below its average value. Upside risk—experiencing a higher than average living standard—is great. But downside risk—having your living standard drop, potentially *a lot,* compared to what you expected— is an enormous concern.

We all face lots of risks, some of which we can control and some of which we can't. In this book, I'm going to pay particular atten-tion to the following important uncertainties:

- earnings risk (the risk that your career or job expectations won't pan out),
- mortality risk (the risk that you'll die young),
- longevity risk (the risk that you'll die well beyond your expiration date),
- inflation risk (the risk that higher prices will reduce the purchasing power of your income and assets), and
- investment risk (the risk that you'll suffer major losses in the market).

These risks can be intimidating to think about, but there are surprisingly effective ways to mitigate each of them.

Here's a personal example: When my mom reached age eighty-eight, I realized that my siblings and I faced a major financial risk. She could, as we hoped, live for many more years—years during which we'd need to support her at a far higher level than had previously been the case. I suggested we buy her an annuity, which is the opposite of a life insurance policy. Life insurance pays off if you die. Annuities pay off if you live.

My brother and sister thought I was nuts. My mom wasn't in the best of health, and her life expectancy was only four years. If we bought an annuity and she passed away in four years or less, much of the money invested in the policy would be lost. I agreed but argued that our far bigger financial risk was that mom would live to, say, a hundred, requiring our support for much longer than expected.

"There's no chance she'll live beyond five years," they said. "Look at the odds."

I explained to them that what counted most was the risk of her *defying* the odds. When it comes to risk, we look at worst-case scenarios. Financially speaking, the worst-case scenario was that mom would live much longer than expected.

My sibs didn't appreciate my antiseptic, analytical tone. But ultimately they got the point, relented, and we bought the annuity. It's a good thing we did. Mom, whom we miss terribly, passed at ninety-eight.

GETTING MORE BANG FOR YOUR BUCK

My third big goal is helping you spend money in ways that will make you happier. To see what's involved, please come with me on a shopping trip to a strange supermarket. In this market, there are no prices posted. You can't tell what a gallon of milk costs, what a six-pack of vegan sausages costs, what a bottle of Hellfire Hellboy Extreme Hot Sauce costs, what a can of fish mouths costs (yes, this place sells some delicious things)—not even what a loaf of bread costs. Nonetheless, your task is to walk through the aisles and decide which groceries to put into your cart. As soon as the combined value of what you've picked exceeds two hundred dollars, the cart, which has sensors, automatically charges your credit card for what you've chosen and bids you a good day.

How would you feel being forced to do such price-blind shopping? You'd be pretty upset. If you don't know what anything costs, you'll buy things that cost more than they're worth to you. You'll also fail to buy things that cost less than they're worth to you. Yes, you'll leave the store with two hundred plus dollars' worth of products but surely not with two hundred dollars' worth of happiness.

Of course, outside of thought experiments, stores post prices. But there are lots of important and expensive things we buy without knowing their true price. They involve personal and lifestyle decisions. Here are a few examples: retiring early, choosing what college to attend, having another child, switching jobs, renovating a house, moving to another state, and getting divorced. Each of these decisions has a precise price (possibly a negative one), measured in terms of your sustainable living standard.

An example will help.

Think about retiring at age sixty-three, rather than at age sixty-seven, from a job with standard benefits. Retiring younger means four fewer years of earnings. It also means four fewer years of employer and employee 401(k) contributions. It means paying for your own health insurance for two years until you're eligible for Medicare at age sixty-five, among other insurance-related costs. It means potentially having reduced Social Security benefits due to your shorter work history and a possibly lower average level of past covered earnings. It also means dealing with a reduced cash flow, potentially leading you to take retirement-account withdrawals, Social Security benefits, or both sooner than would otherwise be the case. If you start taking Social Security benefits early, you'll receive reduced benefits for the rest of your life. Retiring early also means changing your entire course of spending and saving, and thus your future assets, future taxable asset income, and future federal and state income taxes.

You get my drift. Figuring out what it really means financially to retire four years early is complicated. But have no fear. I'm ready and able to tell you what personal and lifestyle financial decisions actually cost so you can better decide which ones to make. If early retirement is one of the items you're picking off your lifestyle grocery shelf, I'm going to help you put a price on it, calculating whether the money you'd earn while continuing to work would be worth a few more years of leisure. If you expect a 10 percent living-standard hit and you learn that it's closer to 20 percent, you may decide to wait a few years to call it quits. On the other hand, if you expect a 20 percent hit and it's just 10 percent, you may opt to retire when otherwise you'd have slogged along.

In short, I'm going to help you buy the most happiness you can afford at a price you understand. Of course, every financial situation is different, but I'll provide enough examples to give you a pretty clear idea of what different personal and lifestyle decisions will cost you.

SOME BOOKKEEPING: ADDING UP MONEY ACROSS TIME

Throughout the book, I'll assume you're going to earn a 1.5 percent nominal return on your savings and will experience a 1.5 percent annual inflation rate. This zero real (after-inflation) return assumption is based on financial conditions as I write this.* It's remarkably convenient. It lets me simply add up inflation-adjusted amounts across different future years. For example, if you're earning $75,000 a year, are ten years from retirement, and your salary will stay fixed in real terms (keep up with inflation), your lifetime earnings equal $10 \times \$75,000$, or $750,000.

FINANCIAL SHOCKERS

We're just getting started, but I've already produced three financial surprises: a lucrative retirement makeover, a means of insuring yourself against living too long, and a powerful method for getting far more happiness without spending an extra penny. To give you an idea of the breadth and depth of the topics we will cover, the following table lists some of the myriad financial shockers coming your way. Understanding their source will be fun and, more important, rewarding.

---

* The prevailing nominal thirty-year Treasury bond rate at the time of my writing is 1.5 percent. The prevailing thirty-year Treasury inflation-protected (inflation-indexed) bond rate is very close to zero. Thus the market is predicting a 1.5 percent long-term inflation rate. US Treasury bonds are generally viewed as among the safest financial assets in the world, in terms of potential default. I'll therefore present calculations assuming that you will invest safely and that inflation will turn out as predicted. If you were instead investing in stocks, I would need to adjust all the results for extra risk exposure. In the end, those adjustments would bring me back to using the safe interest rate in the numerical analyses.

Sampling Money Magic's Financial Shockers

Q: Can it pay to cash out my IRA to pay off my mortgage?
A: Absolutely.

Q: Can I suspend my Social Security benefits and restart them at a higher value?
A: Yes, if you're above full retirement age and under seventy.

Q: Can I set a living-standard floor and invest with only upside living-standard risk?
A: Simple as pie.

Q: Do plumbers make as much as GPs over their lifetimes?
A: Yes.

Q: Can I significantly raise my living standard by moving states?
A: Almost always.

Q: If I lose Social Security benefits from working, will I get virtually all of them back?
A: Almost always.

Q: Can spending aggressively be as risky as investing aggressively?
A: Absolutely.

Q: Should I hold proportionately more stock the richer I become?
A: No. The rich should invest in bonds and the poor should invest in stocks.

Q: Does timing the market ever make sense?
A: Yes.

Q: Do I need more life insurance if we have another child?
A: No, you probably need less!

Q: Should I plan to live to one hundred even if the chances are vanishingly small?
A: Absolutely.

Q: In retirement, should I gradually get out of stocks?
A: No, do the exact opposite.

Q: Are Roth conversions worth it?
A: Definitely, when timed correctly.

Q: Are reverse mortgages cost-effective ways to free trapped home equity?
A: Not at all.

Q: Does it pay to get a master's degree in education?
A: Probably not.

Q: Can retiring at sixty-seven rather than sixty-two make a real difference to my retirement?
A: It can make a huge difference.

Q: If I'm young and single, what's one of my best financial moves?
A: Shack up with mom.

THE GAME PLAN

My goal is to teach you every financial trick I know and leave you empowered to make your own money magic. But first, I'll focus on your making money the old-fashioned way: by working. The same amount of work can result in very different incomes, and thus living standards, depending on your choice of career, so let's start there.

CHAPTER 1

My Daughter the Plumber — The Path to a Dollar-ful Career

You're eighteen and as smart as a whip. You inhale science. Your parents, both doctors, have planned out your life: you're going to a top college, then medical school, then a first-class residency, and, finally, a long and fulfilling career in general practice. They're so sure about your future that they both introduce you as "My daughter the doctor."

Trouble is, you can't stand the sight of blood and aren't really a people person. More important, you can add. And these days, becoming a GP doesn't compute. In fact, after you factor in the exorbitant med-school costs, the decade-long training, the high-priced loans, and the surprisingly low salaries of GPs, a doctor earns roughly the same amount as a plumber.[1] There are medical specialties, like radiology and surgery, that pay more, but they require extra years of training. Plus, these and many other advanced medical fields are rapidly being automated.[2] As for plumbers, their jobs seem safe. There are 120 million buildings in the US, each with its own idiosyncratic piping that isn't in any danger of fixing itself.

Managing your careers well is the most important money trick going. It's the key to maximizing your lifetime earnings and enjoying work to the extent possible. Why do I say "careers" plural, rather than "career" singular? Because you're likely to have several careers and several jobs in each. Between the ages of eighteen and forty-eight, most of us change careers four times and jobs twelve times. We career and job hop for good reason. We're searching for the best long-term match, comparing the potential to do better with the cost of starting over.

There are too many constantly changing options not to keep searching for a new career, even after finding a supposed dream path. The Bureau of Labor Statistics' list of occupations is a window into the enormous opportunities and difficulties in making optimal career and job choices. The BLS lists 867 major career options. Deciding which to pursue and for how long can be overwhelming. You're almost sure to get it wrong before you get it right. By analogy, imagine visiting an ice cream store with 867 flavors. You quickly spot the classics—chocolate, vanilla, and cookie dough. Then you scan the rows of open tubs. Virtually all look and sound delicious. If you could sample them all, you'd surely find your dream ice cream. But a long line of sugar addicts is waiting behind you. With a minute to decide and not knowing what to pick, you ask the clerk for their favorite. In short order, you're out the door, regarding with horror your double scoop of horse flesh, ranked as the grossest of the planet's extant flavors.

Fortunately, you have years, not minutes, to explore your career options. You also have a free, trustworthy online career counselor, namely the BLS. Its Occupational Employment and Wage Statistics (OEWS) program provides detailed information about each of the 867 occupations. (Check out BLS.gov.) You'll find occupations you probably haven't thought of and others you've surely never heard of.

YOU, YOUR DAUGHTER, AND YOUR GRANDDAUGHTER, NANCY

Consider twenty-two-year-old Nancy—she could be a stand-in for you, your daughter, or your granddaughter. Nancy just graduated from Duke with a BA in art history and a mountain of debt. She spent the last month diligently applying to museums across the country for the thirty-seven low-paying internships advertised. To date, she's received thirty-three polite rejections.

Nancy does what we all do in these situations. She panics and asks for help. The first person she consults is Uncle Bob, an ear, nose, and throat specialist. Bob urges Nancy to become a hearing aid specialist (HA). "This field has tremendous potential. The country is aging and aging spells hearing loss."

Nancy checks out the occupation online, which leads her to the OEWS program on the BLS website. Its statistics show that HAs earn, on average, $53,000 per year. That sounds great to Nancy. But is this her best option? Her eyes land on a strange-sounding profession listed just above it: orthotist and prosthetist practitioner (O&P). O&Ps fit people with leg braces and artificial limbs, a bit different from fitting hearing aids but not a drastically different field. Yet O&Ps earn, on average, $73,000 a year—38 percent more than an HA.

Suppose Nancy becomes an O&P rather than an HA. And suppose she earns the $20,000 extra each year, in inflation-adjusted dollars, through a reasonable retirement age of sixty-seven. How much more would that mean to her living standard over her lifetime?

Because prevailing inflation-adjusted long-term interest rates are essentially zero, the answer is simple to compute. Just multiply $20,000 by Nancy's forty-five years of work. This gives a lifetime earnings difference of $900,000. Wow—almost a million-dollar difference in lifetime earnings. For Nancy, it's (sorry for this) an

ah-HA moment. As an O&P, Nancy can retire fourteen years earlier than as an HA and still enjoy the same annual living standard
through the end of her days.

YOUR CAREER'S EARNINGS PATH

Earnings growth is a key dimension of career choice. Unfortunately, the BLS doesn't report earnings by starting age or by years
on a job. But it does report the different pay levels in a career. For
example, the twenty-fifth percentile O&P salary (the salary of an
O&P with the twenty-fifth lowest salary out of one hundred O&Ps)
is $52,000. If we view this as a proxy for entry-level earnings and
the seventy-fifth percentile as a proxy for end-of-career earnings,
we can compare wage growth across careers. Using this estimation,
an O&P's starting salary is about $14,000 higher than an HA's, and
an O&P's late-career salary is close to $23,000 higher. This suggests
that an O&P's salary grows faster during their career.

The BLS website also lets you compare salaries in different cities. Average annual O&P wages in Jackson, Mississippi, are
$123,000—$50,000 higher than the national average. This is the
second-highest city average for O&Ps, after $129,000 in Los Ange-
les. But LA is roughly 50 percent more expensive to live in than
Jackson, according to online cost-of-living calculators. Therefore,
an O&P's living standard in LA is a lot lower than in Jackson.

Tampa, Florida, has the top HA salary, at $77,000. That's a lot
higher than the $53,000 HA national average. Still, if you factor in
salary and cost-of-living differences, an O&P career in Jackson
offers twice the living standard as an HA career in Tampa.

"Are O&P salaries keeping up with HA salaries?" asks Uncle
Bob, skeptical that he hadn't given the best possible advice. "The
HA-O&P difference you're referencing is amazing. But their data
only provide a snapshot. You need to understand what's happening

to the two fields over time. In thirty years, HAs may be earning more than O&Ps."

Bob has a point. The HA-O&P salary differential has narrowed according to the BLS data, which go back over a decade. But the current gap between O&P and HA salaries remains huge. And nothing says the gap will continue to narrow, let alone that HA salaries will ever overtake O&P salaries.

Uncle Bob pushes Nancy yet again. "Have you factored in training costs? Maybe it takes a lot longer to get certified as an O&P than as an HA. And maybe the tuition costs are much higher."

"Sure did," Nancy replies. "Both occupations have similar time and dollar costs. Whichever path I take, I'll need to borrow more money and spend at least a year getting certified. This is why, ah, you were the first person I turned to in my job search. I need a loan."

SEEK AND YOU SHALL FIND

Nancy's excited about her tentative career plan. But now that she's shifted her focus to making money, she's wondering if there's an even better-paying option than becoming an O&P. Fortunately, the BLS has two virtual assistants—an occupational handbook and a career finder tool—that can help narrow her search.

The occupational handbook characterizes each general type of occupation and lets you drill down to see any associated specializations. It also provides quick occupational facts—median pay, education requirements, prior-work requirements, on-the-job training requirements, national employment, and projected employment growth. The career finder tool lets you search for occupations that have particular characteristics, like high average wages.

Unfortunately, the career finder tool can easily go overboard in narrowing the options. To make sure you don't miss a great career, I urge you to slog through all 867 of them. For motivation, think about the big bucks Nancy uncovered by simply comparing O&P with HA. Also, bear in mind that there are far more careers to choose from than the BLS identifies. Even if the BLS occupational categories seem specialized, they are actually highly aggregated.

Take career 11-9033, which references educational administrators, postsecondary. This is a career Nancy should consider. It requires a BA degree and has a national mean wage of $112,000. That's $39,000 higher than the mean O&P wage and $59,000 higher than the mean HA wage. Here's the BLS description:

Plan, direct, or coordinate research, instructional, student administration and services, and other educational activities at postsecondary institutions, including universities, colleges, and junior and community colleges.

Universities post lots of careers fitting within 11-9033. The list includes university department manager, university lab coordinator, undergraduate student advisor, assistant dean of students, academic grants administrator, college budget director, program director, project coordinator, human subjects specialist, and student services manager.

The need for at least shallow occupational dives holds for all careers listed by the BLS. HAs, for example, come in two forms: audiologists and hearing instrument specialists. The former diagnose hearing loss. The latter choose hearing aids to correct the problem.

NETWORK, NETWORK, NETWORK

Career databases like the BLS's can tell you only cursory information about the day-to-day of a job. If you think becoming a grants administrator sounds interesting but you really want to know what it's like, call up your local university and ask to speak to the head or assistant head of the grants department. Explain that you're researching their career and have questions only they can answer. Chances are you'll get lots of advice, maybe even a meeting. Maybe even lunch!

Reaching out to friends, family, and even strangers to learn about careers and ultimately land a job is called, of course, networking. No one knows for sure how many people get hired via networking, but what evidence there is suggests the percentage is well over half.[3] There's also evidence that a large share of jobs never get posted because those trying to hire find it more efficient to work their own networks rather than wade through a large stack of résumés. This means that you'll never even get a shot at many potential jobs unless you take advantage of networking. Think about friends hiring friends and you'll get the picture. As for how best to network, the internet is full of good advice, whether it's properly preparing your résumé, using social media like LinkedIn, offering to help people from whom you seek help, or simply being friendly.

In addition to the traditional form of networking, professional career counselors, online career tools, and headhunters can help. Online tools cost money and many seem to be based on the BLS's free data, so be wary of what you pay for. As for headhunters/job recruiters, they typically collect their fees from employers. You likely have nothing to lose by using them.

DON'T STOP THINKING ABOUT TOMORROW

Fleetwood Mac got it right. Always focus on tomorrow for one simple reason: when it comes to a career choice, the payoff is long-term. Also bear in mind that no matter how appealing a career might look, if you can't do it for very long, it's not going to be the best long-term choice.

Many high-paying jobs come with high burnout and turnover rates. Becoming a corporate lawyer is an example. In your early years you have to work sixty or more hours per week. If you reach age fifty and can no longer hack the pace and get replaced by a twenty-seven-year-old willing and eager to work weekends, your stunning career has just gone south. When picking a career, spend time making sure it has a fair share of gray hairs on board. If not, it could mean that the burnout rate is very high, the work is physically very demanding, or employees are being tossed once they've ripened or, due to seniority-based pay, become expensive.

Our progressive tax system magnifies the price of choosing a high-paying, but likely short-lived, career. Since we pay taxes on an annual basis, the same lifetime earnings bunched into fewer years means higher earnings per year and a higher average annual tax rate, leading to less money you actually have to spend. Remember our comparison between doctors and plumbers. A medical career entails significant earnings compressed into relatively few years, which spells tax bunching. A plumbing career does not. This is one of the reasons that plumbing can provide the same living standard as doctoring.

While burnout is a real danger, it's at least somewhat under your control. However, if your job gets automated, outsourced, or offshored, you will likely have few options other than to find a new career.

Automation is a particularly acute concern in choosing a career these days. Robots will, by some estimates, eliminate half of existing US jobs over the next few decades.[4] It may seem impossible to believe. Then again, it's hard to think of many jobs that robots can't or won't be able to do. They already fly our planes, drive our cars, staff our factories, fill our prescriptions, process our purchases, babysit our children, flip our burgers, vacuum our rugs, remove our gallbladders, rub our backs, and kill our enemies. And consider that plenty of skilled workers have been rendered obsolete by less sophisticated technology than we have today. For example, in 1900, there were more than twenty-one million working horses, most of them involved in transportation and farming. Then came the combustion engine. Today, the number of working horses is less than two million.

Fortunately, you can check the probability, estimated by an economist and a machine-learning expert, of almost any occupation going the way of the horse. The website Replacedbyrobot.info is one place to learn the odds of your career becoming high-tech toast. Interestingly, the site reports that O&Ps as well as HAs (in this case audiologists) are among the least automatable of all professions. Software is certainly used extensively to customize braces and artificial limbs and improve hearing devices, but human clinicians appear indispensable.

Losing your job to outsourcing or offshoring is no more fun than losing it to a robot. Outsourcing means your company hires a third party to do your job. Offshoring means your company replaces you with someone in a different country. Offshoring currently appears the far bigger threat to US jobs. One recent study suggests that a quarter of all jobs could be offshored in coming years.[5] Yikes!

As we saw with automation, the jobs least likely to be outsourced or offshored are those whose tasks are non-repetitive and that require people skills. This includes many jobs in the healthcare industry, like being an HA or an O&P, both of which involve human interaction.

Another way to hedge becoming redundant is to begin your career in an area that's experiencing rapid growth in new businesses—places where new jobs spring up all the time. That way even if you get booted, it will be easier to reboot. Remarkably, half of all new US companies are opting to locate in just twenty of the United States' 3,006 counties, any of which could be a good place to launch your career.[6] Some of these counties are in expensive major metropolitan areas, but some are in more affordable suburban locales.

With so much uncertainty about early termination, how can you factor this into comparisons between what you'll make in various careers? The answer is to multiply each year's earnings by the probability—say 0.8 (80 percent)—you'll last in the career to the year in question. Then just add up all these expected annual earnings amounts, subtract the expected annual costs, and you'll have the expected value of the career. Where do you get these probabilities? Clearly, researching the estimated chance of your career being automated is a place to start. But ask people who are in the field— older people who have a long-term perspective—what they think are the chances their jobs will be around in thirty years.

Of course, crunching the numbers doesn't capture the actual economic and psychic costs of being fired and having your life upended, or the fear factor of working in a dwindling industry. Those are personal factors you can't ignore. But it does get straight what the career or job will pay, on average, given its potential to disappear.

TRADE HIGHER INITIAL EARNINGS FOR FASTER EARNINGS GROWTH

Suppose you're twenty-two and you plan to work through age sixty-seven. Career A offers a great starting salary: $75,000 per year. But it doesn't promise real wage growth, meaning you won't get increases in annual pay that exceed inflation. Career B starts off paying just $60,000, but annual earnings will grow at 2.5 percent above inflation through age fifty (when earnings in most careers peak). Which job pays more, on a total career basis, after taxes?

The winner is career B by a mile. Even though you start out earning 20 percent less, by age fifty you're earning 60 percent more, and you receive this higher pay for the next seventeen years. Your lifetime earnings are 35 percent higher in career B! Be careful, though. Career earnings paths are tilted for a reason. They provide you with an incentive to work harder when you're young to get the big payoff when you're old. But often this means that if you don't work hard enough or produce enough business, your employer will let you go. Moreover, as you begin to earn more, some employers are dishonest and may fire you unfairly to avoid having to pay you the higher real amount they implicitly promised. Getting canned after, say, ten years—the time it takes to reach $75,000 in annual compensation in career B—is awful given that you likely worked yourself to the bone on the basis of a big future salary boost.

FIND A CAREER YOU LOVE AND OTHERS HATE

If career B offers 35 percent more for your services than career A, there's a reason. When a given career's pay rate is boosted due to the job being unpleasant in some way, economists call the extra pay a "compensating differential."

Compensating differentials are common in the labor market. All else being equal—including skills, education, and experience—people with unpleasant, dangerous, nerve-racking, insecure, disturbing, or financially risky jobs get paid more than people with the same skills working jobs with none of these drawbacks. Think again about Nancy and her O&P/HA choice. An O&P position likely pays more because fitting an eighty-year-old with a hearing aid is emotionally far less taxing than fitting a twenty-three-year-old with an artificial arm.

That's the tack Uncle Bob takes in his final effort to convince Nancy to take the HA route. "Nancy, surely you realize why O&Ps are paid more. Every day you'll encounter someone with a very tough physical problem. It will depress you."

Nancy has thought this through. "I hear you. The fact that the O&P job will pay more than an HA job is probably no fluke, and

I'm sure it'll be hard at times. But I'm not most people. I'm atypical. I'd find great personal reward in assisting people as an O&P. Indeed, for me, the compensating differential is just a bonus. I'd prefer to work as an O&P instead of as an HA even if the O&P position paid the same."

"Well, Nancy, I'm glad you're considering all the angles. Maybe a career as an O&P is your best path," replies Uncle Bob.

"Actually, Uncle, once I discovered I could career shop so easily and potentially pull down much more money, I got greedy and kept researching options. I've found something with an even bigger compensating differential. I'm thinking of becoming a mortician. It's a field dominated by men, but there's no reason a woman can't make a killing."

Once again, Nancy has the right idea. She's applying her own personal compensating differential to her search. For her, being a mortician actually sounds fun—she likes the idea of working with people who don't talk back. So not only will she be getting extra pay for doing a job most people wouldn't want to do, she'll also get extra pleasure.

The message here is worth keeping front and center as you find your economic way. The more you like things that most people hate, such as becoming an embalmer, the bigger the gold mine associated with your career search. The trick is to find an occupation you love and, ideally, others hate, and put it at the top of your search list.

HIRE YOURSELF

Going out on your own is not for everyone. But you're not everyone. Otherwise you wouldn't be reading this book. More than 600,000 new businesses are started each year. Lots of them fail. After seven years, only half survive. After ten years, only 30 percent are still operating. Twenty years out, it's 20 percent. So starting your own business is no sure thing, but it can bring enormous rewards. You don't have to be Steve Jobs, who started Apple in his garage and became a billionaire. Plenty of more modestly successful entrepreneurs demonstrate that you can safely and handsomely hire yourself.

Take, for example, Pat and Cara Cairny, two entrepreneurs I met recently. As a youth in Ireland, Pat was a decent student, but college wasn't his thing. Nor was working on his dad's small and struggling farm. At eighteen, he left Cork, Ireland, for Sag Harbor, New York, where his sister Cara was already living, with a job cleaning homes.

My wife and I rented Pat's parents' cottage in Cork. We became friends with their folks overnight and joined them a few months later when they visited Pat and Cara on Long Island. They had told us their kids had done well, but Pat and Cara's actual level of success was startling. Pat, now age forty-five, has a highly profitable construction company. Cara has also done remarkably well with the cleaning company she started.

When Pat arrived from Ireland, he took the first job he found: doing menial tasks at a construction site. Over time, he worked for a series of contractors and learned the building trade. He also discovered he had a gift for design and interacting with clients. For New Yorkers, his accent is a real tonic. After five years, he struck out on his own, hiring extra hands for the middling commissions he could attract. Finally, a friend asked him to design and build a small house. It was a beauty and led to larger projects. When we met, Pat was finishing a thirty-thousand-square-foot beachfront home for a Wall Street magnate. It has all the trimmings: tennis courts, swimming pool, hot tub, Jacuzzi, gym, six-car garage, plus solar panels galore to assuage its owner's climate conscience.

Meanwhile, Cara expanded her business by using the oldest marketing trick in the book: ask your current clients to help you find new clients. As her customer list grew, Cara spent less time cleaning and more time supervising. Before long, her cleaning service morphed into a thirty-five-employee business with seven hundred clients. Cara, like Pat, moved quickly into an upper-income living standard.

Two decades after leaving Ireland and making it big, Pat and Cara are the same down-to-earth people. When I asked them about their success, they said it was luck. They said they just as easily could have started and stayed as waiters in the local restaurant industry. While that may be the case, I suspect their restaurant experiences would have led them to start a food-truck business followed by a small café and, finally, their own restaurant. The Cairnys have too much drive to suppose otherwise.

Although drive was important to their success, it wasn't the key ingredient. The most important thing was insider knowledge. They carefully learned their trades and realized they could provide far better and cheaper services than their bosses were providing. Recall Benjamin Franklin's aphorism *Time is money*. Perhaps for entrepreneurs the saying should be *Specialized knowledge is money*. That knowledge, by the way, doesn't need to be technical; it can be interpersonal. In Pat's case, he certainly needed to learn his craft. But he also needed to fully understand two things: he had a better sense of design than most of the contractors and architects with whom he was interacting, and thanks to his winning personality and sense of humor, he was far better at interacting with clients than anyone in the area. Prudence was also key. Both Pat and Cara knew not to take on debt but instead to let their companies grow bit by bit.

Starting your own business may sound highly risky. But for Pat and Cara, their decisions were fairly safe moves. Actually, working for themselves probably ended up being far less risky than their working for others. Pat and Cara have maximum job security. They can't be fired. They'll never be passed over for a promotion, they'll never get a smaller than expected bonus, and they'll never have to tolerate difficult bosses. Plus, as their businesses have grown, they've earned vastly more than they would've had they remained employees of others.

CAREER ADVANCEMENT USING COSTLY SIGNALING

Clearly, there are excellent reasons for hiring yourself. But there are also ways to control your economic future even as an employee. Consider CJ, a longtime employee and eventual owner of Belmont Car Wash. I used to live near Belmont, Massachusetts, and would take my car to CJ, who even in his sixties was not only loudly instructing the workers but also doing fastidious detail work himself to set an example.

One day CJ regaled me with the fascinating story of his career. He had come to the Boston area in the 1960s, when he was in his early twenties. Finding work as a Black man with only a high school diploma wasn't easy. After months searching, he saw the car wash's "Help Wanted" ad and took four buses to get to Belmont. The owners were dubious, but he persuaded them to give him a try. They told him to show up the next morning at 8 a.m. He got there at 6:30 a.m., wearing a tie and sporting perfectly polished shoes. The owners were impressed by his appearance and asked him how long he'd been waiting. "An hour and a half," he explained.

The next day, the same thing: CJ arrived at 6:30 to start work at 8. Day after day, CJ came to work far too early and far too well dressed, always with spit-polished shoes. What in the world was the point? As he explained to me, he was signaling to the owners that he was reliable, something he had to signal particularly hard because he was Black. The earlier he showed up, the better he dressed, the shinier his shoes, the higher the cost to him, and, therefore, the better the signal. If he had come just ten minutes early to work, well, no big deal. But an hour and a half early day in and day out, and well dressed, with those glistening shoes? Now, that was a very credible signal. It paid off. The owners realized CJ was spending his valuable time and money to convince them that he took the job extremely seriously and that he was committed to working with them for the long term.

CJ's appearance also signaled that he had bigger ambitions than just detailing cars. As a result, the owners immediately started thinking of CJ in a very different manner. In particular, they realized that he could solve a critical problem they faced: finding someone as good if not better than them to run their business while they went golfing. The owners also needed some fresh thinking about advertising, new products, and ways to cut costs. CJ wasn't being paid to solve their problems, but that didn't stop him. He knew that doing so was the fastest way to advance his career. Under his watch, his new marketing strategies, including greeting the customers with a huge smile and remembering their names, more than doubled the car wash's revenues.

Over time, CJ went from being one of many car detailers to running the entire enterprise. When the owners retired, they sold him the business, which he continued to run successfully, putting his three girls through college. This, CJ told me, was his life's biggest achievement. Needless to say, even once he owned the place, his shoes were always shiny.

The strategy CJ hit on was essentially the same as a highly developed, Nobel Prize–winning economics theory describing how costly signaling can convey credibility. As an economist, I was struck that CJ, at roughly age twenty-two, had figured out the essence of signaling theory on his own and had conveyed his signal in such a brilliant manner.

SWITCHING CAREERS LATER IN LIFE

Let's go back to Pat for a moment. What if three bad things were to happen to Pat and his business? Their Wall Street mogul customer goes to jail for financial fraud and can't pay the huge amount he still owes Pat, the sea level rises—a lot—and demand for construction work dries up on the north end of Long Island, and Pat starts losing his sense of humor.

Pat would have to start over. But where and doing what? Picking a career path at forty-five is not like doing so at twenty-two, so his calculus would be significantly different from Nancy's. The biggest differential is that entering a new career at an older age means fewer years to recoup training costs. For example, if Pat aims to retire at sixty-five, he can't spend a decade training to be a doctor—he would be fifty-six before he saw his first paying patient. Similarly, he wouldn't have time to take advantage of careers that offer earnings growth over a high entry-level salary. Consequently, he'd need to look for a career with a quick payoff.

If he did the math for each occupation, adding up all the expected projected earnings and subtracting all the expected projected costs, his short time to recoup any investment would come into play, and he'd be able to see what pays, on balance, and what does not.

RECAP

Here are key career-choice takeaways:

- Today's labor market, with its fast-paced automation, outsourcing, and offshoring, is not your parents' labor market. It's a market in which plumbers can earn as much over their lifetimes as doctors and in which a host of careers you've never heard of deserve your consideration.

- Use the BLS and other tools available, but realize you need to consult more than just databases to research career options. Get help, network like crazy, and figure out how to solve a potential employer's problem. Signal and then signal some more at a clear cost to you to convey that you're going to bring something special to the table.

- Multiply, add, and subtract. Multiply each career's payoffs and costs, year by year, by the probability of your lasting in the career long enough to earn the projected payoffs and pay the projected costs. Then add up, across years, all the expected payoffs and subtract all the expected costs. This will produce a first-order sense of which career will net you the most. But don't ignore a worst-case scenario. You can't just play the odds. What happens on average won't happen to you.

- Compare the expected net costs and your personal compensating differential. This is what you'll need to be paid to choose career A over career B were they otherwise to pay the same.

- If one career pays a lot more for no clear reason, figure out why. Is there more physical danger, more difficult hours, higher training costs, higher burnout, more sexual or racial discrimination, or more commuting time? Be aware of the compensating differential of that career, but don't be afraid to embrace a career you love just because everyone else hates it. That's actually your sweet spot.

- Consider working for yourself. If you start the right business in the right way, it will raise your remaining future earnings and give you unmatched job security.

- Keep thinking about tomorrow. Are you in the best possible career for the rest of your working days? Should you make a switch? Is your current career in danger? In other words, keep your options open by keeping your eyes open. Set a date every few months to do a career review with a spouse, partner, parent, or friend.

- Consider the trends in your career's payoffs and future risks. If you're doing construction on Long Island, keep an eye on the sea level. But also understand that every hurricane will likely be someone else's loss and your gain as you rebuild their home.

- Don't worry about career and job hopping. There are too many options not to shop around. Certainly, the fastest path to a raise is to get a credible outside offer. Bear in mind that career choice is your most important financial investment. With very little extra effort, you can find a career that entails hundreds of thousands of dollars in extra lifetime earnings. That's money magic!

CHAPTER 2

Hang In or Hang Out?—Divining the Right Time to Retire

If you're in your late fifties or sixties and still working, you're likely dying to quit your job and hang out with your retired friends. Or maybe your spouse/partner has already retired and wants some company. Or your kids may be looking for a free, full-time babysitter.

Financially speaking, it's generally far safer and far smarter to retire later—in other words, to hang in with working rather than hang out with others. Still, almost two-thirds of us retire early, between ages fifty-seven and sixty-six.[1]

Few of us think of early retirement as what it is: a decision to take the longest and most expensive vacation of our lifetimes. Putting it this way makes clear that the wonderful benefits of retirement—extra time with the grandkids, the ability to pursue hobbies, the reduction in stress, the freedom to do what you want when you want—all come at a high price, namely the loss of years, if not decades, of earnings.

Of all this book's money tricks, none is simpler than making money by not *not* making money. Retiring early is a decision to forgo money. I want to be clear that there are situations where early retirement is a great option. Some people have carefully planned and can afford to retire early, buying more leisure at a price they both understand and can handle. And, of course, many workers simply have no choice. They run out of physical or psychological steam. Others find their jobs automated, outsourced, or offshored. Still others are illegally let go simply because they're old, only to face age discrimination in finding another job.

Still, the vast majority of people who decide to retire early do so of their own volition. Most people who leave work in the fifty-five to sixty-four age bracket are able-bodied, without disabilities that would prevent them from staying on the job,[2] yet many of them call it quits despite having saved next to nothing.

THE BABY BOOMERS' RETIREMENT DEBACLE

The group that's now retiring early is the massive, seventy-three-million-strong baby boomer generation—people born between 1946 and 1964. Their mostly voluntary decisions to hang it up are surprising, given boomers' limited savings.[3] Indeed, almost half of already-retired boomers have little if any savings.[4] Across all boomers, median wealth is just $144,000—less than three years of median household spending.[5] If boomers had significant private or state or local pensions to rely on, things might look better. But they don't. Fewer than one in three have a pension apart from Social Security, and the average Social Security benefit is less than $18,000 a year.[6] As for those with pensions, many worked for state or local governments that didn't participate in Social Security, precluding their workers from doing so.

Widespread undersaving isn't just a boomer problem. Most workers are saving bubkes. According to a report from Boston College's Center for Retirement Research, half of today's working families risk a major living-standard decline in retirement.[7] The share would drop roughly in half were all workers to retire two years later.

I don't mean to freak you out. Just because millions of retirees have screwed the pooch, to use an old NASA expression, doesn't mean that you personally have saved too little. Nonetheless, you may still be planning to retire far too early or to stay retired when you should get back in the game. Deciding when it's best to permanently throw in the towel requires two things. The first is to realize that, financially speaking, you may live longer than you planned. The second is to understand the magical difference that working longer can make to your old-age pocketbook.

YOU CAN'T COUNT ON DYING ON TIME

The failure of most of us to save adequately is partly due to a widespread misunderstanding of life expectancy. In statistics, the word "expectation" references an average. For example, a fifty-year-old today will die, on average, at age eighty-two. Thus, their life expectancy is thirty-two years. Life expectancy is routinely used to set one's planning horizon. That might seem totally reasonable, but it's frankly nuts.

The chance we'll die exactly at our life expectancy is essentially zero and the chance we'll die within a year of our life expectancy is extremely small. Well over half of those now age fifty will hang in there beyond age eighty.[8] Roughly a quarter will make it to age ninety. Moreover, if you're married or partnered, your family unit's combined longevity is what's most important. Consider a sixty-five-year-old married couple. The probability that at least one of the two will make it to ninety-five is 18 percent.[9]

What about becoming a centenarian—making it to age one hundred or more? It might sound fanciful, but it's not. Your chance of rounding that corner is somewhere between 1 and 5 percent depending on your age and health status. And if you do reach triple digits, you'll have lots of company. By 2050, centenarians will number close to half a million — enough to fill up a good-sized US city. Imagine driving through Kansas City and seeing only centenarians at the wheel.

If you stay healthy, living a century or longer is a tremendous gift. Assuming your descendants procreate early and often, you'll meet not just your great-grandkids but also your great-great-grandkids. What a personal joy. But financially speaking, what a problem. Every year you survive is another year you'll need to feed, clothe, house, and maintain yourself. Given how costs — especially for healthcare, home care, and nursing care — rise with age, the maintenance bit is particularly daunting.

The problem is compounded by early retirement. Suppose you make it to a hundred having retired at what seemed, at the time, a reasonable age: sixty-two. If you started working at twenty-five, that's thirty-seven working years. Surely, thirty-seven years of grinding it out is longer than anyone should have to tolerate a jerky boss, handle a long commute, make nice with annoying coworkers, and surrender a huge chunk of pay to Uncle Sam. But the difference between sixty-two and one hundred is thirty-eight. And thirty-eight exceeds thirty-seven, meaning that if you make it to one hundred, you'll have spent more years retired than you spent working!

Let me pound the metaphorical table: no matter how many times your financial planner or the Social Security system references life expectancy, *you can't count on dying on time.* Averages are not useful in this situation. Therefore, your life expectancy isn't your proper planning horizon.

So what *is* your proper planning horizon? As crazy as it sounds, it's your maximum life span: the oldest age to which you could live.

If you're fifty and your maximum life span is one hundred, your planning horizon should be fifty years, not thirty-two years. That's

56 percent longer! Clearly, getting your planning horizon right will make all the difference in the world to your decisions about how much to save and when to retire for good.

THE FINANCIAL RISK OF LIVING TOO LONG AFTER RETIRING TOO EARLY

Put yourself in twenty-five-year-old Martha's shoes. Martha's appropriate planning horizon is seventy-five years since we'll assume her maximum age will be one hundred. Let's also assume she makes $100,000 in today's dollars through age sixty-two—the age Martha wants to retire. Finally, posit that Martha's savings are invested in safe Treasury bonds, which keep up with inflation but don't provide a real return beyond that.

How much does Martha need to sock away each year until she turns sixty-two to ensure she'll be able to maintain her spending through age one hundred? Martha can spend almost $50,000 annually (in today's dollars) on a discretionary basis right through age one hundred. (Discretionary spending refers to all expenditures Martha makes beyond what she has to spend on fixed—off-the-top—expenses, such as housing, federal and state taxes, and special expenses, which could include tuition payments, alimony payments, car loan payments, etc.) In order to reach that $50,000 goal by sixty-two—even including Social Security benefits and a 401(k) plan—she would have to save $20,000 per year. That's 20 percent of her pretaxed annual earnings, but since the savings would have to come out after necessary expenses like taxes and housing, it's really more like 40 percent of her yearly $50,000 discretionary income. Will Martha have the discipline to save, after giving Social Security and her retirement plan a major chunk of change, namely two dollars out of every five dollars she has to spend on housing, food, entertainment, travel, etc.? Not likely.

So how can Martha plan to save what's needed to maintain her living standard as long as necessary? Let's suppose she sticks her head in the sand and plans to die right on schedule—at her life expectancy, namely age eighty-two. As for living past eighty-two, she has two words: "never happen." This approach dramatically shortens Martha's retirement-planning horizon, cutting her requisite preretirement saving almost in half. It also increases what she can smoothly spend, after taxes, to almost $60,000 a year. Martha previously had to save two dollars for every five dollars she spent. Now it's just one dollar.

Fast-forward and join Martha at her eighty-second combined birthday and going-away party. All her friends and relatives join her as she thanks them for filling her life with love and joy. "But tonight, dearly beloveds, is my last on God's good earth. I've reached my life expectancy. Tomorrow I will be no more."

With this mournful proclamation, Martha bids farewell and falls asleep, fully expecting to awaken before the pearly gates. But when her eyes open, she finds herself right where she bedded down in her fourth-floor walk-up. Martha immediately realizes that she has not a penny left in the bank, having carefully arranged to die as the last dollar was spent. Despondent about her looming penury and worried about missing her heavenly appointment, Martha considers opening a window and jumping.

MAXIMUM AGE OF LIFE IS THE CORRECT PLANNING HORIZON

Fortunately, Martha's economist sister, Margaret, comes to the financial rescue and Martha lives happily ever after, apart from Margaret's weekly reminder: "Martha. You're not a statistic. You're an outcome."

Margaret's got it just right. Every statistic, at its core, is an average of outcomes. When it comes to considering your life expectancy, think of yourself as just one of those outcomes. You may die early or late but never on time. The same is true for everyone with your general characteristics. Your life expectancy is just the average of the eventual death ages of tens of thousands of people just like you.

Since you're going to kick the bucket once and only once, and you don't know when that will be, there's only one longevity outcome to which you need to pay particular attention. It's the financial worst-case outcome—the one in which you live to your maximum age of life. Still, something down deep leads us to assume there is no chance whatsoever of ending up a Methuselah. Our certitude is, no doubt, influenced by pain avoidance. Thinking about becoming very old is—let's be honest—a scary and depressing activity. After all, the longer we live, the less we're going to like what we see in the mirror, the less money we'll have left to spend, and the less we'll be able to do. The emotional pain we experience in contemplating tomorrow may be why so many of us pretend we'll die either early or on time. But we *are* our future self and have no option but to look out for that person.

I can't tell you how many heated arguments I've had over the years about the proper planning horizon, many of them with financial planners. But the argument ends when I add this economics longevity maxim:

Plan to your maximum age, but place a bet on the favorable odds that you'll die before your maximum.

In other words, set your planning horizon at your maximum age even if you doubt you'll make it that far. But spend relatively more when you're young with the knowledge that you'll be forced to spend less when you're old if you keep on keeping on. Yes, if you stay alive, you'll have a moderately lower living standard, but you won't be leaving your future self with absolutely nothing. And there's a good chance that as you make it into the later stages of old age, your ability to spend, at least on physically demanding activities, like traveling, will decline anyway.

To this end, let's return to Martha and see how much less she'll need to save if she plans to live to age one hundred but also plans to have her living standard drop by 1 percent every successive year after age seventy-five. This is a significant early death bet. If Martha makes it to one hundred, her living standard will be 22 percent lower than at age seventy-five, but the trade-off is that she won't have to save quite as much in order to stick with her plan.

How big is the difference? Recall that during her working years Martha has to save twenty cents out of every dollar she earns if she plans to perfectly smooth her living standard right through age one hundred. With a planned post-age-seventy-five living-standard decline, Martha can save less—but not that much less. She now gets to spend 5 percent more each year prior to age seventy-five and needs to save eighteen, not twenty, cents of every dollar earned, which translates into thirty-six, not forty, cents per every dollar spent.

So while a reasonable death bet can slightly change the retirement savings calculus, it really needs to be only a small part of your plan. Are there any bigger parts? Let's see if working longer can make a difference.

THE MAGIC OF DELAYED RETIREMENT

Surely there must be a more efficient way for Martha to ensure her standard of living through the ripe old age of one hundred without saving at a crazy-high rate or resorting to drastic measures. There is, and it's simply not retiring too early.

Martha, as you know, hauls in a healthy one hundred grand annually. Ignoring taxes and other considerations, working an extra five years translates into $500,000 in higher lifetime earnings. That's a huge sum. Even at the extremely aggressive $20,000 per year savings clip we talked about earlier, it would take her twenty-five years to save what she'd make by working just five more years.

Of course, we can't ignore federal and state taxes. They'd take close to $150,000 off the top of the extra $500,000 Martha would earn. But there are two pieces of good news. First, Martha would pick up another $30,000 in employer 401(k) contributions by working five extra years. Second, Martha would avoid another mistake: namely taking Social Security as soon as she can, at sixty-two. By working longer, thereby delaying her receipt of Social Security, her retirement benefit won't be reduced by what's called the "early retirement reduction." Indeed, if she doesn't take benefits until retiring at sixty-seven, she will get her full retirement benefit, netting a whopping $280,000 in additional lifetime benefits if she lives to one hundred!

What does working till sixty-seven do to Martha's sustainable living standard—what she can afford to spend year after year apart from paying taxes? Without the increase in lifetime Social Security benefits, Martha's living-standard improvement is 10 percent. With the increase, it's 17 percent. This is huge. By retiring five years later, Martha can spend 17 percent more year in and year out *for seventy-five years*—starting immediately and continuing through age one hundred.

What does retiring later mean for Martha's required saving during her working years? Does she still need to sock away twenty cents for every dollar she earns to achieve a stable living standard both before and after retirement? No. Her new preretirement saving rate is now twelve cents per dollar earned. That's substantial but far more manageable.

Retiring later would have a similarly positive effect on Martha's lifetime finances regardless of how much she earns throughout her lifetime, and in fact, the effect is magnified slightly at lower income levels. For example, if Martha made $50,000 rather than $100,000 per year, she would get an 18 percent annual living-standard raise rather than 17 percent. And if Martha earned $200,000, the living-standard gain would be 15 percent. The message here is that retiring later is a somewhat bigger deal for low earners, given our country's progressive fiscal system.

RETIRING LATER FOR OLDER WORKERS

Of course, while at age twenty-five Martha has started to lay out a plan for retirement, most folks don't think about retirement seriously until much later in life. If working five more years is such a good deal for a twenty-five-year-old, what does it mean for people who, say, just turned sixty-two and are deciding whether to retire immediately or stick it out till sixty-seven?

Consider hypothetical Nebraska couple Ray and Sue, both age sixty-two and both with jobs that pay $75,000 per year. Combined, they have $1 million in 401(k) accounts and own a modest $300,000 house free and clear. They are proud of their $1 million nest egg. It represents almost seven years of work. But divide $1 million by the thirty-eight years they could live and we're talking $26,000 per year—not quite as impressive when you think about it that way. Now whack that by about 10 percent to account for federal and state income taxes and they're left with a total retirement income only a bit above the federal poverty line. Things look a lot better if we add in each spouse's $23,000 annual, age-sixty-two Social Security benefit. Ray and Sue would then have a total of $72,000 a year to live on. But that's before paying income taxes, Medicare Part B premiums, premiums for a supplemental Medicare policy, out-of-pocket healthcare costs, property taxes, homeowner's insurance, home maintenance, and car insurance. Deducting all these expenses leaves them with about $50,000 a year for everything else. That's $4,167 per month, $961 per week, and $137 per day. Not too shabby, especially for Nebraska. But Sue's mom is in a costly nursing home, and Ray's dad will move into one soon, with both needing Ray and Sue's financial help. This is why the couple is rethinking their early retirement dream.

Working till sixty-seven would mean $750,000 more in combined pretax earnings. It also would mean, as we saw with Martha, higher Social Security benefits once they started. Put these two factors together and the couple's increase in annual spending power would be a striking 33 percent. That's roughly twice the gain Martha would see if she retired late. How come? Because the extra labor earnings will be spread out over far fewer years.

Ray and Sue are middle class, actually, upper middle class. But tens of millions of Rays and Sues reach retirement with even worse savings shortages. We Americans just don't save well. As a group, we seem to think Uncle Sam and our employer's retirement plan will keep us comfortable in retirement. Not the case. Indeed, if Ray and Sue had the median baby boomer wealth of just $144,000 in their combined 401(k)s, retiring at sixty-seven rather than sixty-two would mean a 51 percent higher living standard for the rest of their days!

RECAP

Let me tell you what I told you:

- A surefire way to make money, potentially lots of money from your financial perspective, is simply to delay your retirement.
- It's easy to fall into the trap of thinking that you'll die on schedule, exactly at your life expectancy. Don't be fooled. Virtually no one dies on time.

- Your life expectancy is a statistic—an average. You're not an average. You're an individual outcome in the making.

- Since you're going to die when your number is called, not when a statistician says you should, your life expectancy is of zero value to your financial planning. My advice: fuhgeddaboudit!

- Plan for a longevity catastrophe, dying at what, financially speaking, is the worst possible time: your maximum age of life. The longer you last, the longer you'll need to clothe, feed, house, entertain, and maintain yourself.

- Planning for your maximum age of life is critical to deciding when you should retire. Otherwise, you'll likely save far too little and jump your job ship far too early.

- Setting your planning horizon based on your maximum age of life doesn't mean ignoring the virtual certitude that you won't live that long. Economics counsels placing a death bet as large as is desired. Doing so is easy. Simply spend somewhat earlier in retirement knowing that if you lose the bet and keep on living, you'll need to spend somewhat less in later years.

- These days, with safe investments yielding nothing after inflation, saving for a potentially very long retirement is extremely tough. It requires much more discipline than most of us have. Retiring substantially later than you've planned is surely your best move. If you're young, your required retirement saving will be much less, but it will still be far more than you think. If you're old and you've saved too little, retiring later can represent financial salvation.

- Retiring early typically means taking Social Security benefits early. For most households, this is a ginormous financial mistake.

CHAPTER 3

Social Security — Ten Secrets to Maximizing Your Lifetime Benefits

Social Security is a much bigger financial deal than many of us think. For younger people, it may feel like something that exists only for politicians to argue over. For people in their peak earning years, during the middle of their careers, it may just feel like a vehicle for taking a chunk out of their paychecks. Even for older people, Social Security can be taken for granted. If the government sets the amount of your Social Security benefits, why bother worrying about it? In truth, Social Security is one of the most important, if not *the* most important, financial factor in most people's lives. And you have the power to raise, indeed maximize, your benefits. I'm about to share ten key secrets for turning Social Security into your personal gold mine. Before doing so, let me give you a sense, via a pretend person named Sandy, of its financial importance.

Sandy's a single, childless, fifty-year-old Kansan who earns $50,000 annually, has accumulated three years' worth of earnings in her 401(k), gets a 3 percent employer match on her own 3 percent 401(k) contribution, has half a year's earnings in her checking account, and has a twenty-year mortgage on her $250,000 house. She plans to retire and start taking Social Security at age sixty-two.

Sandy currently has five assets: her remaining lifetime labor earnings, her retirement accounts, the equity in her home (its value less the mortgage), her regular assets (her checking account), and her lifetime Social Security benefits. Which is the largest? Social Security, and by a good margin. Her lifetime benefits, which total $724,000, exceed her remaining lifetime labor earnings of $650,000. The present value of her future 401(k) withdrawals is $191,000. As for her home equity and regular assets, they total only $50,000 and $25,000 respectively.

Thinking of all your future Social Security benefits as your *personal* financial asset, like your checking account, may seem strange. But that's what Social Security is, and once you see it that way, you'll realize that you need to manage the benefits no less than you need to manage all your assets. But why is it your personal financial asset? Because it reflects your paying 12.4 percent of every dollar earned in covered employment—jobs in which Social Security FICA taxes are levied on your compensation. Congress calls half of the 12.4 percent an employer tax and half an employee tax. It does that to make us think employers are actually paying taxes for us and that our personal FICA tax burden is half as big as it actually is. But our bosses aren't our friends, they aren't our parents, and they aren't our rich aunts and uncles. Anything they pay on our behalf comes out of our economic hides in the form of reduced take-home pay. And every dollar of every benefit for which you are eligible is a dollar that belongs to you.* That's why, when it comes to Social

---

* Yes, some will say we have no legal claim to any benefits—they are simply government benefits that can be changed at any time. Social Security lawyers who specialize in helping you get benefits to which you are legally entitled will tell you otherwise. But the issue here is economics, not legalities. All our assets, regardless of whether someone

Security, you need to "get what's yours." Doing so means managing this asset. In Sandy's case, it's the most important asset for her to manage for a simple reason: *it's her largest.*

Now consider 3× Sandy, Sandy's financial clone except that every non–Social Security resource of hers is three times larger. In other words, 3× Sandy earns three times more, has three times more in her 401(k), owns a house worth three times more with a three times larger mortgage, and so on.

3× Sandy's lifetime earnings log in at $1,950,000. Her future Social Security benefits are worth $1,290,000. That's less than twice Sandy's amount. This is benefit progressivity at play. Up to a point, higher earnings produce higher benefits, but the benefits are not proportionately higher. Still, Social Security represents 3×'s second-largest asset.

How about 6× Sandy? Her lifetime benefits are $1,300,000—not much different from 3×'s. However, 6×'s lifetime labor earnings total $3,900,000. Despite the fact that the gulf between first and second place is much larger, Social Security is still 6×'s second-largest asset. The present value of her future 401(k) withdrawals—$1,150,000—is a close third.

When considering our future financial security, we stay up nights thinking about optimizing our lifetime earnings—whether to switch jobs, change careers, retire early. We also worry about retirement-account decisions. Should we contribute more? Should we open a Roth IRA? How should we invest? Will Roth conversions help? When and how should we take the money? What are required minimum distributions about? What most of us don't think about is how to handle our Social Security.

You might say, "But Social Security benefits are set by the

---

calls them private or public, can be augmented or reduced, indeed even confiscated, by Uncle Sam at the stroke of a pen via a spending or tax bill or right of eminent domain.

government. They'll be what they'll be. I can't change them. Why bother worrying about them?"

Actually, there are many ways to turn your lifetime Social Security benefits into a treasure trove.

SECRET 1: KNOW THY BENEFITS

Social Security provides lots of benefits—thirteen in total—most of which you've probably never heard about. Here's the list:

1. Retirement benefit
2. Disability benefit
3. Spousal benefit
4. Divorced spousal benefit
5. Child-in-care spousal benefit
6. Widow(er) benefit
7. Child benefit
8. Disabled child benefit
9. Mother (father) benefit
10. Divorced widow(er) benefit
11. Parent benefit
12. Grandchild benefit
13. Death benefit

Social Security is full of rules, many age based, that limit when and how you can collect benefits and provide benefits to others. Still, there are big bucks available from running the bureaucrats' gauntlet.

Spousal and divorced spousal benefits are provided to current spouses and exes. But the exes can't collect unless they did their time. They need to have stuck it out with you for at least ten years. They don't need to have lived with you for the full decade, let alone shared the same bed. They just need to have stayed legally married to you that long. They also can't have remarried if they want to collect divorced spousal benefits on your record. (If this sounds like provisions written by men, you're getting the picture.)

Child and disabled child benefits are available to young children and any older children who were disabled before age twenty-two. The child-in-care spousal benefit is for your spouse who is caring for your young or disabled child. For your spouse and kids to collect any of these benefits, you need to be taking your retirement benefit. That's not the case for your ex. They can collect divorced spousal benefits provided they, to repeat, spent a decade married to you, you're at least sixty-two, you've been divorced for more than two years, and guess what: *they're single!*

To provide your dependents, exes, and even dependent parents with survivor benefits based on your work record, the first thing you need to do is die. Once you're out of the way, everyone can try to cash in, starting with pocketing your measly death benefit. Survivor benefits are more lucrative than dependent benefits. So make sure your ninety-year-old mom, to whom you've been providing at least half support, knows she can collect a handsome parent benefit—three-quarters of your full retirement benefit—the minute you take your permanent leave.

Widow(er) benefits are available starting at age fifty for disabled widow(er)s and at age sixty for nondisabled widow(er)s. If your spouse takes care of your young or disabled child after you pass, they can collect a mother (father) benefit.

With Social Security, there's always a nasty catch-22. One of these is its maximum family benefit, which limits what your kids, spouses, and parents can jointly collect based on your earnings record. Once both spouses start collecting their retirement benefits, their family benefit maximums are combined. This can relieve the constraint on what can be paid to dependents. If benefits owed to dependents exceed the relevant family benefit max, they'll receive a proportionate split. Fortunately, the split is spelled out in the law. This avoids what would otherwise be a bloody intrafamily fight over your Social Security remains.

Exes who qualify and are single or *remarried after age sixty* (feeling the sexism?) can collect a divorced widow(er) benefit. But what exes get doesn't come out of the maximum family benefit available to surviving spouses and children. Someone in Congress was smart enough to keep your exes and your current spouse far apart when it comes to collecting off dead you.

SECRET 2: USE IT OR LOSE IT

Social Security is a use it or lose it system. If you don't formally request a benefit for which you are eligible, you won't get it. Social Security isn't in the business of letting us know what it owes us, never mind that we have paid FICA taxes our entire working lives for those benefits.

I've had many people in their mid-seventies ask me when Social Security will start sending them their check. That's when I groan and tell them they need to file for their benefit immediately. Waiting beyond seventy to collect won't raise your monthly amount. You'll just lose a month in benefits for every month you wait to apply. They will cut you a slight break, as Social Security will pay you benefits six months in arrears, but that's it. Therefore, someone age seventy-three and a half who hasn't filed and is due a $30,000 annual benefit has already kissed $75,000 goodbye.

More than sixty-four million Americans—almost one in six—are collecting Social Security benefits. They've obviously all made benefit-collection decisions. Many have additional benefit-collection decisions to make. Everyone else has all their collection decisions on their to-do list. Therefore, we're either all in the Social Security decision-making boat or have colleagues, friends, and relatives in the boat. Yet Social Security is rarely discussed in everyday conversation. So you shouldn't count on learning about available benefits by accident.

Here's your primary Social Security homework assignment (recall, I'm a professor!): Identify all the benefits you can collect and when you can collect them. And, it goes without saying, make sure to apply for them on time. Be aware that consulting the Social Security Administration's website or its staff can lead you badly astray. The website is highly misleading. As for SSA staffers, half of what they tell you, from my experience, is either wrong, misleading, or incomplete. There's a reason they do such a poor job. The system is incredibly complicated, and the staff is underpaid, overworked, and undertrained. Unfortunately, they're convinced they have everything right.

Let me tell you about Marjorie; I helped her collect a particular benefit. Marjorie went to her local Social Security office and was told she wasn't eligible. She then contacted me and said she thought she was eligible based on a column I'd written. I told her she certainly was eligible and to return to the office and ask the staffer to call me. Lo and behold, I received a call from the staffer the next day. She proceeded to scream at me for half an hour that I was completely wrong about the benefit in question. I could barely get a word in edgewise, but in the end I managed to say, "Let me make sure I have your name and the name of your office right as I'll be posting a column about this conversation in an hour." She then uttered an oath and hung up on me. Ten minutes later, she called back with an entirely different tone of voice. She'd spoken with her supervisor and now agreed I was right. Would I accept her apology? "Absolutely," I said. I never wrote the column.

SECRET 3: SHOP AROUND

If Social Security provisions can be so complicated (which they are), if the information provided on the Social Security Administration's website can be so misleading (which it is), and if SSA staffers can give such bad advice (which they do), how can you be sure you're getting what's yours?

First, read up on the system. Yours truly coauthored a bestseller on the topic.* Second, shop around. Go to different offices, talk to different staffers on the phone, ask to speak to supervisors, and don't take no for an answer if you're sure you've got it right and they have it wrong. In complex cases involving auxiliary benefits paid to dependents, Social Security has its staffers calculate by hand what you'll get. Given the mistakes they make in the process, you literally may get a better deal down the street. Unbelievable but true. Also, be aware that you can insist on filing for a particular benefit even if the SSA tells you that you aren't eligible. The SSA can't refuse to let you apply for benefits, and by filing you protect your appeal rights.

There are a variety of online tools that you can buy and use (one of which my company provides†). The SSA has its own online calculators. I'd avoid those. They can both under- and overestimate your future benefit. If you're under sixty, the age up to which your past covered earnings are wage indexed, Social Security assumes there is neither economy-wide, average-wage growth nor inflation. If you're, say, forty, their tools can easily understate your future benefits by one-fifth. And if you're working, their tools may assume you will continue to earn at your current level through full

---

* *Get What's Yours*—a *New York Times* bestseller that I coauthored with *PBS NewsHour* economic correspondent Paul Solman and longtime personal finance writer Phil Moeller.

† Maximize My Social Security is my company's tool (Maximizemysocialsecurity .com).

retirement age. If that's not the case, you may wind up with an over-statement of your future benefit.

I'd also avoid free online calculators, which fully justify the expression "quick and dirty."

SECRET 4: WAIT TO COLLECT

Suppose Sandy, 3× Sandy, and 6× Sandy retire at age sixty-two as planned but make one crucial change to their Social Security collection strategy. They wait till age seventy to begin collecting their retirement benefit. Does this affect their lifetime benefits? It certainly does. It raises each Sandy's lifetime benefits by hundreds of thousands of dollars!

Sandy gets an increase of $267,520. That's more than a quarter of a million shiny greenbacks! Imagine Sandy walking out her front door and seeing an eight-story-high stack of one-dollar bills — all hers for the spending. For 3× and 6×, the increases are $474,616 and $476,010, or close to half a million dead presidents towering fifteen stories high on their front stoops.

Let me explain where all this free Social Security money comes from. As we've covered earlier, benefits are reduced if you take them early. The reduction is roughly 7 percent for every year you collect before your full — also called "normal" — Social Security retirement age (sixty-seven for those like Sandy, who were born in 1960 or later). The precise reduction is five-ninths of 1 percent per month for the first thirty-six months of reduction and five-twelfths of 1 percent for any remaining months of reduction. In addition, starting your retirement benefit beyond Social Security's normal retirement age generates delayed retirement credits (DRCs). These are benefit increases of 8 percent per year (two-thirds of 1 percent per month) for each year you wait to start collecting. DRCs only accumulate through age seventy, so, as recently mentioned, your benefit won't be larger if you wait beyond seventy to collect.

The reductions for taking benefits early and the increases for taking them late are called actuarial adjustments. They are meant to compensate for getting benefits for more years, on average, if you started benefits early. But the calculations governing the reductions and increases were made decades ago, when interest rates were high and people didn't live as long. These days, the Social Security Administration overpays us at an astounding rate for being patient.

The retirement benefit for each Sandy will be roughly 76 percent higher if they start collecting at age seventy rather than at age sixty-two. Take 3× Sandy: If she starts receiving her benefit at sixty-two and makes it to one hundred, she'll receive $32,008 per year in each of the following thirty-eight years. If she waits till seventy, she'll collect $56,364 annually for the following thirty years. That's where the $474,000 difference comes from.*

You're now allowed to scream *"Wow!"* Sandy can effectively score more than five years of extra labor earnings simply by waiting eight years to apply for her Social Security retirement benefit. For 3×, the benefit pickup is equivalent to more than three years of labor earnings. For 6×, it's more than one and a half years' earnings.

But what about taxes? Are there extra taxes on the extra benefits? There are, but there's also an offsetting tax advantage that makes the extra benefits essentially tax-free. First, some background: You pay federal income tax on half of your benefits if your total income (calculated as adjusted gross income plus nontaxable interest income plus half of your Social Security benefits) exceeds

---

* But should you place full value on benefits you may not be likely to collect? The economics answer is an unambiguous *yes* as a matter of financial arbitrage. A guaranteed stream of real (inflation-adjusted) Social Security benefits is no different from a stream of equal-sized coupon payments from a Treasury-issued inflation-indexed bond.

$25,000 ($32,000 if you're married) and is less than $34,000 ($44,000 if you're married). If your total income exceeds $34,000 ($44,000 if you're married), another 35 percent of your benefits becomes taxable. Unlike most provisions in the federal income tax, these thresholds aren't indexed for inflation. So over time, as each generation earns more and receives more dollars in benefits, a larger share of Social Security recipients—heading to 100 percent—will face federal income taxation on 85 percent of all their Social Security benefits.

Having your benefits repossessed by Uncle Sam is no fun. (There are other expressions.) But the delay in receiving benefits produces a subtle offsetting tax reduction. While waiting till age seventy to collect benefits, the three Sandys spend the bulk of their regular assets. This means that in their sixties their taxable income is lower because they aren't collecting benefits, and after age seventy their taxable income is lower because they don't have as much taxable regular-asset income. This smoothing of their taxable income puts the Sandys in lower tax brackets—so low that the extra benefits entail, on balance, virtually no extra lifetime taxes.*

Waiting until seventy to receive Social Security isn't feasible for everyone. Many people take Social Security early or at full retirement age because they have no option—they have nothing else to live on. Others need to activate child, disabled child, child-in-care spousal, or spousal benefits. Yet others know for sure their remaining days are strictly numbered due to health conditions. But here's my Social Security plea: before making any moves, figure out the strategy that maximizes your household's total lifetime benefits. Bear in mind: *Deciding when to take Social Security may be among the most important financial decisions you ever make.*

---

* Another plus is that you would need to be an even higher earner than 6× before you'd have to pay Kansas state income taxes on your Social Security benefits. As for the other states, only twelve tax Social Security benefits.

One warning: If you're planning to begin collecting Social Security at seventy, expect to receive a scam phone call a few months before your seventieth birthday. It won't be an illegal scam call. It will be an official scam call from the Social Security Administration itself. They may have changed their policy by the time you read this, but currently, people close to seventy are receiving offers from the SSA to begin their retirement benefit retroactive to six months from the date of the call. The carrot dangled is getting a big check equal to six months of past-due benefits. The scam offers are also made when someone close to seventy calls the SSA to request that their benefits begin at seventy.

Taking this deal will cost you the remaining monthly DRCs until you hit seventy plus the additional six months of DRCs. For example, suppose you're four months away from reaching seventy. If you take Social Security's deal, they'll send you a check for six months of benefits based on what you would have received had you started taking your benefit six months ago. Going for their "deal" means losing ten months of DRCs. Your benefit will be lower, *forever,* by 6.67 percent. When they twist your arm to take their offer, the SSA won't necessarily mention that it comes with this permanent benefit loss. That's why it's a scam—it's good for the SSA but bad for you.

I first heard about this con in my dentist's chair. I asked him about his plans for taking Social Security, not realizing he was already over seventy. "Oh, I waited till seventy." Several minutes of drilling later, he said, "Actually, the people at Social Security were really great. They called me a couple of months early and offered to give me six months of benefits for free. I was really impressed. They gave me the maximum benefit and the extra six months' check." At that point, I had to decide whether to burst his bubble. He had no idea that the check he was getting and would be getting every month was less than would otherwise have been the case. I decided that he might be able to warn someone else, so, yes, I told him he'd been scammed. My bill ended up higher than expected.

If you're still several years from turning seventy, it's also reasonable to be concerned about whether the government will make good on the benefits you're owed. Social Security's long-term finances, like those of the federal government in general, are abysmal. The system has an unfunded liability—the present-value difference between all projected future outlays and all projected receipts—of $53 trillion.[1] That's roughly two and a half years of GDP. No one knows how this red ink will be covered. Certainly, cutting the benefits of current or near-term retirees would be very difficult to enact politically. Still, even a major permanent cut of, say, 20 percent starting around 2030 wouldn't reverse the general prescription to wait till age seventy to collect your retirement benefit. Yes, the advantage of waiting would be smaller, but it would remain huge. Why? Because you'll face the benefit cut either way.

SECRET 5: BEQUEATH HIGHER BENEFITS

Waiting to collect Social Security benefits provides yet another potential bonanza available to Sandy—or actually to Sandy's spouse. It comes in the form of survivor benefits. Consider 3× Sandy and add a spouse, Jane, with the same birth date but an $11,696 annual age-sixty-two benefit—about one-third of 3×'s.

If 3× passes away at seventy, having taken her benefit starting at sixty-two, Jane will start receiving 3×'s check instead of her own.* That's an annual increase of $25,805—pretty good money. But if 3× waits till seventy to collect, the increase is even bigger. Jane's

---

* The SSA will describe this as Jane's receiving her own retirement benefits plus excess survivor benefits equal to the difference in 3×'s age-seventy benefits and Jane's age-sixty-two benefits. But the simple description is that Jane will receive Sandy's full check when Sandy dies.

$11,696 annual payment flips to $56,364, for an increase of $44,668. If Jane makes it to age one hundred, she'll end up having collected $565,890 more in survivor benefits than if 3× Sandy had taken her benefits early.

Even if Sandy and Jane were divorced, Jane could still stand to collect the same benefit under certain circumstances. What's true for surviving spouses is also true for surviving ex-spouses, provided the ex was married to the decedent for at least ten years and is either single or got remarried after age sixty. So even if Sandy had multiple exes, they could all potentially benefit from Sandy's waiting till seventy to collect.

What happens if you die between full retirement age and age seventy without ever starting your Social Security? Spousal and divorced spouse survivor benefits are based on the retirement benefit you would have collected had you started collecting in the month you died. And if you die before full retirement age without having started collecting your retirement benefit, the SSA will use your full retirement benefit to figure survivor benefits. If you started collecting before kicking, Social Security will use a complex formula, called the RIB-LIM (retirement insurance benefit limitation), that makes survivor benefits higher in some cases, if you took your benefits closer to full retirement age.

What about survivor benefits afforded to young children and children of any age who were disabled prior to age twenty-two? Do these benefits also depend on when you start collecting your own retirement benefit? The answer's actually no. These survivor benefits are based on your full retirement benefit, not on the actual retirement benefit you collect before you die.*

Here's a sad but true story about how delaying Social Security retirement-benefit collection can matter to lower-earning surviving

---

* The same holds for parent benefits.

spouses. I attended a dinner party some years back and started talking with Brian, a sixty-eight-year-old heart surgeon I had never met. Brian had learned from the party's host that I wrote about Social Security. After a couple of minutes of pleasantries, he startled me with the news that he'd been diagnosed a month earlier with pancreatic cancer and had at most two years to live. I expressed my deep sympathy. Next Brian relayed that he'd been waiting till seventy to collect Social Security. But when he got the diagnosis, he went to the local Social Security office and told them his situation. They told him that since he had very little time left to collect, he should take his retirement benefit immediately and that they'd pay him six months of benefits retroactively. He agreed and had just received a check.

I asked Brian whether his wife, Pam, worked and whether the SSA staffer had asked him about her earnings history. "No, I was always on call. So she stayed home bringing up our three children. And, no, the staffer didn't ask if I was married."

I then told Brian that the good folks at the SSA had given him terrible advice. "If you wait to collect and make it to seventy, Pam will receive a 16 percent higher monthly survivor benefit, adjusted for inflation, for the rest of her life. Getting her higher lifetime survivor benefits is far more important financially than starting your retirement benefit now. Fortunately, you have a year from the time you start receiving a benefit to withdraw the application for it. You'll need to return the money you've received. But you'll get a Social Security do-over. And whatever delayed retirement credits you end up receiving yourself, Pam's check will be permanently higher as a result." Brian got the point and said he'd withdraw his application.

The moral here is that maximizing your family's benefits can be at odds with maximizing your own benefits. This arises in other situations as well. Suppose you reach age sixty-two with a young or disabled child and a spouse who cares for the child. Once you start collecting your retirement benefit, they can collect a disabled child benefit and a child-in-care spousal benefit. Thus, your waiting to collect more for yourself will reduce your family's lifetime benefits. Your optimal move in this situation is generally to wait, but not all the way to seventy. Note, however, in the case of a disabled child who is collecting a Supplemental Security Income (SSI) benefit and/or a disability benefit based on their own work record, every dollar of the Social Security disabled child benefit you provide them in the course of collecting your retirement benefit will reduce the sum of their SSI and their own disability benefit by a dollar. Therefore, for parents of disabled children collecting SSI and/or their own disability benefit, waiting till seventy will likely remain best.

SECRET 6: SUSPEND AND RESTART

After reading the last few secrets, you may be kicking yourself for having taken your retirement benefit too soon. However, if you're between full retirement age and seventy, you can reduce the damage by suspending your benefit and restarting it at seventy. When you restart, you'll receive a bump up to your retirement benefit that accounts for the DRCs you accrued during the months your benefit was in suspension.

Unfortunately, when you suspend your retirement benefit, you also suspend any benefits that your spouse or children are collecting or could collect based on your work record. Once you restart your retirement benefit, their benefits will also restart, but they will remain at their former values apart from an inflation adjustment. Unfortunately, there are no DRC-type actuarial increases for benefits other than the retirement benefit.

SECRET 7: GENERALLY IGNORE THE EARNINGS TEST

This is a really important secret. If you elect to receive Social Security benefits before the year in which you reach full retirement age, Social Security will reduce your benefits by fifty cents for every dollar you earn above what's called the exempt amount. In 2021, the exempt amount was $18,960. Once you reach January 1 of the year you'll turn full retirement age (sixty-seven for anyone born in 1960 or later), the amount you lose for every dollar you earn above the exempt amount drops to thirty-three cents, and the exempt amount itself jumps to $50,520. On the first day of the month you turn full retirement age, the earnings test comes to a glorious end, meaning there is no benefit loss associated with earning more money.

Piled on top of all the other taxes we face, these age-dependent earnings tests can feel beyond egregious. To see why, suppose you're sixty-three, you lost your $50,000 per year job six months ago, and you've started collecting your reduced, $20,000 annual retirement benefit. Six months later your old boss calls and wants to rehire you. Returning to work seems to make absolutely no sense. After paying Social Security and Medicare (FICA) taxes, federal income taxes, state income taxes, and losing $15,880 in Social Security benefits, you're left with about $20,000 for a year's work. This represents a 60 percent tax. Why work hard only to pay 60 cents of every dollar in taxes?

Fortunately, this Social Security earnings test is, for most people, largely a terrible ruse. It's a ruse because when you look carefully, it almost entirely disappears. It's terrible because most people don't realize this and decide not to go back to work. Consequently, they lose loads of money by not making money they think is exorbitantly taxed when it's not.

The earnings test basically disappears due to another Social Security provision, which most people have never heard about. It's called the "adjustment of the reduction factor." The reduction factor refers to having your benefit reduced due to taking it early. In principle, the benefit reduction should be applied only to months in which you actually collected your benefit early. If you lose months of benefits due to the earnings test, then, philosophically, your benefit reduction should not include those months. In other words, the degree of early retirement benefit reduction should be reduced. And that's what happens. But this reduction in the reduction occurs with a lag—when you reach full retirement age. At that point, Social Security increases your benefit on a permanent basis by enough, in most cases, to make you almost exactly break even.

Here's an easier way to grasp this bizarre taking-from-the-right-pocket-and-giving-to-the-left-pocket: Suppose you filed for early retirement benefits on your sixty-second birthday, and that same day you were offered and took a very high-paying job—high enough to wipe out all your benefits via the earnings test straight through that month when you turned full retirement age, at which point you permanently retire. Due to the adjustment of the reduction factor, your benefit at full retirement age will be no different whatsoever had you never filed for the benefit at sixty-two!* In other words, you aren't penalized for going back to work. Furthermore, once you reach age sixty-seven, full retirement age, you can suspend your retirement benefit and restart it in the month you turn seventy. The age-seventy amount will also be no different had you never filed back at age sixty-two.

The reduction factor applies not just to your own retirement benefit but also to other benefits you may have taken early and lost

---

* By the way, you would end up in the same place had you withdrawn your application for retirement benefits within a year of starting to collect what turned out, after the earnings test, to be nothing.

due to an earnings test, including spousal, divorced spousal, widow(er), and divorced widow(er) benefits—all of which (with one important exception we'll get to) are reduced if taken early.

The major caveat to what I've just said is that if you switch to a higher benefit, say your widow(er) benefit, at full retirement, the fact that your retirement benefit has been raised won't be of any help since, effectively speaking, you won't be collecting it down the road. In this case, the earnings test does represent a horrific tax on working. Given this, your best move may be to take your retirement benefit early and call it quits, work-wise.

SECRET 8: IF ELIGIBLE, COLLECT FREE SPOUSAL BENEFITS

A big change was made to Social Security law in 2015 that presented those born before January 1, 1954, with a benefit treat: the ability to collect a spousal benefit while letting their own retirement benefit accumulate DRCs. There's a catch, of course. The partner of the person claiming the spousal benefit needs to be taking their retirement benefit. For example, consider a sixty-nine-year-old wife born in 1953 with a sixty-two-year-old husband. If the husband files for his early retirement benefit and the wife files just for her spousal benefit, she'll collect half her husband's full (not early) retirement benefit for one year before filing for her own retirement benefit at seventy (assuming it's larger than her spousal benefit). Suppose the husband's annual full retirement benefit is $30,000. While waiting until seventy to collect her maximum retirement benefit, the wife can collect $15,000 for a year.

Most eligible couples have no idea this free money is available. A couple of years ago, on a flight back from a conference, I was seated next to a seventy-two-year-old Harvard economics professor who is viewed as among the top macroeconomists in the world. I'll call him Frank. At some point it dawned on me that (a) Frank was collecting his retirement benefit and (b) his wife might have been born before January 1, 1954. I asked. Sure enough, his wife was just old enough and had just reached full retirement age. In a few seconds, I made Frank more than $50,000, whereupon I suggested he take my wife and me to dinner (which he did).

The point of telling you about Frank, apart from making clear that this money magic trick is real, is that the spouse collecting their retirement benefit can be older than the spouse filing for just their spousal benefit while letting their retirement benefit accumulate DRCs.

Unfortunately, this money trick won't be available after January 1, 2024. It will be phased out because anyone born before January 1, 1954, will already have reached age seventy. That said, it may still behoove a higher-earning spouse to take their retirement benefit early in order to start their older or younger low-earning spouse's spousal benefit early. The same argument holds true for activating child and disabled child benefits.

SECRET 9: SEQUENCE WIDOW(ER) AND RETIREMENT BENEFITS

Consider Janet, a retired widow who's celebrating her sixty-second birthday by going to the local SSA office to finally get what's hers. Janet's not sure what benefits are available. But a friendly staffer tells her the best move is to apply for all the benefits she can collect: her retirement benefit and her widow benefit.

Unfortunately, the staffer gave her the worst possible advice.

To see why, let me fill in the hypothetical details. Let's assume Janet's early retirement benefit is $2,000 per month and her widow benefit is $2,001 per month. If Janet follows the staffer's advice and applies for both benefits, she'll get the larger of the two—in this case, the $2,001 widow benefit—*for the rest of her life*. That is, she'll never collect her own retirement benefit for which she dearly paid in FICA taxes over a very long and trying career.* Her lifetime benefits will be $2,001 per month for thirty-eight years (to her assumed maximum age of one hundred), or $912,456.

If the staffer actually understood the way retirement and widow benefits work, they would have given Janet the following correct advice rather than engage in what effectively constitutes gross financial malfeasance.

File now for your widow benefit and wait until seventy to start collecting your retirement benefit. You are free to do this. You aren't compelled to file for both benefits at once. Between now, when you're sixty-two, and eight years from now, when you're seventy, you'll collect the $2,001 widow benefit. Then starting at seventy, you'll file for your retirement benefit. Rather than its current value of $2,000 per month, it will be $3,520 per month, 76 percent higher. That's because it won't get zapped by the early reduction factor and it will be increased by your accumulating delayed retirement credits.

Since the larger of the two benefits from age seventy on will be $3,520, you'll collect that amount from age seventy through age one hundred. Sure, you may not make it that long, but late-in-life benefits have major value because you might. That's $2,001 per month for eight years plus $3,520 per month for thirty years, for a total of $1,459,296. That's $546,840 more in lifetime benefits than taking both benefits at once.

So why do I think it's unlikely that an SSA staffer would give Janet that well-informed advice? Is the SSA so incompetent or so malevolent as to allow widow(er)s to lose vast sums—in Janet's case more than

---

* Yes, Social Security will claim she's collecting her $2,000 retirement benefit plus a $1 excess widow benefit. But if her retirement benefit were only $1,000, they'd claim she was receiving it plus a $1,000 excess widow benefit. In both cases, her total check would equal $2,000 per month, i.e., the widow benefit.

half a million dollars—by simply signing an application with an extra benefit incorrectly/mistakenly checked off? You bet it is. In 2018, the SSA's inspector general issued a report accusing his own shop of using this method to reduce widow(er) benefits by $132 million and counting.[2] The SSA's watchdog called on the system's administrators to fix this problem and consider compensating widow(er)s who had been deprived of lifetime benefits. So far nothing has been fixed and no one has been compensated. Nor do we know how these "mistakes" came to pass. It may be that people like Janet requested just the widow(er) benefit but were filed for both by a staffer. This could reflect carelessness, incompetence, malevolence, or all three.

Had Janet understood the mistake, she could and should have returned to an SSA office and asked them to verify in writing that she was receiving only her widow benefit and that she was not in their system as having ever filed for her retirement benefit. She also should have specified in the remarks section of her application (and photographed it) that she was restricting her benefits application to her widow benefit and that she would not file for her retirement benefit until a later age.

Though it was the case for Janet, I want to be clear that taking your widow benefit first and your retirement benefit second is not always optimal. It may be best to start your retirement benefit at age sixty-two and take your widow benefit when it peaks—when waiting longer to collect it provides no advantage. This would be the case when the widow(er) benefit is a lot larger than the retirement benefit. For widow(er)s whose deceased spouse either never collected their retirement benefit or did so after reaching their full retirement age, the best time to take the widow(er) benefit is at full retirement age—when it will no longer be reduced due to being taken early. For widow(er)s whose deceased spouses took their retirement benefit before they died and did so early, the widow(er) benefit can peak up to three and half years before full retirement age because it's calculated based on the complex RIB-LIM formula I previously mentioned.

Please read that last sentence five times over. If you, say, take your retirement benefit at sixty-two and wait five years to take your widow(er) benefit at full retirement age, thinking it will max out then, but it actually maxes out when you're age sixty-four and a half, you may lose thousands if not tens of thousands of dollars by waiting beyond sixty-four and a half. You may follow this errant course after reading something on the SSA's highly misleading website, listening to some grossly uninformed/undertrained staffer, or doing what your financial planner, who should know better, says. If you fall into this boat—widowed in your early sixties, with a deceased spouse who took their retirement benefit early—do spend the time to get this right.*

SECRET 10: RAISE YOUR BENEFITS BY EARNING MORE

We've touched on how the amounts of Social Security benefits can vary based on how much money you made during your career, but it's important to understand how the amounts are determined so you can ensure you're getting the most money possible.

Each of the Social Security benefits you can collect (or provide to others) is pinned to what's called your primary insurance amount, or PIA. In calculating your PIA, the SSA ranks all of your past covered earnings—earnings throughout your career on which you paid FICA taxes. But before doing the ranking, they adjust your pre-age-sixty covered earnings to take into account intervening

---

* My company's tool, Maximizemysocialsecurity.com, costs next to nothing—forty dollars—and may be your only means of getting this 100 percent right. Yes, this sounds like an ad. But my sense is that all the other tools do actuarial valuation, treating you as if you're an average, not an outcome—something no well-trained economist would endorse.

growth in average wages in the country.* Covered earnings after age sixty are not indexed. They are just entered nominally in the ranking. Therefore, if you work after age sixty and earn a lot in dollars due to either your own or economy-wide real-wage growth or inflation, your post-age-sixty earnings will have an oversized influence on your PIA.

Once the SSA has all your past covered earnings—the indexed earnings up to age sixty plus the unindexed earnings after age sixty—ranked from top to bottom, they average the highest thirty-five values to form your average indexed monthly earnings (AIME), which is then used to figure your PIA. There are lots of complicated details involved in that process, but the key thing to realize is that if you keep working, you can raise your AIME and thus your benefits. The SSA calls this the recomputation of benefits. The administration's recomputing of your benefits occurs every year you're receiving your retirement benefit. To give an extreme, but entirely valid, example, say you unretire at age eighty-eight to work at a high enough paying job for it to rank among your top thirty-five annual earnings. A year later, the SSA will raise your AIME, your PIA (which, recall, depends on your AIME), and your retirement benefit (which depends on your PIA). Your retirement-benefit increase will be over and above that year's cost of living adjustment (COLA).

Now, let's suppose you have five *single* ex-husbands, each of whom served his ten years with you and is collecting a divorced spousal benefit based on your work record. For this to happen, they each had to have earned fairly little and, in any case, much less than you during their working careers (or they did work on which they

---

* For example, if you reached age sixty in 2018, your covered earnings when you were thirty-seven back in 1995 would be blown up ("indexed"), prior to being ranked, by a factor of 2.11—the ratio of US average coverage earnings in 2018, namely $52,145.80, to the average in 1995, namely $24,705.66. As for covered earnings after age sixty, they're just entered nominally—they aren't indexed.

didn't pay FICA taxes). Whether they were professional gigolos or just couldn't make a living, they all are benefiting from your Social Security earnings. And to stop inter-ex Social Security benefit wars, each ex's benefit has no impact on what the others can collect. So when you earn more at eighty-eight and kick up your PIA, voilà! Each of your exes receives a higher divorced spousal benefit for the rest of their days. Furthermore, once you give up the ghost, the exes who survive you will each collect a higher divorced widower benefit, even if they remarry (provided it's after age sixty).*

The ability to earn more and raise your PIA as you age is particularly important if your earnings in the past were low or sporadic (though it's worth noting that if you have a far-higher-earning current or former spouse and won't likely collect on your own record, raising your own PIA by earning more might not matter much or at all). It can also be important if you're a high-earning older worker — someone who earns above the SSA's covered earnings ceiling.†

If you have a spotty covered-earnings track record, it may include lots of low numbers or even outright zeroes. By earning more, regardless of how old you are, you can replace these weak spots with a positive or higher value. This will raise your AIME, and thus your PIA.

Let me illustrate the potential importance of this secret. Say you're a single, sixty-year-old Louisianan who intends to retire next year. You currently earn $27,000 and your wages have been keeping up with the national average. You were married a dozen times in the past but never for the ten years needed to collect on your exes'

---

* If they remarry before age sixty, they can begin collecting divorced widower benefits from you once their new spouse meets their maker. Indeed, if they have multiple deceased exes or spouses, to whom they were married when their spouse died, they can collect on the one delivering the highest widower benefit.

† The ceiling is the highest amount of earnings on which Social Security taxes are assessed. In 2021, it was $142,800. This amount rises over time based on the growth of economy-wide average wages.

Social Security. Because you didn't work while raising the children, you only started earning and contributing to Social Security at age forty-five. Hence, you've put in the ten years needed to secure the forty "quarters of coverage" required to get a Social Security retirement benefit. Fortunately, you inherited some money—half a million dollars from your favorite ex—and plan to live off that through age seventy, when you'll take Social Security.

What happens if you work an extra year? Your lifetime Social Security benefits will rise by $9,288, or more than a third of a year's pretax earnings. Stated differently, you can get a one-third pay increase during retirement by working one extra year. Of course, you and your employer will need to pay additional Social Security payroll taxes. They'll total $3,348 for the year. Even so, working the extra year will net you $5,940—a 77 percent return on your extra Social Security tax payment!

Next, suppose you were able to earn the Social Security ceiling amount next year as opposed to not working. Doing so would raise your lifetime benefits by an amazing $98,310. The combined employer plus employee Social Security tax bill would exceed $17,707, but you'd still net a bundle. Indeed, that single extra year's work would raise your lifetime Social Security benefits by almost one-quarter!

Now consider an alternative history of Social Security covered earnings. Suppose you've always earned above Social Security's earnings ceiling and you're currently over age sixty. Further assume your current-year earnings also exceed the ceiling. If this year's ceiling is more than prior ceilings, which is almost guaranteed, your AIME will rise, as will your PIA, as will your retirement benefit whenever you take it. This may not be immediately obvious, but it drops out of Social Security benefit math. Okay, but does this increase in real benefits matter much? Yes and no. In present value, you'll increase your lifetime benefits by roughly $4,500. This is far less than the roughly $17,707 in extra Social Security payroll taxes you'll pay. But if you were going to work anyway, it's a very nice bonus.

There's one other important way to raise your benefits by earning more, which applies to the roughly 15 or so percent of workers who spend part of their careers in employment not covered by Social Security. These are primarily state and local employees, such as teachers, whose jobs are exempt from Social Security payroll taxation. These non-covered workers typically receive pensions from their employers. But if they earn their forty quarters (ten years) of credits by working in the covered sector, they can collect a Social Security benefit as well. Such workers will have fairly short covered earnings histories and appear to the SSA's highly progressive PIA benefit formula as low-wage workers deserving of a disproportionately high benefit.

To avoid being overly generous to workers with non-covered pensions, Congress adopted the Windfall Elimination Provision (WEP), which kicks in once you start receiving your non-covered pension. Being "WEP'd" means having your AIME run through a less generous PIA formula. Your loss in benefits from being WEP'd is limited to half of your non-covered pension or half of the pension the government imputes from your non-covered 403(b) or similar retirement plan.

But here's an important thing: the extent to which you're WEP'd depends on your number of years earning a substantial amount in covered employment. The amount of earnings needed in 2021 to have a year of substantial earnings was $26,550. You're fully WEP'd if you have twenty or fewer years of substantial earnings. Between twenty and thirty years the degree to which you're WEP'd declines with each additional year of substantial earnings. After thirty years, you're no longer WEP'd. Thus, there are ten years during which your substantial earnings add a kicker to your retirement benefit.

As for spousal, divorced spousal, widow(er), and divorced widow(er) benefits received on your decedent spouse or ex-spouse (to whom you were married a decade), they are reduced by a different provision—the Government Pension Offset—if you receive a non-covered pension.* The reduction is two dollars for every three dollars of your non-covered pension or the pension the government determines your non-covered retirement-account balance will provide. There is one pretty easy way to escape the GPO. Just work for sixty months—they need not be consecutive months—in a federal, state, or local government job, which is covered by Social Security. You'll be fully and forever exempted from being GPO'd!

RECAP

For most of us, Social Security is our biggest or second-biggest economic asset. It's also one we can increase dramatically if we play our cards right. Let me bottom-line my Social Security secrets:

- Social Security has thirteen benefits, most of which you've probably never heard of. With Social Security, it's use it or lose it. If you don't file for a benefit for which you're eligible, you'll be giving up free money. Your job is to get what's yours.
- The system isn't making you a gift in providing you benefits. You earn them by making a hefty 12.4 percent FICA contribution on every dollar earned up to a high ceiling. Regardless of how the government labels these contributions as

---

* Pensions earned abroad do not trigger the GPO in the case of widow(er) benefits.

between employee and employer, they all come out of your financial hide.

- You need to formally file for any and all benefits. Social Security won't notify you when you become eligible to collect a benefit. At best, they'll pay six months of missed benefits in arrears.

- Shop around. Check with more than one Social Security Administration office and run yourself through a highly detailed online tool to discover whether you're eligible for one or more of the thirteen benefits, or if your family, friends, and even exes you care about are collecting what's theirs. I recommend my company's tool, but others may get things right.

- Social Security provides an enormous incentive to delay collecting your retirement benefit. This is the system's biggest pile of gold. It's not a myth at the end of a rainbow; it's real. You just need to exercise some patience in choosing when to spend the trivial amount of time required to file for your benefits.

- Waiting to collect a higher retirement benefit will also provide surviving spouses and qualifying ex-spouses with higher widow(er) benefits. The gain to your survivors can be so great that it makes sense to sacrifice your own lifetime retirement benefit to raise theirs.

- If you took your retirement benefit too early, you can suspend it starting at full retirement age or any age prior to seventy and restart it prior to or at age seventy. Don't fall for the SSA's con job and take your retirement benefits earlier than seventy at the cost of a permanently reduced monthly benefit.

- For most workers, the earnings test has very little if any impact on their lifetime benefits because what's lost is recouped in the form of permanently higher benefits starting at full retirement age. So don't let the earnings test necessarily deter you from going back to work if you retired or lost your job and were forced to take your Social Security retirement benefit early.

■ Those born before January 1, 1954, may be able to collect a free spousal benefit. There are several million baby boomers who can still pull this off and make a small killing. Most likely they have no idea because Social Security has done nothing to let people know they're eligible to collect a free spousal benefit provided they qualify.

■ Properly sequencing widow(er) and retirement benefits is critical for maximizing your lifetime benefits as a surviving spouse or qualified surviving ex-spouse. Social Security has—out of ignorance, mistake, or malice—conned thousands of widow(er)s out of hundreds of millions of dollars. It's also ignored its own inspector general's report calling on the system to use its internal data to determine which widow(er)s it expropriated and appropriately compensate them.

■ Depending on your work history, you may be able to substantially raise your lifetime benefits by working longer in covered employment. For some people, earning more later in life can produce an enormous return on the extra Social Security payroll contributions they make. Anyone earning above the earnings ceiling beyond age sixty will, due to Social Security's benefit math, automatically raise their PIA and all benefits based on it above and beyond the annual COLA. If you're being WEP'd, earning above the substantial earnings limit may reduce the WEP's impact.

CHAPTER 4

Give Yourself a Tax Cut — Top Tax-Saving, Retirement-Account Moves

As lamented previously, we Americans are, as a group, terrible savers. But our failure to save individually and collectively (our national saving rate was, pre-COVID, abysmally low, too) is nothing new. Congress, going back decades, recognized the problem and devised an elaborate retirement-account and merit-goods-account saving system to bribe us to save above and beyond what we're socking away in Social Security.

Lawyers are heavily overrepresented in Congress, and lawyers can't help but make things as complicated as possible. It's in their professional DNA. They've certainly left Social Security a complete user's nightmare. Ditto for our crazy quilt of retirement-account systems. The one I've highlighted thus far is the 401(k) plan, which is set up and managed by your employer. But let me now run the gamut: traditional IRAs, Roth IRAs, spousal IRAs, Keogh plans, SEPs, simple IRA plans, simple 401(k) plans, payroll deduction IRAs, 403(b) plans, profit-sharing plans, defined benefit plans, employee stock-ownership plans, 457 plans, solo 401(k) plans, nondeductible IRAs, Roth 401(k) plans, Roth 403(b) plans, Roth 457 plans, and, well, that's enough. Please grab some coffee!

Each plan comes with its own provisions, restrictions, contribution limits, and eligibility requirements. Learning the retirement accounts for which you qualify and how to best use them can lower your lifetime taxes. This, obviously, permits higher lifetime spending. In this chapter, I'm going to describe the two basic types of retirement accounts, the source of their tax breaks, and how you can move money between different types of retirement accounts to maximize your tax advantage. Then we'll move from the terribly dry but vital rules and regs (which you can skip and return to later) to the really fun part: showing you how much money can be pulled from this particular magic hat. This includes, for most employees, pocketing a massive, no-extra-work-required bonus from your employer, called the "employer match."

Taking advantage of the employer match is possibly the simplest money magic trick in the book. The average matching contribution to an employee's retirement plan is more than 4 percent of their pay. Yet a quarter of the workers eligible for this free money don't participate in their employer's plan. Let me proclaim this no-brainer:

If your employer offers to give you money for free, take it.

Once I've walked you through retirement accounts, I'll discuss HSAs (health savings accounts), cafeteria plans, and 529 plans. These are accounts earmarked for certain types of spending. They let you, within prescribed limits, spend money you've saved on "merit goods," like education or healthcare, which the government likes and wants to subsidize via tax breaks. In the case of HSAs and cafeteria plans, the tax breaks are 100 percent, meaning the earnings you allocate to them aren't taxed at all.

I realize that the dull retirement-account nitty-gritty, which I'm about to cram into your frontal lobe, is partly already there. But retirement accounts are Uncle Sam's personal invitation to cut your taxes, and I want to ensure you don't miss any opportunities to do just that. This means walking you through the two main types of retirement accounts you can use to minimize your lifetime taxes, the ways you can move between them, and the degree to which you can legally use them to cut your taxes.

TAX-DEFERRED AND ROTH RETIREMENT ACCOUNTS

Retirement accounts break down into two basic types: tax-deferred and non-tax-deferred. The bulk of retirement-account assets are in tax-deferred accounts, often called traditional (regular) IRAs. The exceptions are the non-tax-deferred IRAs that carry the name of their sponsor, former Delaware senator William Roth. Roth IRAs make up about one-tenth of all IRA assets.[1]

Employer-sponsored 401(k) retirement plans also permit employee and employer matching contributions. They come in two varieties—tax-deferred and Roth. The 401(k) is a type of defined contribution (DC) plan, which means employers and the government regulate what is contributed. DC plans have, in recent decades, largely replaced defined benefit (DB) plans, in which certain retirement benefits are guaranteed.

DB plans used to be ubiquitous among large companies, but today they're a dying breed, except the plans sponsored by unions, state and local governments, and the military. About half of private-sector workers have access only to a DC plan. Thirteen percent have access to both a DB and a DC plan. Four percent have access only to a DB plan. The remaining thirty-two percent work for companies that don't sponsor retirement plans period.[2] Clearly, DC plans—most commonly 401(k)s—account for most of our tax-deferred economic resources. Once funds are placed in your DC account, you can invest the money within limits set by your employer. In contrast, you can invest your IRA assets pretty much as you like. With DB plans, to which contributions can be much greater, what you'll receive is determined by a formula, not how well particular investments perform.

So how does a tax-deferred account work? Contributions to these plans can be deducted from your taxable income, meaning you don't have to pay income taxes on the money you save at the time you save it. You also can invest the money. Depending on the type of account, you can park it in mutual funds or exchange-traded funds (ETFs), which are collections of underlying securities, or you can invest in individual securities, including stocks, bonds, real estate trusts, gold and other commodities, rental property, options (within limits), land, even cryptocurrencies, like Bitcoin. When your investments pay off, no tax is immediately due. This is called "inside buildup." It means that none of the dividends, capital gains, interest, or other investment income flowing into your account will be subject to taxation as long as the money stays in the account.

The trade-off, however, is that when you take withdrawals from a tax-deferred account, you have to pay taxes on what you pull out. Furthermore, you do so without preferential tax treatment. For example, though the dividends and capital gains tax rate is now less than ordinary income tax rates, dividends and capital gains that have accrued in your 401(k) are, when withdrawn, taxed at the same rates used to tax labor earnings.

There's another catch to tax-deferred retirement accounts: once you reach age seventy-two or seventy and a half (if you reached that age by January 2020), you have to start withdrawing at least the required minimum distribution (RMD). The RMD is calculated by dividing your account balance in a given year by a life expectancy factor for that year. At age seventy-two, the factor is 25.6. At eighty-two, it's 17.1. Therefore, if you have $1 million in a traditional IRA at seventy-two, you will need to withdraw $39,062 that year. At eighty-two, the RMD on $1 million is $58,479.

THE ROTH DIFFERENCE

In contrast to tax-deferred accounts, contributions to non-tax-deferred Roth accounts can't be deducted from taxable income, meaning you still have to pay taxes on the money you save at the time you save it. Like tax-deferred accounts, Roth contributions accumulate tax-free. But unlike tax-deferred accounts, your eventual withdrawals aren't subject to taxation. Since you already paid tax on that money when you saved it, it won't add to your taxable income when you take it out. Roth accounts also aren't subject to RMDs (a point we'll return to later).

Part of the deal with both tax-deferred and Roth IRAs is that the money you save is tax advantaged because it's earmarked for retirement. So if you withdraw money from a tax-deferred IRA before age fifty-nine and a half, you'll have to not only pay taxes on the money but also generally face a 10 percent penalty. For Roth accounts, you can always withdraw your contributions tax- and penalty-free. But withdrawals before age fifty-nine and a half of any income earned in a Roth are taxed and penalized, unless the withdrawals are for education, a first-time home purchase, or birth or adoption expenses. After fifty-nine and a half you can withdraw Roth income penalty-free as long as five years have passed since you established the account and contributed to it.*

---

* This doesn't have to be the Roth account from which you are withdrawing.

As I'll describe shortly, there are limits on what you can contribute to IRAs. If you exceed the limits, you can still contribute, up to a second limit, to a traditional IRA, but your contribution will no longer be tax-deductible. Still, money contributed to a nondeductible IRA will receive the inside buildup advantage, accumulating tax-free. Furthermore, as mentioned previously, only the accumulated asset income will be taxable when you withdraw from such accounts.

ANNUITIZING YOUR RETIREMENT ACCOUNTS

Whether you have a tax-deferred or Roth retirement account, you can use the proceeds to purchase an annuity. Annuities, again, are payments that continue until the recipient passes. Annuities can be single life (until you cease) or joint survivor (payable until the passing of you or your spouse, whichever occurs later). They can include a guarantee period. And they can be graded, meaning they will increase annually. How you design your annuity—the features you include—determines the payout and the conditions when it ends. Unfortunately, none of the annuities available on the market are inflation indexed. Graded annuities are said to provide inflation protection, but that's hokum. Inflation protection is when the amount you receive rises by 50 percent when prices rise by 50 percent. It's not piddling—say a 3 percent "graded" increase that is independent of the actual inflation rate that prevails.

Apart from the inflation risk, annuities shine in providing longevity protection. The basic deal, for a single person to keep things simple, is you invest and earn a high nominal return if you continue to live and nada if you die. So it's a gamble. But if you don't need money when you're dead, which you surely don't, there is no downside. Most people don't annuitize their retirement accounts. This is rather surprising. The transaction fees aren't the cause. They're fairly reasonable. The reluctance appears to reflect our overconfidence we'll die young, a concern with inflation, and the risk that the insurance company selling the annuity won't last as long as we do. The surety of early death is financial wishful thinking. Concern with insurance company default can be handled by buying multiple annuities from different insurers. And inflation, as I'll soon describe, can be hedged by acquiring a nominal obligation, like monthly mortgage payments whose real value declines when prices rise.

I recommend you rethink annuities, particularly the new annuity kid on the block: QLACs, which stands for qualified longevity annuities contracts. You can invest up to 25 percent of your tax-deferred retirement accounts to a maximum of $135,000 in a QLAC. In exchange, you'll get an annuity that begins at a future date. Since you may kick before making it, the QLAC payout will beat a regular annuity payment. Thus, if you're seventy and sure you'll live for the next, say, fifteen years, but not thereafter, buying a QLAC that kicks in at eighty-five (the latest age you can start taking payments) may provide excellent protection against living beyond eighty-five. One other nice thing about QLACs: the money you invest in them is exempt from RMDs! The major concern with QLACs is inflation risk, which is compounded because the nominal payments are deferred.

CONTRIBUTION LIMITS — IRAS AND 401(K)S

Although you can contribute at any age to an IRA account, whether traditional or Roth, the federal government sets limits on how much you can contribute. It also limits what you can contribute to an employer-sponsored retirement account, like a 401(k). The limits depend on the type of account. In 2021, the total you could put into a traditional IRA and a Roth IRA *combined* was the lesser of

$6,000 ($7,000 if you were over fifty) and your 2021 labor earnings, which the IRS calls "taxable compensation."*

There are also upper income limits on contributing to a Roth IRA. For single people in 2021, if your modified adjusted gross income (MAGI) exceeded $140,000, you couldn't contribute. Between $125,000 and $140,000, the amount was limited. For married couples, the limit applied to a MAGI between $198,000 and $208,000.† One nice thing is that you can contribute to IRA accounts no matter your age, and as mentioned previously, you can actually contribute more once you're over fifty.

For 401(k)s, in 2021, the contribution limit was $19,500 ($26,000 if fifty or older). For example, if you're forty-five and you work in a high-paying job, you could put $19,500 in total into your 401(k) and your Roth 401(k). Even if you worked for multiple employers, your 2021 total contribution limit, across all plans, was the same $19,500 ($26,000 if fifty or older).

CAN YOU CONTRIBUTE TO A TRADITIONAL IRA IF YOU HAVE AN EMPLOYER-BASED RETIREMENT PLAN?

If your income doesn't exceed a specific amount, what you can contribute to traditional IRA accounts does not affect what you can contribute to your 401(k) accounts, and vice versa. However, the income limits get complicated. You need to carefully read the IRS rules to make sure you get this straight for the year in question.[3] In 2021, if you had an employer-sponsored plan, regardless of its type,

---

* Taxable compensation includes wages, salaries, self-employment income, and taxable alimony. It doesn't include income earned on assets, such as interest, dividends, capital gains, or rent.

† A good reference here is the IRS's "Amount of Roth IRA Contributions That You Can Make for 2020," https://www.irs.gov/retirement-plans/plan-participant-employee /amount-of-roth-ira-contributions-that-you-can-make-for-2020.

you could fully deduct contributions to a traditional IRA if your modified adjusted gross income (MAGI) was $66,000 or less. If you're married, the MAGI limit was $105,000 if both spouses had employer plans ($198,000 if one spouse had an employer plan). You could make partially deductible contributions if you were covered at work and are single with a MAGI between $66,000 and $76,000. If you're married, and both you and your spouse have a work-related plan, partially deductible contributions were permitted if your MAGI fell between $105,000 and $125,000 (or between $198,000 and $208,000 if one spouse had a work-related plan).

If you exceed the MAGI limits, you can still contribute to a traditional IRA, *but only on a non-tax-deductible basis.* However, bear in mind that there's still an independent limit of $6,000 ($7,000 if you're over fifty) on total IRA contributions, whether to traditional IRAs (made on a deductible or nondeductible basis) or to a Roth. Non-deductible IRAs can be converted to Roth IRAs. Such *backdoor Roths,* like straight conversions, let the rich avoid the Roth income-based contribution limit.

In sum, regardless of its type, if you or your spouse have an employer-sponsored retirement plan, deductible traditional IRA contributions are MAGI related, age related, and year related. If you don't have an employer-sponsored retirement plan, the IRA contribution limit (Roth and regular combined) is simply the direct IRA contribution limit.

CAN YOU CONTRIBUTE TO A ROTH IRA IF YOU HAVE AN EMPLOYER-BASED RETIREMENT PLAN?

Roth IRA contribution limits don't depend on whether you have an employer-sponsored plan. The sum of your Roth, traditional IRA, and nondeductible IRA contributions can't exceed the IRA contribution limit, and as noted, the Roth contribution is separately limited based on your MAGI.

SPOUSAL IRAS

If your spouse doesn't work but you do, your spouse can still have their own IRA. However, the amounts contributed to their account can't exceed the individual IRA contribution limits, and your combined contributions can't exceed your own earnings. If you have a retirement account at work, your spouse's IRA contribution limit is based on the same MAGI formula as your own IRA contribution.

LIMITS ON EMPLOYER CONTRIBUTIONS TO YOUR RETIREMENT ACCOUNTS

Having your employer put money in your tax-deferred accounts is better than contributing the same amount yourself. That's because the employer's contribution is not subject to payroll taxes—the Social Security and Medicare tax known as FICA. In contrast, your own contributions aren't excluded from FICA taxation.

When you withdraw from your retirement account, none of the withdrawals are subject to FICA taxation. This makes sense for withdrawals based on your own contributions. After all, you've already paid payroll taxes on them when you originally made the money. But withdrawals based on your employer's contributions *never* get hit by the FICA tax. That's a sweet deal, as the employer's portion of the FICA tax—tax that you effectively pay—is 6.2 percent, which is half of the combined 12.4 percent due on pay up to Social Security's taxable maximum. As for the 2.7 percent Medicare portion of the FICA tax, the employer's share is 1.45 percent on pay regardless of how much you make.

Employer contribution limits depend on the plan. In 2021, the 401(k) limit was whatever was smaller: 25 percent of your pay or $58,000 ($64,500 including the maximum catch-up contribution of $6,500 if you're age fifty or older). But this limit is further reduced by what you contribute to the plan. In 2021, for example, if you personally contributed $18,000 to your 401(k) (whether tax-deductible or Roth), with the employer limit at $58,000, your employer could contribute only the $40,000 difference. And the total of your and your employer's contributions to an employer-sponsored plan can't, in any case, exceed 100 percent of your compensation.

With a simplified employee pension (SEP) there are no employee contributions. The maximum employer contributions are set in 2021 as 25 percent of employee compensation or $58,000. There is no catch-up provision for older workers.

ROTH CONVERSIONS — FORMAL AND INFORMAL

As we've just discussed, tax-deferred accounts let you postpone paying taxes. Roth accounts do not. In either case, your contributions are taxed, just at different times—either on the way in or on the way out of your retirement accounts. For reasons we'll get into shortly, it can be advantageous to convert one type of account to the other—generally going from a tax-deferred traditional account into a non-tax-deferred Roth account. This is called a "Roth conversion."

Under a Roth conversion, you can withdraw money from a tax-deferred account, pay the taxes you owe on the amount withdrawn, and then immediately contribute the amount to a Roth account. For example, if you withdraw $50,000 from a traditional IRA, you'll have to pay taxes on the $50,000, but you can simultaneously make an extra contribution of $50,000 to a Roth, independent of current contribution limits.

For people close to retirement, doing a Roth conversion is very simple. If you're over fifty-nine and a half, you can simply withdraw money from a traditional IRA and contribute to a Roth IRA the same amount (or even a different amount—often people use some of the withdrawn money for the tax bill). This is called an "informal Roth conversion." However, if you're below age fifty-nine and a half, you have to pay a 10 percent penalty on tax-deferred retirement account withdrawals under most circumstances—not ideal for the financially conscious.* That said, there is a process called a "formal Roth conversion" that allows people below fifty-nine and a half to make an exact dollar-for-dollar transfer from a traditional IRA into a Roth.

You can even do a Roth conversion from a 401(k) or similar employer-provided tax-deferred account as long as your employer permits this in their plan. Also, if you leave your employer, you can roll over your employer tax-deferred account into a traditional IRA and then do a conversion down the road.

Though it's not as common, you can also move money the other way, from a Roth to a tax-deferred account. Just withdraw funds from the Roth and use them, up to the legally permitted limit, to add to your tax-deferred account. As an example, suppose you have $100,000 in a Roth IRA and you want to contribute $5,000 this year to your traditional IRA. Also suppose that for cash-flow reasons you can't afford to contribute without tapping into your Roth. You can grab the $5,000 from the Roth and you'll be able to gain a $5,000 deduction.†

---

* There are a number of ways to get around the 10 percent penalty on early tax-deferred withdrawals, regardless of their use. The easiest is to withdraw the same amount of money each year for five or more years. You can also avoid the penalty if you use the funds to pay for large medical expenses, purchase health insurance after being laid off, cover college costs, fund (up to $10,000) a first-time home purchase, handle disability expenses, or deal with military service costs. Finally, there's no penalty if the withdrawal is from an inherited IRA. See this article: Emily Brandon, "12 Ways to Avoid the IRA Early Withdrawal Penalty," *U.S. News & World Report,* December 15, 2020, https://money.usnews.com/money/retirement/slideshows/ways-to-avoid-the-ira -early-withdrawal-penalty.

† This is, of course, no different from contributing $10,000 to the IRA from your earnings and withdrawing $10,000 from the Roth to deal with your cash-flow problem. As the saying goes, a dollar is a dollar. But no matter how you describe what goes

USING RETIREMENT ACCOUNTS TO TIME YOUR TAX PAYMENTS

So what's the point of a Roth conversion, which makes your taxable income higher now and lower later? And what's the point of going the other way—contributing more to a tax-deductible account and reducing your taxable income now and raising it later? The point is to lower your lifetime taxes. Doing so involves your tax bracket.

If you're like most people, your tax bracket will be lower when you're retired, sometimes dramatically lower, since you won't be earning money at a job. Your tax bracket could also be lower now and higher later. For example, you could be currently unemployed but expect to be recalled to your old position or find a new job in a year. In this case, putting money in a Roth account will ensure the income used to make contributions is taxed at your current low tax rate, not your future high tax rate. If your tax bracket is temporarily low, you want to pay taxes now, not in the future. That's where contributing to a Roth account makes sense, as does a Roth conversion.

So far I've been using the term "tax bracket" to reference the federal plus state income tax rate you face on additional taxable income. But for retirees, their taxes from additional income can also be greatly affected by federal income taxation of Social Security benefits and the assessment of higher Medicare Part B premiums based on your MAGI as calculated two years in the past.

Uncle Sam's taxation of Social Security is quite convoluted but very important, particularly for the rich. In 2020, if your MAGI, including half your Social Security benefits, exceeded $25,000 if

---

down, your Roth account is reduced by $10,000 and your traditional IRA account gains $10,000.

you're single, or $32,000 if you're married, up to half of your Social Security benefits were subject to federal income tax. And if your MAGI exceeded $34,000 if you're single, or $44,000 if you're married, up to 85 percent of your benefits were taxable. High-income households faced a 31 percent taxation of their benefits. To repeat myself, these thresholds aren't inflation indexed. Thus, eventually, all retirees will face taxation on 85 percent of their Social Security benefits.

The high-income Medicare Part B IRMAA (income-related monthly adjustment amount) premium is a similar type of tax on the elderly. The 2021 baseline Part B premium was $1,782. In 2021, a person who is single on Medicare with a MAGI in 2019 of between $88,000 and $110,000 (between $176,000 and $222,000 if married) faced an extra $712.80 annual premium (per person).* For those with determining incomes above the next threshold, the premium increased by another $1,069.20 per year. And there are three more thresholds to go! These thresholds are also unindexed for inflation.

If you're in a low federal income tax bracket and, say, you withdraw taxable retirement assets thinking you'll save taxes, be careful. You may trigger Social Security or higher Social Security benefit taxation as well as higher Medicare Part B premiums in two years. Thus, Roth conversions may make sense for retirees who aren't yet taking Social Security and aren't yet enrolled in Medicare. But for retirees who are doing one or both of these things, Roth conversions, particularly large ones, may make little or no sense.

---

* IRMAA is imposed with a two-year lag: your income two years ago determines your IRMAA. Note that traditional, but not Roth, IRA withdrawals add to your MAGI.

TAX-FREE INSIDE BUILDUP

What's the advantage of having assets earn income inside either type of account on a tax-free basis? By deferring your tax payments, you get to earn money on what you owe the government.

Suppose you're about to pay Uncle Sam $10,000 in taxes, and he says, "Thanks, but I'm feeling generous. Hold on to the $10,000 and invest it. In thirty years, you can pay me taxes on whatever total amount you end up with." Sam's offering a good deal: a loan of the $10,000 plus the ability to wait to pay Sam when your tax bracket is lower. Let's assume you contribute $10,000 to your IRA this year. Let's also assume you're in, and will remain in, the 30 percent tax bracket. Finally, assume you can safely invest the funds at 3 percent. If you invest tax-free for thirty years, you'll end up with $20,094. If you have to pay a 30 percent tax along the way on the 3 percent return, you'll end up with $16,813. With a 1.5 percent long-term interest rate—the situation currently—the difference is smaller: $14,509 versus $12,984. Although this nets a smaller amount, inside buildup is still very valuable even when interest rates are low.

Another way to describe inside buildup is as a shelter for your asset income from taxation. This brings me to a tax advantage of Roth accounts that is rather subtle and I'm not sure generally recognized. Recall that when you contribute to a Roth, you pay taxes on your contributions via standard income taxes on your earnings as you make them. But this means that over time you have less in the way of nonretirement assets. Stated differently, a larger share of your total assets—your nonretirement and retirement assets—will be represented by retirement accounts and, thereby, sheltered.*

---

* This is for a given path of contributions, which you're going to place in either a tax-deferred or a Roth account. If you realize that contributions to tax-deferred accounts are taxed on withdrawal, you might contribute more to the tax-deferred account to cover those extra future taxes.

SHOW ME THE MONEY

How big are the lifetime spending gains from using retirement accounts? Let me answer by way of a young man named Jerry.

Jerry's twenty-five, earns $50,000, and, since he's just starting out in life, has no assets whatsoever. Jerry lives in New Jersey, is self-employed, and has set up a traditional IRA into which he's just started to contribute $3,000 per year, or 6 percent of his earnings. Let's assume that Jerry's salary and contribution keep pace with inflation. Let's also assume that Jerry earns 1.5 percent on his IRA contributions and that the inflation rate is also 1.5 percent. Finally, Jerry will start withdrawing from his retirement account at age seventy-two, when required minimum distributions begin.

What will be the lifetime payoff to Jerry if he contributes 6 percent of his annual earnings to his IRA until his retirement at age sixty-seven but does not withdraw anything before age seventy-two? In present value, it's a whopping $39,403. That's a pretty good chunk of change—roughly a year's after-tax earnings. Think about this. By spending an hour setting up an IRA and scheduling automatic contributions from his checking account, Jerry can afford the same permanent lifestyle but retire a year earlier.

If Jerry makes the same 6 percent contribution to a Roth instead of a traditional IRA, the increase in lifetime spending is much smaller: $11,440. This makes sense. Jerry's tax bracket when he's young is a lot higher than when he's old. Contributing to a Roth helps him shelter the return on his savings—the tax-free inside buildup just discussed—but it doesn't allow his contribution to be taxed at a lower rate.

The lifetime spending gains from using a traditional IRA or a Roth IRA would pale in comparison to the gains he'd receive by switching to an employer who will match his 401(k) contributions. With an employer matching his 6 percent for a total of 12 percent, the gain would be $150,231 — more than four years of disposable earnings. You might not be impressed by this figure. After all, if Jerry's new job comes with a 6 percent raise, of course he's going to be much better off over the course of forty-two years. However, as with most employers, their contribution is based on Jerry's contribution. So perhaps think of it as Jerry first joining a company that offers an employee match, then independently deciding to take advantage of it. In this case, the payoff from using the retirement account is vastly larger due to the employer match. The lesson, of course, is to pick up loose dollar bills. In other words:

Contribute to your retirement account at least what's needed to secure your employer's match.

3× JERRY

Consider 3× Jerry, who makes $150,000 a year and contributes 6 percent to a 401(k). His lifetime spending gain is $58,421. That's serious money but not nearly as much as what you might have expected. The reason has to do with the size of the reduction in tax brackets when he's old. There is a much smaller tax-bracket difference between young and old 3× Jerry than that of regular 1× Jerry. The drop for 1× Jerry is roughly 80 percent. For 3× Jerry, it's roughly 40 percent. If we consider a 500,000× Jerry, the drop in tax bracket is nonexistent. Someone with such high income would be in the top tax bracket their entire life. Therefore, for a very rich person, the only gain from using a retirement account would be inside buildup.

If 3× Jerry contributed to a Roth 401(k) instead of a standard 401(k), his gain would be $66,746. How come the gain in a Roth beats the same amount contributed to a deductible 401(k), when for 1× Jerry it was the reverse? Here's why: 3× Jerry needs to save proportionately more than 1× Jerry because Social Security's bene-fit formula is progressive and he can't depend on it for retirement support to the degree that 1× Jerry can. Saving more means, other things being equal, higher assets, higher taxable asset income, and, thus, landing in a higher tax bracket when old. Therefore, the sheltering of assets from taxes in old age is more important for 3×, and that's what the Roth does particularly well.

As for the value of contributing in the context of an employer match, the lifetime spending gain would be $288,078—more than two years of after-tax earnings. Yes, the absolute gain from 3× Jerry's contribution to a 401(k) is almost twice that of 1× Jerry's, but 3× earns three times as much. This reflects 3× Jerry's far higher retirement tax bracket. So for 1× Jerry, joining his employ-er's 401(k) is, relatively speaking, a much bigger deal. Another way to say this is: lower-income workers have relatively more to gain than higher-income workers from participating in tax-deferred employer-matched retirement accounts. This, like so much else you're reading in these pages, contradicts conventional wisdom.

THE RISK OF FUTURE TAX HIKES

Let's stick with 3× Jerry and return him to his old job, where he contributes to a 401(k). And let's assume that taxes rise permanently by 25 percent precisely when he starts taking retirement-account withdrawals at age seventy-two. His gains are now only $29,612—about half the amount they would be without the tax hike. This makes sense. The tax-bracket advantage of using tax-deferred accounts is having your retirement withdrawals taxed at a lower rate. But that's less the case if tax rates are one-quarter higher when you retire.

In contrast, the tax hike actually raises the gain from contribut-ing to a Roth, which would now be $78,577. Why is the gain so much better in a Roth? The answer is that the future tax hike is going to happen whether or not 3× Jerry participates in a 401(k). And anticipating this entails him saving more. As a result, the no-contribution baseline involves more asset accumulation and more asset-income taxes as Jerry ages, particularly in retirement. This, in turn, means lower lifetime spending. But sheltering assets from income taxation is where the Roth shines. The increase in lifetime spending in contributing to a Roth is higher because lifetime spending under the Roth is being compared with lower lifetime spending without it. This, in a nutshell, is why the Roth does even better in the context of future tax hikes than one might think.

ROTH CONVERSIONS

Next, let's take a quantitative look at Roth conversions with pretend Jean. Jean's sixty-one, earns $100,000, and plans to retire when she turns sixty-two. She's sitting on $2.5 million in a traditional IRA and $500,000 in regular assets. Her plan entails starting smooth retirement-account withdrawals as well as Social Security benefits at sixty-five.

Suppose Jean does a $500,000 Roth conversion this year, while she's still working. This is a really bad move. Roth conversions move taxes to the present, which for Jean means a time in which she's working and in a high tax bracket. Doing a Roth conversion this year will raise her lifetime taxes by $16,335. That's a quarter of what Jean will make this year after tax. In terms of lifetime spending capacity, Jean would do equally well by working three-quarters of the year and calling it quits. She'd not only enjoy the same living standard as she'd have doing the Roth conversion but also gain an extra quarter-year of retirement.

The smart move is for Jean to postpone the conversion until she retires. Jean's tax bracket will be considerably lower at ages sixty-two, sixty-three, and sixty-four. Then it will rise as she takes her retirement-account withdrawals and Social Security benefits. If Jean converts $100,000 per year in those three years to take advantage of her otherwise low tax bracket, she'll lower her lifetime taxes by $42,038.

Clearly, timing is crucial when it comes to Roth conversions. But if the timing and the amounts converted are properly planned out, the conversions can have significant financial value.

Jean could also achieve a similar effect by choosing alternative dates on which to start smooth withdrawals from her traditional IRA. In Jean's case, if she doesn't want to do a Roth conversion or make any other retirement moves, the best age to start her traditional IRA withdrawals is not sixty-five but sixty-two. This will deliver an $11,251 reduction in lifetime taxes, again by her taking advantage of the low tax brackets between sixty-two and sixty-four. That's about one-fourth as good as doing the yearly Roth conversion we just talked about, but it's still significant. And if Jean needs more money during those lower-income years, there's nothing that says she needs to Roth convert. She could, for example, simply withdraw $100,000 annually from her traditional IRA between ages sixty-two and sixty-four and make no Roth contributions at those ages, starting smooth withdrawals of what's left at sixty-five.

TIMING ROTH CONVERSIONS AND WITHDRAWALS

When you're beginning to draw from retirement accounts, is it better to draw from Roth or traditional accounts first? And when should you consider a Roth conversion? The answers to these questions flow from three goals: one, to smooth your tax brackets over time; two, to accumulate assets on a tax-free basis (inside buildup); and, three, to smooth your living standard.

Unfortunately, trying to satisfy any one of these goals can make it more difficult to satisfy the others. You'll want to shoot for a happy medium. When interest rates are low—as is the case as I write this—the first goal is more important than the second. But the third goal is always paramount. Depriving yourself significantly in the present in order to party in the future—a future you may not be around to see—is not necessarily worth the tax savings and higher future living standard.

Take George, who is sixty-five. George was a moderate earner before he retired last year. He has $1.8 million in a traditional IRA and $100,000 in regular assets. George is going to hold off until age seventy to take his $30,000 annual Social Security benefit. And he's waiting until seventy-two, when RMDs kick in, to start smoothly withdrawing from his IRA.

George's base plan presents severe cash-flow problems. Between sixty-five and seventy, he will have $18,670 per year to spend. Between seventy and seventy-two, he'll have $37,997. And after seventy-two, the amount jumps to $78,997. Were George able to borrow against his future Social Security benefits or IRA withdrawals, he could have a smooth living standard. But he can't. Consequently, he's forced to live off his regular assets prior to seventy, then for a few years he can add in his Social Security benefit, and then finally begin smooth IRA withdrawals.

George's base plan's lifetime spending is $2,551,418. But when he realizes how pinched he will be in the short term, he does what most people do. He files for his Social Security retirement benefit earlier than he had planned. This improves George's consumption smoothing. He will now be able to spend $38,529 through age seventy-two and $72,600 thereafter. But that's far from smooth, and due to taking Social Security early, the associated reduction in lifetime spending—$96,760—is considerable.

What if George sticks with his original plan of taking Social

Security at seventy but starts smooth IRA withdrawals at sixty-six? This lowers his lifetime taxes and raises his lifetime spending by $72,191 relative to his base plan and by $168,951 relative to his taking Social Security immediately. This is a huge difference. Unfortunately, while this third plan does a better consumption-smoothing job, it's still not perfect. George's smoothest possible spending path jumps from $55,241 before age seventy to $72,926 thereafter.

As a fourth plan, George decides to withdraw $80,000 from his IRA each year between sixty-six and seventy and withdraw the balance smoothly thereafter. This raises George's lifetime spending even more—by $73,629—compared to the base plan and smooths out his annual spending at a permanent $70,599. Now George has the best of two worlds: more lifetime spending and no spending bottlenecks as he ages.

The next question is whether George can do even better with a Roth conversion. Say George converts $30,000 a year through age seventy. His lifetime spending would be $79,455 higher than it would be with his base plan. That's a very small—roughly $6,000— extra improvement, but, hey, every bit helps. It does, however, require that George spend somewhat less before age seventy. The reason is clear. Roth conversions require paying extra taxes sooner than would otherwise be true. And this puts pressure on a person's cash flow.

Let's tweak the numbers a little more to see how George would fare were he to do a Roth conversion of $50,000 in each of the next four years and take $60,000 per year out of his IRA on a non-conversion basis. This plan leaves George with $82,827 more than the base plan in lifetime spending. But it reintroduces cash constraints since George will have to pay more taxes prior to age seventy. George's annual spending prior to seventy is $46,596, after which it jumps to $72,457.

For George, virtually all the gains from smoothing tax brackets can be obtained by just making withdrawals from taxable retirement accounts. Doing so can also alleviate cash constraints and improve consumption smoothing. Going beyond this by doing a Roth conversion will save a bit more in lifetime taxes but at the price of potentially severe cash constraints and their associated consumption disruption.

However, as we saw with Jean, the problem with Roth conversions causing or worsening cash constraints doesn't arise if your household has considerable regular assets. For example, if George had $1 million in regular assets, rather than $100,000, he'd face no cash constraint between sixty-five and seventy. Also, absent any IRA withdrawals during those years, he'd be in a very low tax bracket. In this case, Roth conversion would come at no consumption-smoothing cost to George and, if done at scale, could really help shelter George from future asset-income taxation.

The key point in thinking about regular assets is that only the income earned on them, not the principal (corpus or basis), is taxable. But the principal of the household's regular assets—$100,000 in George's case—largely governs whether the household will face cash-flow pressure from Roth conversions. In sum, Roth conversions are of most value to those with substantial regular assets relative to the amount of assets in their retirement accounts. Again, this is because you have enough money on hand to cover the extra taxes such conversions entail. Being well stocked with regular assets goes hand in hand with being rich. But whether or not you're rich, if you find yourself at the point of retirement with sizable regular assets relative to your retirement accounts and lifetime Social Security benefits, Roth conversions may be just the ticket. Although let me reiterate: keep an eye on how moving taxable income into different years affects both your Social Security taxation and your Part B premiums two years afterward.

TAP SOCIAL SECURITY OR YOUR 401(K) FIRST?

Tucked into the earlier weeds was a money magic eye-catcher that probably didn't catch your eye. It's the potential gain from taking retirement-account withdrawals early in order to delay taking Social Security benefits. I ran into this issue when I was writing a nationally syndicated personal finance column for a couple of years on the side.

One day my editor, Scott, told me he was done, calling it quits, heading out to pasture, retiring. Scott, then sixty-five, was perfectly healthy but had seemingly burned out from one day to the next. He claimed it wasn't working with me, although my wife raised an eyebrow. Anyhow, in keeping with my general view that voluntary retirement is financial suicide, I did my pushy best to keep Scott tied to his laptop. No luck. Then, as we were saying farewell, Scott told me he was going to start Social Security right away so he could keep his 401(k) invested in the market.

"Hold on, Scott. I think that's a big mistake. Shoot me over your numbers and I'll take a look."

Sure enough, Scott was about to throw away close to $85,000. But getting him to see this wasn't easy. Scott had been editing personal finance columnists his entire career. But none, before me, was an economist. One of our specialties is valuing risk. Scott wanted to delay 401(k) withdrawals to make a killing in the stock market. But the stock market is extremely risky, as I'll soon describe. Once you adjust for risk, its return is far below what you can earn by investing in not taking Social Security benefits early. (Think of taking them early and then handing them back—investing them—to get a higher benefit starting at seventy.)

The risk adjustment couldn't be simpler. You just look at yields on Treasury inflation-protected securities, or TIPS, which are the safest security going. Since people are free to invest in stocks and

TIPS, the yield on TIPS tells you what people are willing to pay to avoid the risk in stocks. The TIPS yield is thus the stock yield adjusted for risk and can be compared directly with earning an equally safe real return by "investing" in Social Security (if you're patient).

If this chapter teaches nothing but the general value of taking retirement-account withdrawals before taking Social Security, I will be a happy author.

MERIT-GOODS EARMARKED SPENDING ACCOUNTS

Let's now turn to merit-goods accounts. My favorite are HSAs— health savings accounts. Money you put into an HSA isn't subject to federal income tax, the FICA tax, or most state income taxes. Plus, provided you spend your accumulated assets on healthcare expenses (co-pays, deductibles, co-insurance, medical care, vision care, dental care, or even over-the-counter medications), the withdrawals are tax-free as well. If you spend your HSA on things that aren't covered, like cosmetic surgery, the associated withdrawals are treated like an IRA withdrawal—taxed and potentially penalized if taken before age fifty-nine and a half. Thus, HSAs can, at a minimum, be a means of effectively expanding your IRA contribution limit.

You don't have to work to contribute to an HSA. But you do need to be enrolled in a health insurance plan with a high deductible, aptly named a high-deductible health plan (HDHP). Whether or not you're working, you can set up your own HSA if you're in an HDHP and don't have an HSA through your employer. However, if you form your own HSA and have labor income, your contributions won't be exempt from FICA taxation. They will still be spared federal and, generally speaking, state income taxation. There's also a connection between enrollment in Medicare and HSA contribution deductibility. If you're enrolled even just in Part A, the hospitalization part of Medicare, you can continue to contribute to your HSA, but you have to pay taxes on the contributions. Unfortunately, if you're sixty-five or over and receive or start to receive a Social Security benefit of any kind, you'll automatically be enrolled in Medicare Part A.

The 2021 limits on HSA contributions were $3,600 for you and $7,200 for your family with an extra $1,000 catch-up allowance for those fifty-five or older. Given these limits, is joining an HSA a good money magic move? Let's go back to our New Jersey–based friend Jerry, who is twenty-five, single, and earns $50,000 annually. The HSA limit is 7.2 percent of his pay. Since Jerry's in roughly the 30 percent tax bracket, taking account of federal income, FICA, and state income taxes, contributing to the HSA throughout his working years is worth 2.13 percent of his pay, or $1,065 dollars annually. Multiply this by Jerry's forty-two years of expected work and we're talking $44,730 in additional lifetime spending by participating in his employer-sponsored HSA plan—about 1.3 years' worth of after-tax earnings. In other words, by participating in his company's HSA, Jerry can maintain his same living standard but retire 1.3 years earlier. We've found yet another enchanted money-maker.

If you're not covered by an HSA-eligible insurance plan, a company-sponsored flexible savings account, or FSA, can cover current-year outlays on healthcare, dependent care, premiums for health plans not offered by the employer, and several other minor outlays. FSAs enjoy the same tax treatment as HSAs but are less generous and also more restricted with respect to the timing of outlays. These restrictions effectively eliminate the potential for inside buildup. Medical FSAs are the most common. They cover a host of health-related expenses, ranging from dentures to vasectomies.

The other major merit-goods plan is the 529 plan, which covers education-related expenditures, specifically tuition, fees, books, supplies, and equipment (think laptops!). The tuition can be for any accredited college, university, or vocational school in the US and for some foreign universities. Contributions to 529 plans aren't given any federal tax break, but they do receive state tax breaks in certain states. There is inside buildup and no taxes on withdrawals used for qualified expenditures. Thus, 529 plans behave, for tax purposes, very much like Roth IRAs. There are two types of 529 plans: prepaid tuition plans, which are offered in ten states, and savings plans. The prepaid tuition plans insure the beneficiary of the account (you, your spouse, or your children) against future tuition hikes but lock you into a particular choice or set of choices of college.

RECAP

Retirement and merit-goods accounts let you lower your lifetime taxes by moving taxable income to years when you're in a low tax bracket (tax-bracket smoothing), by deferring your taxes (tax-free inside buildup), and by targeting your spending on healthcare and education, which are tax subsidized. As for specific takeaways, here's my list:

- Over the years, Congress has legislated a crazy quilt of retirement plans.
- Retirement plans can be personal, such as IRAs or Roth IRAs, or company sponsored, such as 401(k)s. Retirement plans are primarily tax-deferred or non-tax-deferred Roth defined-contribution plans.
- Your contributions to tax-deferred plans are income-tax-deductible but not deferred from FICA taxation. Your employer's contributions to your plan are deferred from both income

and FICA taxes. Plan assets accumulate tax-free, but withdrawals are subject to federal and potentially state income taxes. They are not, however, subject to FICA taxation.

- Contributions to Roth IRAs aren't deductible. Plan assets accumulate tax-free, and withdrawals, with some exceptions, aren't taxable.

- Annual contributions to IRAs, whether a Roth or a traditional IRA, are subject to an overall limit and can't exceed your labor income. Roth IRA contributions are further limited or precluded entirely if your modified adjusted gross income is too high. There are additional income-related limits on contributions to traditional IRAs if you or your spouse participate in an employer-sponsored retirement plan.

- Roth conversions let you expand your asset balances in Roth IRAs. A dollar-for-dollar conversion entails an equal-sized withdrawal from an IRA and a contribution to a Roth IRA. The withdrawal triggers income taxation. Employers may also permit conversions from their tax-deferred to their Roth plans.

- There is a global limit on how much you can contribute to all employer-provided retirement plans combined. And there is a higher global limit on the sum of your combined employee contributions to your plans and your employer's combined contributions to your plans.

- Smoothing tax brackets across years, tax-free asset accumulation (inside buildup), and Roth conversion can be highly useful tools for significantly reducing lifetime taxes, particularly if your tax bracket will change substantially over time. But be aware that moving taxable income across years can trigger higher Social Security benefit taxation as well as higher future Medicare Part B premiums.

- If you have a relatively large amount of regular assets, you can benefit the most from a Roth conversion because you can use those assets to cover the extra tax payments without having to reduce your spending.
- Merit-goods spending accounts, including HSAs, FSAs, and 529 plans, can also reduce your lifetime taxes. Contributions to, accumulation in, and withdrawals from HSA and FSA plans are tax-free; 529 plans are taxed like Roth plans.
- Starting retirement-account withdrawals early in order to postpone taking Social Security (when doing so otherwise makes sense) can conjure up a *huge* pot of gold compared to doing the opposite.

CHAPTER 5

Get House Rich—Shack Up with Mom and Other Smart Housing Moves

House poor" is a common expression used to describe people who are spending too much on housing, leaving them with too little to spend on everything else. But it also can refer to people who are getting too little housing bang for their buck. This chapter's goal is to make you house rich, ensuring you end up with the housing you really want at the price you can really afford. I'm going to take you through a range of housing issues, including how to calculate the true price of a home, how to define your housing market, whether owning beats renting, why a mortgage is a financial and tax loser, how using your retirement-account money to pay off your mortgage can pay off big-time, the hidden tax break in homeownership, how homeownership can reduce longevity risk, the advantage of cohabitation (including shacking up with Mom), the gains to downsizing, and the best way to free trapped equity, which may entail using an expensive mechanism called a reverse mortgage.

To start things off, let me relate my own transition from house poor to house rich. It's a story with a good ending but, as you'll see, not one I'm particularly proud of. I'm typing these words in a small, very old house that my wife and I recently bought. It's in Providence, Rhode Island—a good hour's commute from my day job at Boston University. We sold our two-bedroom condo in Boston to buy it. When I say very old, I'm not kidding. It was built in 1720. You can tell its age from the low ceilings, the cracked wooden beams, and the single chimney serving four fireplaces.

I didn't want to move. Boston's a far more exciting city than sleepy Providence. From our old place, I could get to the office in ten minutes. Plus, I loved the building—an 1880 brownstone with high ceilings and large windows looking onto a lovely street. I was sure that moving into a museum—in Providence, no less—was a mistake.

The debate began. "I'll miss Boston." "You'll love Providence." "The commute's too long." "You mostly work from home." "I love high ceilings." "You'll adjust." "Boston has a world-class orchestra." "We never go."

The arguing continued until my wife calculated the difference in housing costs. It was unbelievable. The new (very old) house was half the price of our condo and had 60 percent more square footage. Per square foot, the house was a third the price of the condo! Plus it had a basement and a small yard.

My wife's beating me at my own game—economics—irked me. I couldn't imagine the housing market was so screwed up as to make comparable quality housing in Providence so much cheaper than in Boston. Yes, many people share my preference for Boston, but I never expected the compensating differential could be that big. Consequently, I had never checked the housing-price difference between the two cities.

After light dawned, yet again, on Marblehead, we bought, sold, and moved. Once in Providence, I realized my wife was right about everything. The low ceilings were no big deal. The house's age gave us a meaningful mission: preserving a small part of US heritage.

Our neighbors couldn't be nicer (we'd met no one in eight years in our Boston hood). And Providence was, well, peaceful. All of a sudden, when adjusting for quality, the square-foot price difference felt even greater than a factor of three.

I told friends and relatives about the huge housing-price differential between the two cities. "Oh, weren't we clever to figure this out?" I effectively proclaimed. Then I realized I was bragging about having made a colossal financial mistake by living in Boston for so long. Yes, it was good to stop dramatically overpaying for housing. But we'd been doing that for eight long years! I'd forgotten my adage: The easiest way to make money is not to lose it. Overpaying for anything is losing money.

That brings us to this chapter's first get-house-rich secret:

Don't overpay for housing.

Calling this a secret is ridiculous. You know this. Everyone knows this. But overpaying means failing to comparison shop. That was our mistake. We hadn't kept an eye on our housing market. We had been shopping blind. The secret within the secret, though, is figuring out how to correctly compare the cost of two very different homes. This is tricky even if the two homes are of equal quality and size. How, for example, do you compare costs if one's a rental unit and one's a unit you'd buy and occupy? I'll explain straightaway.

Just like it was for us, it's likely that housing is the largest item in your budget. Before we moved, we were spending about 25 percent of our disposable income on housing. We're now spending half that amount. Thus, the move raised our living standard *for the rest of our lives* by about 12.5 percent. This happy as well as painful confession provides the second get-house-rich secret:

Keep tabs on your housing market.

WHAT'S YOUR HOUSING MARKET?

Staying in the market means continually checking housing costs in all the places you might live, whether we're talking homes you'd buy or rent. But what's your housing market? It's certainly broader than it once was, because in this telecommuting age, there's no need to live where you work.

After writing that last sentence, I took a break to work on a column with an editor who lives in Hong Kong. As we were talking in real time, separated by half the planet, it struck me that I could have been in Hong Kong and she in Providence. Work-wise, nothing would have been different. Actually, if I could do all my teaching, research, and meetings remotely, I could live anywhere in the world as long as there was a fast internet connection.

Does that mean Hong Kong is part of my housing market? Arguably yes. But not really. Moving twelve time zones would mean saying too many goodbyes to too many friends and relatives. These days the location of your friends and relatives may be the most important factor in determining your housing market. This is why we've been advertising Providence to our buddies and kids. We want our circle to move here. Then again, they may subscribe to comedian George Burns's quote that "happiness is having a large, loving, caring, close-knit family in another city."

Just to be clear, I'm not suggesting you treat searching for the best housing deal like a full-time job. But spend more time than I spent. Take a few hours per month reviewing the prices in your housing market.

CHOOSING YOUR HOME

Choosing a home is tough sledding. Houses, condos, and rental apartments differ in price, square footage, layout, charm, location,

HVAC system, appliances, utility costs, street noise, access, parking, taxes, insurance, risk (flood, fire, earthquake, wind), security, needed repairs, and more.

To further complicate things, many aspects of the perfect home are subjective. There's no objective calculator that will accurately weigh how charming you find a particular house. And sometimes what feels undesirable to others makes the perfect house for you. Just like Nancy discovered when planning her career track as a mortician in chapter 1, the search for the perfect home involves compensating differentials. I was skeptical that the compensating differential created by cheaper housing in Providence would make up for leaving Boston. But once I learned more about Providence, it was clear that both the location *and* the price were pure upside. That's the beauty of compensating differentials—they can be negative as well as positive.

So how do you compare houses and factor in compensating differentials? Let's say you're considering houses A and B. Suppose B's price is $53,000 higher than A's. Ask yourself if you owned A, how much you'd be willing to pay to swap it for B. If the answer is less than $53,000, stick with A.

What if you have three house choices: A, B, and C. Now decide what you'd be willing to pay (which could be a negative amount) to move from A to B. Also determine what you'd be willing to pay to move from A to C. These are your compensating differentials. They don't depend on what it actually would cost to buy any of the three houses; they depend on how much you would *want* to live in B or C compared to A. Once you've done this, lower B's and C's prices by these compensating differentials. (If the differential is negative, you'll arrive at a higher number.) Now you have the total cost of each of the three houses, including their compensating quality differentials, and can compare which house is cheapest taking all factors into account.

Let's say B costs $80,000 more than A, but you like B $40,000 better. Then, in total, B costs $40,000 more than A and A wins out. Now suppose C costs $80,000 less than A, but you like A $100,000 more than C. Despite the sticker price, for you, C is actually $20,000 more expensive than A. A wins again. As a third example, suppose, after factoring in compensating differentials, B beats (is cheaper than) A by $35,000 and C beats A by $60,000. C is the right choice.

There's an old saw that economists know the price of everything but the value of nothing. I'd put things differently and broaden it to us all: *Before factoring in compensating differentials, we know the market price of everything but the personal price of nothing.* Clearly, not everything comes with a price tag. For compensating differentials, we need to come up with our own values-based prices. Before adjusting the price of a home we should, however, include all factors that can readily be priced. For example, if the commute from B to work will cost $13,000 over the rest of your career, add that to the cost of the house.

You get the point. Include everything you'll need to directly pay for that's connected to homes A, B, and C. If A is your current location, pretend you're buying it from scratch. The list of dollar add-ons includes commuting costs, property taxes, insurance, repairs, maintenance, security systems, gardening, utility costs, state- or country-specific taxes, and your financing loss (not the same as your mortgage payment, as we'll discuss shortly). Once you've added all tangible extra costs to the prices of A, B, and C, subtract from B and C the extra amount you'd give to live there rather than in A — their compensating differentials. Then compare total prices.

COMPARING THE COSTS OF OWNER-OCCUPIED AND RENTAL HOMES

Is it better to rent or own? There are two ways, neither simple, to compare the cost of renting versus buying. One way is to think of the house you own as a rental unit and consider how much you're effectively paying its landlord (you) as rent. This pretend rental price is called "imputed rent," which you can compare with what rental units of the same quality would cost you. Economists make imputed rent calculations in determining how much annual GDP (gross domestic product) is being produced or provided in the form of housing services by all occupied houses each year across the country. Imputed rent can be determined by directly measuring what similar homes would rent for. Or it can be indirectly calculated by adding up what you'd need to charge a renter for you to be willing to hold the property as an investment. The components here are property taxes, homeowner's insurance, maintenance, and forgone after-tax interest, less any expected real-price appreciation.*

Or think about it the opposite way: treat a rental unit as a home you'd buy. I prefer this way because the formula for imputed rent can get a little hairy. Value your rental apartment as something you could permanently rent. This pretend permanent asset can then be compared with homes you might buy.

Let's start with the easy case that you're considering renting home C for the rest of your days. Then it's like buying a house, where the price is the present value of your rental payments plus the

---

* This formula means you'd be indifferent about renting your place at its calculated imputed rental value or selling it and investing the proceeds and earning the same after-tax real return.

extras, like utility bills, which you're also going to include in figuring the adjusted prices of A and B.*

This discussion brings me to an important final point about comparing the total present-value cost of either buying or renting a home, or a sequence of homes. If you plan to sell your home and then buy or rent another, the present value of the proceeds of the sale needs to be subtracted in figuring the cost of this housing plan. In addition, you'll need to add the present value of your future home purchase or rental payments and all their attendant costs. You're, in effect, comparing different housing-path strategies.

What about your final move from a house you own through the end of your days? Should the present value of your projected, distant terminal house sale—actually, its bequest—reduce the total price of the house you're considering buying? It should. You're reaping a benefit from bequeathing your house, and this reduces your cost of this housing-path strategy.

MORTGAGES AREN'T PART OF THE BASIC COST OF HOUSING

How on Earth can an economist say mortgage payments aren't a fundamental part of housing costs? Let me give you an illustration. Imagine you face no taxes and have $1 million in the bank. Also, assume you can borrow at the same interest rate that you can earn on your savings. In other words, your mortgage rate is exactly the same as you can earn on your assets. Finally, assume you're buying a $500,000 house.

---

* But what if you plan to rent one place for four years and a different place thereafter? In this case, form the present value by calculating the entire projected path of rents at both places. And if you'll rent and then buy? Add the present value of the short-term rent to the present value of the future purchase price and other costs you'll likely pay on your future home.

There are lots of ways you could arrange your purchase. The most straightforward is to buy the house with cash. Just fork over the $500,000 and you'll have the house plus $500,000 left in your checking account. Your net worth—the value of all your real (physical) assets plus your financial assets minus your financial liabilities (debts)—remains $1 million, comprising the $500,000 house and the $500,000 checking account less zero debt.

Alternatively, suppose you finance the house purchase by borrowing $400,000—taking out a $400,000 mortgage. You now have a house worth $500,000, you have $900,000 in assets ($100,000 having been used as a down payment), and you have a $400,000 financial liability (the mortgage). Add up your assets, subtract the mortgage, and, voilà!, your net worth remains $1 million. Nothing would change if you borrowed a different amount, say $200,000. Your net worth would still be $1 million.

Since it's possible to have hugely different-sized mortgages, own and occupy identical houses, and have exactly the same net wealth, what does your mortgage have to do with the cost of buying the home? The answer is absolutely nothing. Let's record this as a secret.

Mortgage payments are not part of the cost of owning a home.

The word "mortgage" is just one of many names for a loan. There are student loans, credit card loans, car loans, payday loans, business loans, home-improvement loans, home-equity loans, and more. The only reason we associate mortgages with homeownership rather than, say, student loans, is that we can lose our house if we don't make our mortgage payment.

When a bank or other financial company grants you a loan, they ask for some assurance that you'll repay. This is called collateral. If you take out a car loan, for example, they put a lien on your car. In other words, they put their name on your car's title, so you can't sell it without their permission. Your car is their collateral. The word comes from medieval Latin. *Co* means "with." And *lateral* means "side." Together it references a loan that comes with a side condition. You don't repay, we drive off with your Tesla and give you the finger out the window.

Different kinds of loans are collateralized in different ways. Student loans may be collateralized by your future earnings. Don't pay and we'll garnish your wages. We'll even go after your Social Security benefits once you receive them (shocking but true). And mortgages are collateralized with the house you buy. You can also use your house to collateralize a small business loan. Yet no one would suggest the cost of purchasing your home includes your future business loan payments.

Because mortgages are collateralized with your house, their repayment has come to be viewed as a cost of the house. But you're still just borrowing money — what you do with that money doesn't have any necessary connection to purchasing or living in a house you own. Nor does it necessarily have anything to do with the cost of a particular home.

Another way to see this is to suppose you and your clone have the same house, but you have a larger mortgage that requires you to make larger monthly mortgage payments. Would this produce any difference, financially speaking, between you and your clone? No, as the examples earlier indicated — you'll both be occupying identical homes and you'll both have exactly the same net worth. It's no different from you and your clone having the same amount of money, but your clone has half in her right pocket and half in her left pocket, whereas you have it all in your left pocket.

All this said, there is one caveat we need to consider when we translate those hypotheticals into the real world: mortgage interest rates are higher than safe interest rates on investing. As I write this, the thirty-year mortgage rate is 3.2 percent. The interest rate on thirty-year US Treasury bonds is 1.5 percent. The difference is 1.7 percentage points.*

No one would borrow at 3.2 percent to lend at 1.5 percent. That's a surefire way to lose money. When we see people taking out mortgages, with their high interest rates, it's because they don't have the cash to buy their house outright. This is what's meant by being cash constrained. Paying an annual finance charge to own a house, measured by the product of the annual interest rate differential — that 1.7 percent — and the outstanding mortgage balance, is an extra cost, like the extra cost of commuting to and from that home. You'll need to add the present value of this extra cost for each home you might buy, *which is not the mortgage payment per se,* to understand the total cost of owning each house. To summarize this secret:

Mortgage interest rate differentials, not mortgage payments per se, add to housing costs.

MORTGAGES ARE NOT YOUR FRIEND

Because of mortgage interest rate differentials, mortgages are financial losers. They're not nearly as bad as credit card balances, student loans, or payday loans, whose interest rates are far higher, but they're still something to be avoided when possible. As with all consumer loans, mortgages are losers because their safe interest rates are far higher than you can safely earn on your savings. This is why paying off household debts, starting with the highest interest rate debts, is your best investment. It's entirely safe and it provides you a for-sure, above-market yield.

---

* Both rates are strictly comparable because they are both safe, meaning "for sure." You have to pay your mortgage for sure, assuming you won't default. And Uncle Sam for sure has to pay you interest on its thirty-year bonds, assuming Sam won't default.

Think about it. If you have $100,000 that you can invest right now in a bond earning 1.5 percent, you'd have $1,500 in interest income over the course of a year. But if you had a $100,000 debt at 3.2 interest that you could pay off right now, you'd save $3,200 over the course of the year in interest payments. On balance, you'd make $1,700 *with no risk whatsoever* by investing in debt repayment rather than investing in the bond.

Mortgages are not only financial losers but also tax losers. Before the passage of the Tax Cut and Jobs Act (TCJA) of 2017, mortgages were generally viewed as beneficial for tax purposes because you could generally benefit from deducting the interest component of the mortgage payment. TCJA changed that calculation by roughly doubling the standard deduction in 2021 to $25,100 for married couples and $12,550 for singles and limiting the eligibility of interest deduction to mortgages below $750,000. Because of those changes, very few people are able to take advantage of the mortgage interest deduction. When they itemize deductions, including their mortgage interest deduction, the total now almost always amounts to less than the standard deduction. Therefore, borrowing to buy a home provides no tax break for the vast majority of households.

Okay, the tax break of mortgages is basically gone. But why does that mean mortgages are tax losers?

Forget mortgage interest rate differentials, and go back to assuming you can invest at the same rate as the mortgage interest rate. And suppose you have $500,000 in cash to buy your house, but you take out a $300,000 mortgage so you only have to put up $200,000 and you have $300,000 left over to invest. Compared to buying the house outright, you've just raised your tax bill. The interest you earn on your $300,000 investment is taxable, and the interest you pay on the $300,000 you borrowed is not deductible since you'll almost surely take the standard deduction. Things get even worse when you put mortgage interest rate differentials back in the mix.

These problems with mortgages lead us to another get-house-rich secret:

Avoid mortgages to the extent possible.

CASHING OUT YOUR RETIREMENT ACCOUNT TO PAY OFF YOUR MORTGAGE

If mortgages are financial and tax losers, is there a way to reduce or eliminate them and would doing so help your finances? The answers are yes and possibly.

Meet Sam and Danielle, who live in Maryland. Sam's sixty-one, Danielle's fifty-five. Sam's just been laid off from his $150,000-a-year job, but he expects to be rehired in a year. Danielle earns $50,000 working for the federal government. Both will retire at sixty-seven, when they'll start Social Security.

The couple has $1.7 million in traditional IRAs, Sam has $400,000 in a Roth IRA, and they have $100,000 in their checking account. As for housing, they own a home valued at $600,000 with a thirty-year mortgage of $400,000 on which they are paying 3.65 percent interest—far north of the 1.5 percent thirty-year Treasury bond investment rate.

Sam set up his Roth account more than five years ago, so he can withdraw all of it tax-free. If the couple uses Sam's entire Roth account to pay off their mortgage, their lifetime spending will rise by almost $96,000, or about two-thirds of their combined annual after-tax earnings!

The source of this huge gain is the interest rate differential. In the first year alone, the couple was going to earn $6,000 on their

Roth by investing in thirty-year Treasury bonds. But their mortgage interest payments were going to total $14,600. This $8,600 differential will decline over time as their outstanding balance falls and as inflation erodes its real value. Still, you can tell that $96,000 is in the right ballpark for their lifetime spending gain. You can assess your own gains from paying off your mortgage, or at least prepaying it over time. Just add up your real (inflation-adjusted) annual counterparts to the $8,600 over the remainder of your mortgage.

Note that there's no risk whatsoever in conducting this transaction. One safe (for-sure) asset, the Roth, is being used to pay off another safe (for-sure) liability, the mortgage. But when Sam and Danielle consider doing this, they wonder if it wouldn't be better to leave the $400,000 in their Roth and invest it in the stock market. Historically, the stock market has yielded 6.5 percent above inflation. That's miles higher than the roughly zero percent real return on the thirty-year Treasury bonds that Sam and Danielle are currently invested in.

Sam and Danielle should be careful of what they ask for. As I have already belabored and will discuss further in chapter 9, the stock market is extremely risky. Historically, investing in stocks for very long periods of time—thirty or more years—has paid off handsomely. But the stock market can drop and keep on dropping. And nothing guarantees a turnaround before you run out of money.

The fact that the risk premium—the difference between the average real return on stocks and that on short-term Treasury bills—is, as I write this, roughly 6 percentage points reflects the extreme riskiness of the market. The market is, in effect, saying that once you adjust for risk, its real return is zero—the prevailing real return on thirty-year TIPS.

Nonetheless, Sam and Danielle may want to bear the risk and

invest more in stocks. But it's possible for them to have their cake and eat it, too. Even if they use their Roth to pay off their mortgage, they can allocate a larger share of their regular IRA assets to stocks. This will give them the extra stock-market exposure they seek while they still reap the $96,000.

But what if Sam and Danielle had every penny of their Roth and traditional IRA assets in the market? Using their Roth assets to pay off their mortgage would necessarily reduce their total holdings of stock. But Sam and Danielle need to understand that by not paying off their mortgage, they are effectively borrowing money to invest in the stock market. Compared to the position of having no mortgage and no Roth, holding a mortgage and a Roth invested in the stock market is little different from borrowing $400,000 to invest in stocks. Having such a leveraged position is even riskier than just investing in the market. If the stock market collapses, your net worth will fall by an even larger percentage. Why? Because your assets fall, but your liabilities stay fixed.

Is the outcome different if Sam and Danielle use their regular (traditional) rather than their Roth IRA to pay off their mortgage? Doing so requires paying taxes on the withdrawal. Paying those taxes would also affect the couple's cash flow. To avoid this problem, they might withdraw $600,000, giving them enough money to cover the extra taxes. In this case, their lifetime spending gain is just over $90,000. This is a bit short of what they'd get if they paid off their mortgage by cashing out Sam's Roth account.

But how can this be? Shouldn't the gain be far smaller given the need to pay taxes on withdrawals from regular IRAs? No. The couple's regular IRA assets will be withdrawn and taxed at some point. And, as discussed in chapter 4, it's best to have withdrawals occur when tax brackets are low; in other words, to engage in tax-bracket smoothing. And recall, Sam's been laid off.

In sum, regardless of which account is tapped, the secret here is:

Cashing out your retirement-account assets to pay off your mortgage can be a big winner.

WHY IT'S BETTER TO OWN THAN RENT

There's a little-known tax advantage to owning a home that has nothing whatsoever to do with having a mortgage. The tax advantage to homeownership is subtle. Consequently, most people aren't likely aware of this secret:

Homeownership is a tax shelter.

To make clear what's at play, consider two clones, Trudy and Trudy. Each Trudy is the exact physical, emotional, financial, and slightly psychotic copy of the other. The Trudys own identical houses across the street from each other. Though they each own a house, each Trudy lives in the *other* Trudy's house and pays rent to her counterpart.

Why set up this construct? If each Trudy is living in an identical house and each receives and pays the same rent, why should we care? Because when the Trudys rent to each other, the rental income each receives is taxable. However, if they simply live in their own homes and, in effect, pay rent to themselves rather than the other Trudy, that rental income (which you'll remember is called imputed rent) is not taxed. By not taxing imputed rent, the government provides a tax advantage to owning over renting. Economists call this tax advantage a subsidy to homeownership.

How big is the subsidy? Assume that Trudy and Trudy are age thirty, that both will earn $75,000 annually till their retirement at sixty-seven, and that each contributes 4 percent to her IRA. Let's also assume that they charge each other market rent of $16,920 per year, inflation adjusted, on their $300,000 homes.*

As expected, if Trudy and Trudy occupy their own homes, rather than rent to each other, their lifetime taxes are lower by close to $48,000, meaning their lifetime discretionary spending is higher by essentially the same amount. This roughly 1.6 percent increase in lifetime discretionary spending accruing to each Trudy isn't earth-shattering. But it counts.

What's the comparable gain if the Trudys earn $50,000 annually, own $200,000 homes, and rent, at the market rate, from each other? The gain from kicking each other out and moving into their own homes is now much smaller, as they're in lower tax brackets — just $11,000 in reduced lifetime taxes, equaling 0.7 percent of their lifetime discretionary spending. Still, that's not nothing.

How about the Trudys with $150,000 annual earnings who own $600,000 houses? There's a very sizable $108,000 gain — representing roughly a year's after-tax earnings and a 3.3 percent rise in lifetime discretionary spending for each!

How do the two Trudys learn about the tax break from homeownership? Luckily, they have a nasty legal battle, with each accusing the other of stealing her identity. In the ensuing melee, Trudy stops paying rent to Trudy, and vice versa. This leads to mutual evictions and, consequently, occupancy of their own homes, thereby lowering their taxes.

If housing comes with this tax break, but renting does not, why does anyone rent? In other words, why doesn't everyone buy their rental units from their landlords and own, not rent? The answer is

---

* This is, to the dollar, the amount the clones will spend on housing every year over their lifetimes whether they rent or own.

transactions costs, moving costs, and cash constraints (no down payment). College students aren't going to buy an apartment only to sell it four years later, paying large real estate agent fees on both ends. People aren't going to buy a house in a new location based on a new job that may not work out. And low-income people may not have the down payment needed to qualify for a mortgage. In addition, governments, including the federal government, often subsidize the development of rental units, particularly for low-income households, making renting cheaper than owning, as developers lower rents to attract tenants who can let them reap tax breaks.

My message, in general, is to go home-shopping with a bias toward buying with cash, not renting. Having more of your money parked in your home is a way to shelter it from federal and state asset-income taxation. This is particularly the case if you're a moderate to high earner. Therefore, along with the other adjustments you need to make when comparing the monetary costs of buying versus renting, make an adjustment that incorporates paying less federal and state income taxes when you buy.

HOW HOMEOWNERSHIP CAN REDUCE LONGEVITY RISK

Owning a home comes with risks, from floods to fires to wind damage to earthquakes. But these can generally be handled via homeowner's insurance. And when viewed from another angle, owning a home is actually a great way to reduce one of the biggest risks we face: living too long in a world in which the price of housing can rise. If you're, say, seventy and have found your dream location near your grandchildren, renting for the rest of your life runs the risk of rent hikes without the possibility of your fixed income increasing. In contrast, if you own your own home, home prices can soar or collapse, but you'll be insulated. Since you are neither buying nor selling your home, who cares what the housing market does? Your housing consumption is guaranteed *through the end of your days*. If this sounds like a real version of an annuity, it is. It's inflation-proof real income, provided in the form of housing services—services that don't end until you say sayonara.

The other reason to hold on to your house is as a security blanket against large end-of-life medical expenses. The big medical expense that's not covered by standard health insurance is long-term care, be it assisted-living or nursing-home care. The tricky question is how to extract the value of your home to cover these costs.

In the case of assisted-living and nursing-home care, the standard practice, for middle-class and even upper-middle-class households, is to sell your house and use the proceeds to pay for entrance into a nice facility. However, given how expensive decent eldercare facilities are, you'll likely quickly run out of funds if you have an extended stay. But long-term care facilities typically have a workaround. They suggest you sell your house and use the proceeds to pay them as a private-pay resident until your money runs out. In return, they promise that when you're broke and able to qualify for Medicaid, they will continue to let you live in the facility, billing Medicaid for your room. In short, your home—actually the equity in your home—becomes your entrance fee into a nice old-age home.

That brings us to another get-house-rich secret:

Homeownership provides longevity insurance plus a ticket into decent long-term care.

This suggestion to use your "trapped equity" as a reserve to buy into a better Medicaid facility runs counter to the standard counsel conveyed to those who seem likely to require unaffordable long-term nursing-home care. The advice is to gift your assets to your children at least five years in advance so Medicaid can't claw them back to help pay for your care. These are tricky decisions that depend in large part on your relationship with your children or other caretakers. But having gone through this with two parents, I can tell you there is a market for entry into better facilities and thus a good potential use for trapped equity even if you'll ultimately be living in a facility that accepts Medicaid.

EXTRA WAYS TO BE HOUSE POOR NO MORE

Thus far I've focused on methods for determining where to live and how to pay for housing. But there are additional ways to get house rich, such as sharing housing costs via cohabitation, renting out your home, reducing your housing costs via downsizing, and extracting trapped home equity.

Shack Up with Mom!

Consider Hester, a sixty-five-year-old mom, and Peter, her thirty-year-old son, both of whom are single, live by themselves, and are having a tough time making ends meet. Neither is all that fond of the other, but both realize that two can live far more cheaply than one. Plus, Hester can cook and Peter can do physical chores. After many second thoughts, Hester and Peter move in together. Once they do, both of their living standards instantly and dramatically jump due to economies of shared living. This involves sharing not only shelter but also electricity, lighting, heating, air-conditioning, the dishwasher, the washing machine, the dryer, the iron, the hair dryer, video games, the piano, the Christmas tree, the sound system, the toolbox, artwork, laptops, the TV, the printer, the outdoor grill, furniture, leftovers, and so on. They also can make shopping cheaper by buying in bulk.

If Hester and Peter were financial and physical clones and could truly live as cheaply as one person living alone, moving in together would double their living standard! But since each needs their own room and clothes and other personal items, their gain from cohabiting is smaller. Still, the advantages are considerable. My estimate is that two people cohabiting can typically live as cheaply as 1.6 people living separately.* It implies that shacking up with another person will raise each person's living standard by 25 percent. That's pure money magic, setting aside both the loss of privacy and the gain of companionship.

Young Americans—those eighteen to twenty-nine—are increasingly aware that shacking up is a moneymaker. A majority are now living with their parents.[1] This is a massive sea change from the way things were in 1960. Then, only 29 percent of young Americans camped out with Mom, Dad, or both.[2] The counterpart of this change in living arrangements is that older Americans, actually one in five, are now living with their kids and, possibly, their grandkids.[3] Sure, rooming with your folks likely won't entail proportionate sharing of dollar expenses. But if your parents or grandparents really seek your companionship, the living arrangement can be viewed as you paying your fair share of rent and them paying for your company. The net payment is, then, what you actually fork over for board.

If two can live more cheaply than one, can three live more cheaply than two, etc.? Absolutely. The more people you can cram into the same space or a space that's not far larger, the cheaper it is per person to pay the cable and all other household bills.

But as more and more people join your commune, expect war to break out due to the "free-rider" problem—each person failing to

---

* This estimate is informed by a study from the Organisation for Economic Co-operation and Development's Project on Income Distribution and Poverty. See OECD, "What Are Equivalence Scales?" [n.d.], https://www.oecd.org/els/soc/OECD-Note-EquivalenceScales.pdf.

do their share of the work involved in group living (let alone agree-ing on the same Netflix series to watch). Everyone's attitude becomes "Someone else will clean the toilet and do the dishes." The moral here is, pick your roommate(s) carefully. But also know that there is an enormous potential financial gain from living with others, whether or not romance or family ties are involved.

To summarize this housing secret:

Shacking up, even with Mom, is a very powerful way to safely raise your living standard.

Renting Out Your Digs

Another way to lower your housing costs is to rent out your home on a part-time basis. Airbnb and similar online companies have made this very easy. A cousin of mine lives near the beach in Los Angeles. As house prices, insurance costs, and property taxes soared, the imputed rent from occupying her house became unaffordable. One option was to sell and find cheaper housing in the burbs. The other was to transform her garage into a studio apartment and rent out her house on Airbnb. She chose that route, and over five years, she has pulled in enough income to significantly upgrade her studio apartment as well as the house. Since Airbnb rents are very high in her part of LA, she can rent her place during the year and garner the same financial gain as if she had a full-time roommate. But this arrangement gives her much more privacy and lets her rent to larger-sized families who don't want an unfamiliar roommate while on vacation.

Our friends Rob and Abbey don't have a garage they can con-vert into a bungalow, but they still realized their Boston apartment would rent for a good price. They also realized they could work remotely. Seemingly out of the blue, they decided to put their apartment up for rent for six months, packed up their five-year-old, and hopped on a plane to Fiji. Six months and twelve countries later they returned from a trip financed almost entirely by their Boston apartment rental.

What's interesting in my cousin's and Rob and Abbey's stories is not that they could rent out their places and do something with the proceeds, but that the imputed rent—the rent they were, in effect, having to pay to themselves for occupying their homes—was so high that it could, over time, pay for something as significant as major renovations or a trip around the world.

The lesson is:

If your actual or imputed rent is unaffordable, or at least more than you want to pay to your landlord (you), subletting or renting to others is a real option.

By the way, what's true of your home is also true of your car. My friend Roger uses an Airbnb-type service to make money on his car, which otherwise stands idle most days. He and his friend also Airbnb their places on different days and bunk with each other when one has a renter. Not sure what Roger will rent out next. I'm thinking his dog.

Downsizing: The Power of Half

If it's not practical to share your housing or rent it out, consider downsizing to less costly housing that still suits your needs. Americans have large homes. In fact, nine out of ten recently constructed homes have three or more bedrooms. Having lots of rooms when you're raising kids makes sense. But when they've left the nest? That's a prescription for overspending on housing. Yes, holding on to a house gives you a built-in safety net—a store of value that you can eventually swap for entry into a long-term care facility as previously discussed. But every year you pay too much in imputed rent—the sum of property taxes, homeowner's insurance, maintenance, and forgone after-tax interest—is a year you've wasted money. Paying for something you don't need to mitigate a specific future financial risk isn't necessary. There are other ways to deal with long-term care needs. One is to buy long-term care insurance. A second is simply to hold financial assets, including, for that matter, real estate, but indirectly in the form of real estate investment trusts (REITs).

A third is to arrange for your children to care for you if you need assistance short of skilled nursing. Such an arrangement can be quid pro quo. For example, you might downsize, then use freed-up equity to provide your children with down payments to buy their own homes. In exchange, you can make it clear that you expect them to take care of you if you need help down the road or simply live longer than expected. This is, in effect, organizing an implicit, intra-family insurance arrangement. You provide an up-front gift or name your kids in your will. If you die earlier than expected without having incurred substantial living or healthcare expenses, they make out. If you die later than expected or experience large out-of-pocket expenses, they help you with either money or direct physical care and you make out.*

Once you've figured out your long-term care plans, you can focus on how much downsizing can gain you in terms of a higher living standard. To see what's involved, take Peggy and Michael Green, a sixty-five-year-old couple who just retired with $2 million

---

* One of my earliest, coauthored research papers showed that even families with two or three members can provide most of the gains available from purchasing formal longevity insurance. The paper is called "The Family as an Incomplete Annuities Market," written with Avia Spivak. See https://kotlikoff.net/wp-content/uploads/2019/04/The-Family-as-an-Incomplete-Annuities-Market-March-7-2007.pdf.

in their 401(k)s, Social Security benefits of $2,500 per month for Peggy and $1,500 per month for Michael, and a million-dollar, four-thousand-square-foot, four-bedroom house. Their house, which they plan to leave to their kids, is free and clear of any mortgage.

Annual property taxes, insurance, and maintenance equal $7,500, $3,500, and $3,000 respectively. Their pretax interest and inflation rates are, as in prior examples, 1.5 percent. They live in Sacramento, California, and therefore face California's state income tax along with the federal income tax.

Here's the question: By how much would Peggy and Michael's lifetime discretionary spending rise were they to downsize to a two-bedroom place that costs $500,000 and requires half the expenses? To not bias the answer, let's assume the couple will leave their new home to their kids, plus an extra $500,000, so their bequest will remain at $1 million—the same amount they now plan to leave, just with more cash and less home equity.

Under these assumptions, downsizing their housing by 50 percent raises the couple's remaining lifetime discretionary spending by $154,990. That's 5.8 percent more discretionary spending, year in and year out through age one hundred if they live that long, or $4,428 more annually. This is a shockingly large amount of money—more than three years of Social Security benefits. It's not the result of finding a far cheaper housing market—the way my wife and I did. It's not the result of releasing $500,000 in trapped equity, since Peggy and Michael still plan to bequeath $1 million. It's the "power of half," in this case living on half rations with respect to living space. Truth be told, Peggy and Michael aren't using even half of their four-thousand-square-foot home. They visit their kids in Nevada, never step foot into three of the four bedrooms, and eat dinner in their kitchen. Their dining room hasn't been used since, well, forever.

By halving the size of their home, the couple cuts their imputed rent in half. Recall that forgone, after-tax interest is a component of imputed rent. But nominal interest rates are so low that the real return—the return after inflation—from investing in safe long-term Treasury bonds is, at this writing, zero. In other words, there is currently no way to make a real return after taxes on standard safe, long-term Treasury bonds. This makes the imputed rent—the cost of Peggy and Michael sitting in their very big home—smaller than it would be otherwise. In normal times, with, say, a 3 percent nominal return (meaning safe investments would yield 1.5 percent over inflation), imputed rent for Peggy and Michael would be higher. In fact, all else being equal, were the nominal interest rate 3 percent, the percentage increase in living standard from downsizing would be twice as large: 10.6 percent. In absolute terms, the Greens would pick up the equivalent of 5.3 years of Social Security benefits *free of tax.*

Does the power of half hold if all of the Greens' numbers are half as large? Yes. The 5.5 percent living-standard gain is almost unchanged. What about a three-times-richer version of the Greens, in which both Peggy and Michael receive the maximum Social Security full retirement benefit of $3,011 and their other numbers are three times larger? The percentage gain in this case is 6.1 percent. Downsizing by half seems then to deliver the same percentage payoff up and down the income scale.

That brings us to the downsizing secret:

If your nest is empty, downsizing can pay off big-time, particularly when interest rates are high.

Moving to a Low-Tax or No-Tax State

There are forty-two states, including the District of Columbia, with income taxes. The states that don't tax income are Alaska, Florida,

Nevada, New Hampshire, South Dakota, Tennessee, Texas, Washington, and Wyoming. If you live directly on the Massachusetts–New Hampshire border, you can, theoretically, move across the street and save 5 percent of your pay, which you'd otherwise surrender in Massachusetts income taxes. Things are more complicated, of course. Land values in New Hampshire may be higher in light of the state's tax advantage. And amenities, like the school system, might be better in Massachusetts. But who knows? You may be childless and happy to live in a tall five-decker with no yard. So moving across the street could be your path to a small bonanza.

Another potentially huge consideration in deciding what home in what state is best for you is estate taxation. In addition to DC, eleven states levy estate taxes: Connecticut, Hawaii, Illinois, Maine, Massachusetts, Minnesota, New York, Oregon, Rhode Island, Vermont, and Washington. Another five states, Iowa, Kentucky, Nebraska, New Jersey, and Pennsylvania, tax inheritances. And one state—Maryland—taxes both estates and inheritances.

If you have significant wealth you're likely to bequeath, be careful about spending your golden years in states with estate taxes. The federal estate tax kicks in for estates above $11.7 million. But the thresholds are much lower for states. In Massachusetts, for example, it's $1 million. And the Massachusetts estate tax rate rises from 0.8 percent to a whopping 16 percent. In Hawaii and Washington, the top rate is 20 percent.

As for inheriting wealth, if that's on your radar and you're a remote relative or a non-related heir, establish your home outside Nebraska. The state will tax your inheritance by as much as 18 percent!

Freeing Up Trapped Equity

For the baby boom generation, which as we've discussed is very poorly prepared for retirement, spending their home equity is likely to be a necessity. The problem with equity trapped in your house is liquidity—you can't get at it until the house is sold, which may be when you're deceased. You need that money now, not after your salad days are over. That's the consumption-smoothing goal.

Downsizing can certainly help. Consider Peggy and Michael once again, but this time let's have them plan to spend the home equity they'll release when downsizing rather than set it aside for a future bequest. Now their living-standard increase is 25.8 percent higher, with the absolute gain in lifetime spending totaling $692,261. This is the equivalent of more than fourteen years in combined pre-tax Social Security benefits. If the Greens have half as much in resources, their percentage gain is 25.4 percent and their absolute gain is $348,177—still an enormous amount of cash. If the Greens have three times more resources, apart from collecting their maximum full-retirement benefits, the percentage gain is even higher—an amazing 39.8 percent with an absolute gain of $1,984,374 (the percentage gain for the rich is larger because, given the maximum level of Social Security benefits, trapped equity is a larger share of total resources).

But what it you refuse to move, don't need to keep your home equity as a long-term care reserve, and don't have kids or other heirs to whom you wish to leave your house? What can you do to un-trap and spend at least part of your home equity? You can try to free up equity by borrowing on your home, taking out a conventional mortgage or refinancing to a larger mortgage, with the hope of dying before you repay. This appears to let you spend more in the near term, but it's not that simple in practice. If you borrow and spend and fortuitously die before the mortgage is fully paid, you'll have succeeded at spending more before that date, with the bank getting repaid from the sale proceeds of your home. The mechanism is standard. Your bank places a lien on your house when you take out your mortgage. This means that the bank stands first in line for the moolah received when the house is sold.

But what if you die after the mortgage comes due? To make things concrete, suppose you're single, age sixty, no kids or other heirs, and take out a twenty-year mortgage. Then, if you make it to eighty, you will have spent twenty years paying back more money than you could have earned by safely investing the mortgage proceeds. All you will have done is lose money over the twenty-year period. Of course, as soon as you receive the mortgage you can party with its proceeds. But down the road you'll need to pay for doing so in the form of reduced consumption. You could also borrow to invest, say, in stocks. But borrowing on expensive terms to invest at risk is, well, risky. If your stocks tank, you'll still have to repay the mortgage and will likely be forced to reduce your future consumption even more. Either way, you'll be going against your consumption-smoothing grain and paying a good penny for the privilege. Moreover, at eighty you'll likely still have the same amount of trapped equity, in real terms, as you had at sixty. There's also the small point that unless you're still working, you're not likely to be able to take out a regular mortgage. Nor, for that matter, will you likely get access to a significant equity line of credit. This is where reverse mortgages come in.

Reverse Mortgages

Reverse mortgages (RMs) are specifically designed to help you un-trap home equity. They are rather complicated. And complicated financial products are generally designed for a specific purpose: to separate you from your money and other valuables, including your home. On the other hand, RMs are heavily regulated by the Federal Housing Administration. Virtually all RMs are FHA home equity conversion mortgages (HECMs). Surely if Uncle Sam is involved they must be safe for public use, right?

This, unfortunately, is too much magical thinking even for this book. Please recall just three of the scams Uncle Sam is running with Social Security—duping widow(er)s out of potentially hundreds of thousands in lifetime benefits, calling us up as we get close to seventy to bribe us to take what we likely won't realize are lower annual benefits, and failing to provide retroactive benefits, apart from six months, if we learn we're eligible for them too late. This third scam is the most egregious. After all, via years of 12.4 percent combined employer-employee payroll tax contributions, we paid for those benefits we weren't told about and, therefore, failed to collect!

Uncle Sam is, unfortunately, shorthand for politicians, and politicians, particularly those in charge of financial regulation, get their campaign bread extremely well buttered by banks and other financial companies. Just check out the major donors—past and present—to the House Committee on Financial Services. The message is clear. US financial regulation is bought and sold by Wall Street.

Knowing Uncle Sam all too well, I have done my homework on RMs. Here's my bottom line:

Unlike conventional mortgages, reverse mortgages do let you use trapped equity to repay the amount borrowed, but they do so at a very high price and significant risk.

Comparing Reverse and Regular Mortgages

RMs are like regular mortgages with six main exceptions. First, you have to be over sixty-two to qualify for one. Second, you can't borrow as much as you would with a regular mortgage.* Third, an RM has higher interest rates than a regular mortgage. Fourth, an RM comes with higher fees. Fifth, an RM lets you defer repayment until the house is sold, triggered by your vacating the property either vertically or horizontally. And sixth, you can't be evicted from your home unless you fail to cover its carrying costs—property taxes, homeowner's insurance, and maintenance. This is true regardless of whether your RM has gone underwater.

Compared with a regular mortgage, the first four differences—the age requirement, the smaller loan amount, the higher interest rate, and the higher fees—make RMs worse. The fifth difference—deferring payment—lets you, in effect, increase your loan over time. It also gives you more immediate cash to spend since you don't need to make monthly mortgage payments. As for the sixth difference—being able to stay in your home after it's sunk beneath the waves, meaning the amount borrowed accumulated at interest exceeds your home's value—you'll have to live a long time *and not move* for this to happen. Also, the higher the RM fees and interest rate, the sooner this so-called advantage arises. But once you're underwater on your RM, you'll be, in effect, renting from the lender at a below-market price. You'll need to cover only carrying costs, not market rent, which would include the owner's forgone real interest.[†] Yet if that rate is zero, which it is as I write this, there is no actual rental break if you live and stay long enough to go underwater on your RM.

An RM, to repeat, will give you extra spending power, paid from

---

* The maximum amount you can borrow on an HECM RM is the product of x and y: x is a percentage that ranges from 52.4 percent at age sixty-two to 63.8 percent at age eighty-five, and y is the smaller of the value of your home and a cap (the HECM principal limit)—$822,375 in 2021. If you have an existing mortgage, it can't exceed half your home value. If it's less, the HECM is used to pay off your existing mortgage, leaving less available for you to directly receive.

† I'm assuming your home's price will keep even with the rate of inflation.

your home equity while you remain in your home. In this respect, it appears to resolve the trapped equity problem. But since it gives you relatively little to spend in exchange for a large chunk, if not all, of your home equity, it's, to use an old British expression, not worth the candle.

Let me encapsulate my concerns about RMs with two parables that intentionally exaggerate RM costs in order to raise your antennae. I'm describing RMs in different financial terms than are used in actual RM transactions to get at the essence of the deal. Both feature Lou, a single, childless, sixty-two-year-old retiree, and Sue, a newly minted Harvard MBA.

LOU LOSES A BET

One day, while Lou is mowing his lawn, his neighbor Sue ambles over and says, "Hi, Lou. That's a really nice million-dollar house you have. You know, Lou, I checked the public record, and, gee, you own your house free and clear. Congrats. I also heard you're retired. Congrats, again. Still, Lou, I'm worried about you. From the looks of your clothes, car, and waistline, you seem strapped for cash. Given my elite training, I've figured out how to help. Sign here and I'll pay you $500,000 for your house right this minute. Yes, I know your house is worth twice that. But here's the cool thing: I'm going to let you live in your—well, *our*—house for as long as you want or can. I won't move in until you move out or are carried out. In the meantime, all you'll need to do is pay the property taxes, keep it insured, and handle its maintenance. If you fail to cover these carrying costs, well, I'll need to evict you."

Wow, Lou thinks. *A Harvard MBA.* He immediately signs on the dotted line. But in bed that night he tosses and turns, worrying that he'll need to move sooner than expected. Sure enough, at 5 a.m. sharp Lou has a stroke. Fortunately, he's able to squeeze his medical alert button before passing out. The ambulance takes Lou to the ER and, later, to his new lifetime residence—a nursing home. Sue, awakened by the sirens, watches when they strap Lou to the gurney. She tells the EMTs not to worry. She'll lock up her house.

Lou's just lost half a million dollars—money that could have bought him entry into a nicer nursing home or paid for a bevy of private aides. And if we modify the story and have Lou die from the stroke, his heirs inherit half a million dollars less. Sue finagled Lou into an extremely expensive RM structure.

LOU "WINS" THE BET

In a parallel universe, Lou, unbeknownst to Sue, is nobody's lunch meat. He's not even his own lunch meat, as in: You are what you eat. Lou, you see, is vegan. He's shabby because he likes the grunge look. As for his beat-up Beetle, it's his pride and joy. After cutting the deal with Sue, Lou spends the next thirty-eight years doing what he always does—exercising like crazy and eating sprouts, tofu, beans, tempeh, nuts, etc., morning, noon, and night. On his one-hundredth birthday, Lou chokes on a snack of chives and raw oats, squeezes his button, and drops dead. Sue, now graying around the temples, hears the sirens, and rushes to the ambulance, screaming, "Amen!"

In this alternative, happier fable, Lou gets to spend $500,000 more over the next thirty-eight years than he would have otherwise and dies where he'd like: at his kitchen table. And Sue? She has had to wait thirty-eight years to occupy "her" house.

Lou might claim he won the bet. Not in my view. Lou gets to spend only half of his trapped equity.* And his heirs—his niece and nephew—end up with a $500,000 shorter end of the stick.

Actual RMs use different language to describe the deal between Lou and Sue. In RM lingo, Lou borrows the $500,000. But as soon

---

* With higher than the prevailing zero real rates, Lou would have extracted more than half his trapped equity.

as he vacates the property, whether voluntarily or involuntarily, the house is sold to pay the outstanding RM balance (the $500,000 plus unpaid RM fees and closing costs, all accumulated at the combined RM-plus-mortgage-insurance interest rate). If the home's sale price exceeds the RM balance, Lou or his estate will receive what's left over and the loan payoff proceeds are figuratively what goes to Sue. If the sale price is less than the RM balance—the RM is underwater—the entire proceeds from the home sale will go to the RM lender, figuratively Sue.

Let me summarize my issue with RMs:

If you move or die too soon, reverse mortgage lenders will help themselves to a goodly share of your trapped home equity.

Of course, nothing says you have to move. But if you want to move and choose not to due to the cost of repaying your RM, the RM will have locked you into something you no longer want to do: stay in your current home.

These troubling moving cases—"I have to move, but paying back the RM will leave me bereft" and "I have to move, but I can't because repaying the RM is too expensive"—sour me the most about RMs. But I became less concerned when I learned about a type of RM called an HECM for purchase.

HECM for Purchase

Say you take out an RM and then need to move after fifteen years to be near your kids. Also suppose the RM repayment leaves you with too little money to purchase an equivalent home. You can get an HECM for purchase that can help get you into the new home. And, as with your first type of RM, this new loan requires no repayment.

Thus, if your HECM RM borrowing percentage is 60 percent, you can get 60 percent of the proceeds to buy a new house. The remaining 40 percent plus the costs will be yours to cover. In short:

An HECM for purchase can soften the blow of RM repayment if you must move.

To be clear, taking out one RM is expensive enough. Now we're talking about taking out another. And there's nothing that says the second RM will pay off, either. You may need to move more than once over the rest of your life. And if you're underwater when you have to move, you'll have no equity left to buy into a quasi-decent nursing home or to use for a down payment in conjunction with an HECM for purchase loan.

Many people who take out an HECM RM do so to pay off their mortgage, not necessarily to purchase a new home. They are delighted to get out from under the monthly payments that are strapping their cash. But this doesn't make HECM RMs any cheaper. This said, using RM proceeds to pay off existing debt is more prudent than using it to increase consumption.

Ways to Take the Proceeds of an RM

An HECM RM offers six options for taking RM proceeds, either in full or in part. The interest rate you'll be charged on RM-borrowed proceeds as well as on unpaid RM costs is either fixed or flexible. Flexible means it can rise, to your possibly major detriment.

Of the six options, the only one that comes with a fixed rate involves immediately taking all potential RM proceeds in a lump-sum payment. The fixed rate will be higher than the variable rates charged on the other options, but it'll also be safer.* Your second option is to receive fixed monthly payments that continue until you die—effectively, an annuity, which will provide higher payments due to the potential of your dying young. Annuities are, of course, insurance policies against excessive longevity. Your third option is to receive fixed payments for a fixed number of months. The remaining three options each entail your taking out a line of credit with either (a) no payments, (b) payments in the form of an annuity, or (c) fixed payments. The amount held back as a line of credit can be exercised at the borrower's discretion.

RMs If You're Married

If you're married and considering an RM, make sure both you and your spouse are on the deed, and my advice would be to wait until both spouses are over sixty-two to do the deal. An HECM RM, in this case, will be based on the younger spouse's age. If your spouse is under age sixty-two, there are a host of small-print conditions that you'll need to meet to ensure that if the qualifying spouse—the one over sixty-two—dies, the surviving spouse won't land on the street with their stuffies.[4] Let me red-flag this:

> **If your spouse is under sixty-two and you're considering taking out an RM, before signing up, review with a top lawyer what the treatment of your spouse will be if you die.**

HECM RM Payouts and Inflation Risk

If you take your RM payout in a lump sum and invest it in Treasury inflation-protected securities (TIPS) or other assets that are explicitly

---

* Of course, if you take your money and run right to the neighborhood casino, that's actually far riskier than the other options. Also, be aware that RM borrowers are often accosted by scammers, who somehow learn they have free cash they may wish to "invest."

or implicitly inflation protected, you'll be safeguarded in three ways. First, your payout will be protected. Second, you will avoid having inflation erode the real value of the investment, as would happen with an RM payout. Third, inflation will erode the real value of what you'll need to repay when you move thanks to the fixed nominal interest charges associated with a lump-sum RM withdrawal.

In contrast to the lump-sum payout, which has the potential to reduce your exposure to inflation, the other five methods of withdrawals come with variable interest rates, which will surely rise with inflation. Indeed, they can expose you to more inflation risk if their interest rates rise with inflation but your house value does not. Of course, if you live in your home long enough to drown your RM—put it underwater—the impact of inflation on real repayments won't matter. In general, my mantra here is this:

Taking HECM RM payments in a lump sum reduces your exposure to rising interest rates and provides a natural hedge against inflation.

Preserving the Value of Your House with an HECM Line of Credit

There is a subtle, but valuable, form of insurance provided by an HECM line of credit (LOC). An LOC will grow at a variable interest rate—the same rate at which your RM payments and costs will accrue. Here's the cool thing: Suppose you simply take out an HECM LOC and don't take any payment, at least not initially. Let's assume the LOC is for $480,000. Also suppose that over, say, the next twenty years, your home's value stays fixed, at $800,000, in nominal terms (that is, it declines year after year in real terms), whereas the LOC rises to $1 million. At that point you can exercise the option to convert your LOC into an RM. You can, for example, take $1 million in a lump sum even though your house is worth only $800,000. In this case, your RM will immediately be underwater. If you move the day after you take out the RM, you'll walk off with the $1 million and the lender will walk off with your $800,000 home. Thus:

An HECM line of credit provides insurance against a decline in the real value of your home.

The cost of an HECM LOC is considerable. In the case of my wife's and my house, which is worth roughly $750,000, the cost would be roughly $15,000. That's a high price to pay to insure against a major drop in our home's real value. But were we really nervous about the possibility of its value not keeping up with inflation, it would be worth considering.

HECM RM Fees

It's no wonder we're facing such a high cost of taking out an HECM RM or an HECM LOC. Both come with a boatload of large and small fees, for counseling, appraisal, origination, servicing, initial mortgage insurance, annual mortgage insurance, title insurance, survey, credit report, escrow, document preparation, pest inspection, courier, flood certification, and more. Collectively, RM fees can easily add up to almost 7 percent of the amount borrowed. This is more than you'd pay on a conventional mortgage. This is the bad news. The slightly redeeming fact is that different RM lenders set their fees differently. So you can and should shop around to find a lender with the lowest fees available.

Potential Gains from an RM

To see the potential value of an RM to one's living standard, suppose you're a married, sixty-two-year-old, retired, Massachusetts-based couple. You have a home worth $450,000 and no mortgage. Each of you receives $2,000 per month from Social Security. Your only other asset consists of a combined $500,000 in regular IRAs. Apart from paying $10,000 annually in housing costs (property taxes, maintenance, and homeowner's insurance) and paying taxes (including Medicare Part B premiums), you have no fixed expenses.

Let's assume you have no children or anyone else to whom you'd like to leave your house. Then, without doubt, you have $450,000 in trapped equity. Say you take out an RM loan for $235,800 and receive the proceeds as a lump-sum payment. Also assume that you both live to one hundred. The RM raises your lifetime spending by $239,000, or 14 percent. That's a decent increase. But this is also the best-case scenario. And this is the key: By the time you reach one hundred, your house will be almost underwater. Consequently, you'll have extracted only 52.4 cents per dollar of your trapped equity. That's a very high price, in my mind way too high, to pay for the RM, and this is the best-case scenario.

Potential Risks of an RM

What happens if you reach, say, eighty-five having taken out the RM and unexpectedly have to move? Assume your house is still worth $450,000. After paying off the RM, including fees and real interest, you'll be left with about $100,000. Essentially, you'll have used up $350,000 of your $450,000 in home equity. At this point, you can go for an HECM for purchase and get into a house worth roughly $275,000. Thus, your house quality will have dropped by almost 40 percent. And if you have to move again in, say, ten years, you'll be left with only $75,000 in home equity out of the original $450,000. Your next, and let's assume final, HECM for purchase loan will get you into a house worth $180,000, implying a 60 percent drop in housing quality relative to where you started. And this scenario assumes that your and other nominal house prices stay fixed. But if yours stays fixed and other house prices rise, the quality of your housing will really plummet.

Here's the point:

> If you have to move and your house's value hasn't kept up with the inflation rate underlying your HECM RM interest rate, you may find yourself handing over your house to the lender (think Sue) with no wherewithal to cover your ongoing housing expenses.

Leaseback: A Better Way to Free Up Home Equity

The easiest way to free up home equity is simply to sell your home and rent. Ideally, sell your home to your kids or another close relative and lease it back from them. Give them a good price in exchange for their not raising the rent faster than inflation. Or specify a formula under which the rent partially adjusts for increases in property taxes or nationwide rents. If you invest the proceeds in long-term TIPS, your home sale proceeds will be protected against inflation and can be used, in part, to pay your lease.

This arrangement can be legally formalized. As such, a leaseback can be organized with anyone, including a bank. Why the FHA hasn't supported this straightforward solution beats me. Maybe the banks don't want to have to deal with a plumbing leak at 11 p.m. on Sunday night or get into landlord-tenant disputes. This is where parents and children, who love each other, have an advantage. The mutual caring limits the scope for bad behavior, like skipping town without paying rent.

How does this solution differ from an RM? First, it releases essentially all your home equity. There are also no fees. Plus, you get to stay in your home as long as you want. And you're not penalized if you need to move.

Buying into a continuing care retirement community is another way to free trapped equity. In this case, you'd sell your home and hand over a chunk of the proceeds to the facility plus pay a monthly fee in exchange for their agreement to provide you with housing, meals, entertainment, and transportation, as well as home-health and nursing care for the rest of your days. Such communities, because of their large numbers of residents, can provide better terms for their services than if each person were to purchase them separately. The reason is their services can be provided in the form of an annuity. Those who live long get the benefit of the up-front payments of those who die young.

RECAP

Your home is your castle. But as with most of the twenty-five thousand castles in Europe, it may not pay for you to live there—at least not on your own. Here are my housing money secrets:

- Don't spend years overpaying for housing like I did.
- Define and research your housing market.
- Compare purchase and rental prices on a systematic basis, taking your personal compensating variations into account.
- A mortgage isn't a basic housing cost. Instead, it's a financial and tax loser. Pay yours off or down ASAP.
- Cashing out your retirement assets to pay off your mortgage may make you a bundle.
- Homeownership is a major tax shelter. It has nothing to do with mortgages.
- The housing services from a home you own represent a real annuity, which provides insurance against excessive longevity. Your home's trapped equity is also a potential entrance fee to a nice long-term care facility.

- Sharing housing costs can dramatically raise your living standard. Shacking up, Airbnbing, and leasing or subleasing—these are all ways to split costs and save money.

- Downsizing can release lots of trapped equity and dramatically raise your living standard.

- Reverse mortgages are expensive means to un-trap your home's equity. They expose you to moving and home price risk. If you have to move, an HECM for purchase RM can help you buy a new home. But each time you move and take out a new HECM loan you incur high fees that compound at a high borrowing rate. While quite expensive, an HECM line of credit represents a unique way to insure yourself against a major decline in your home's resale value.

- Selling and renting is a straightforward way to release essentially all your trapped home equity. But if you want to live in your home, you'll need to rent from your buyer. Your children would be ideal buyers with whom you can make this leaseback arrangement. Using your home equity to buy into a continuing care retirement community is also worth considering.

CHAPTER 6

Marry for Money—The Oldest Financial Trick in the Book

I've had an exciting time; I married for love and got a little money along with it.

— *Rose Kennedy*[1]

Marrying for money may sound crass, but it's one of the oldest financial practices. Babylonia's Code of Hammurabi, written c. 1750 BCE, makes clear in its bride-price and dowry laws that marriage has long been what it remains today: a matter, in large part, of money.

A bride-price meant paying something—maybe a cow, maybe a piece of land, maybe gold coins—to buy a wife, with the payment going to the future bride's family. The Babylonians sold brides at auction. In fact, it was illegal to buy a bride without bidding for her in a competitive process.[2] Often, though, the auctions would go in reverse, with the bidders paying a negative price. That meant the bride's family had to pay the groom (or the groom's family) a dowry to close the deal. If, all things being equal, brides were in short supply relative to demand, the bride-price would be positive.

Thankfully, for most societies in the years since Hammurabi, literally placing a prospective spouse up for inspection on an auction block is no longer the norm. However, many marriages across the centuries have been arranged informally between parents, often with the help of a marriage broker—a matchmaker. Whatever coat of varnish has been put on the practice to make it seem more palatable, one thing is clear: prospective brides and grooms have been commoditized and, indeed, often treated no different from parental chattel.

Times change. In most modern-day societies, young people have the final say over whether and whom to marry. Indeed, they can leave their intended at the altar. Yet these rights to choose and refuse didn't eliminate the marriage market; it just changed the buyers and sellers. Rather than parents offering their children up to the highest bidder, prospective partners are selling themselves and buying others in an increasingly teched-up relationship market. Tinder, Match, Bumble, Hinge, OkCupid, eharmony, EliteSingles, SilverSingles, Zoosk, and OurTime are a sample of the many dating sites that now facilitate love at first click.

Though there's no immediate exchange of funds (other than perhaps a membership fee), these sites place you on a virtual auction block, where you display and convey your full set of wares—your age, education, personality, background, income, race, religion, physical appearance, likes, dislikes, talents, pets, children, and so on. These composite characteristics are what you bring to the marriage barter market. The barter is not your everyday swap of two plump chickens for twenty juicy sausages. Instead, you're offering to merge your pluses and minuses with someone else's. If all goes well, there will be a quick date over coffee, then a few lunches, then a couple of dinners, then some excursions, then a sleepover, then a weekend trip, more sleepovers, then a meeting with the parents or children, then cohabitation. Before you know it, you're happily married or partnered till death do you part... or at least for a while.

My task in this chapter is not to tell you how best to meet the love of your life. I've no expertise on that matter. My goal is to make sure that you barter for a spouse or partner understanding the true economic resources you and your connubial or partnering wannabes are bringing to the table.

Economic resources can be positive or negative. Positive resources include regular assets, retirement accounts, houses and other real estate, vehicles, current and future labor earnings, current and future pensions, current and future Social Security benefits, and so on. Negative resources could be debts (be it mortgages, credit card balances, or student loans), alimony, child support, child college support, parental support, maintenance due on real estate, an unpaid tax liability, and the list goes on.

In focusing on money, partnering, and marriage, I'm not claiming that money is the only or even the deciding factor in coalescing. For most of us, love transcends money. But we humans have the capacity to fall in love with lots of people. And there's no shame in targeting your swooning on someone who can provide you with a higher living standard.

Let me put it this way: If Gail and Kate are the same in all respects, except Gail earns twice as much as Kate, don't flip a coin. Go for Gail. You won't be the first. People have been going for Gail since time immemorial. Now that I've made your decision for you, let's get deep into the advantages of hitching your wagon to a wealthy partner.

THE GAINS FROM MARRYING YOURSELF

Marrying means shacking up and thereby reaping the economies of shared living—the power of which we discussed in the previous chapter. It also means shacking up with the other person's finances, so marriage has to cover this major cost. If you could marry a clone of yourself it would be far easier to decide whether to tie the knot.

Yes, intimacy would be hyper-weird. But you'd know for sure everything there is to know about your mate. You wouldn't have to balance all the uncertain positives against all the uncertain negatives.

Let's consider clone marriage to get a clear sense of marriage's economic value without having to weigh additional factors, including differences over life's big choices, like window treatments. For simplicity, I'm going to assume that economies of shared living are perfect when it comes to housing—that two spouses can be housed for the price of one. As for other components of consumption, I'll make the same reasonable assumption we made in the previous chapter—that two can live as cheaply as 1.6. If all consumption of goods and services, including housing services, were based on this 1.6 factor, two clones could increase their living standard by 25 percent simply by living together. This 25 percent reference point will be useful as we continue.

Net taxes also deserve advance mention because of what's called the marriage tax. This refers to the fact that net taxes levied on a married clone couple can be more than twice the net taxes levied on each of them were they single. If every adult in the country were, for argument's sake, single and were then to marry themselves, the net marriage tax would average more than 4 percent. In other words, nationwide clone marriage would, on average, mean more than a 4 percent reduction in everyone's living standard relative to the world in which everyone stayed single.*

Despite this small but nontrivial net marriage tax, most Americans were married in the past, are married now, or will be married in the future. The share of Americans sixty-five and older who never married is only 4.4 percent. For those between forty-five and sixty-five it's higher—7.5 percent. This may augur a trend away

---

* This figure was calculated by a group of economists, including yours truly, using data from a nationwide household survey conducted by the Federal Reserve.

from marriage. Even so, we're still miles away from, say, Iceland, where marriage is rare and "living in sin" is standard practice.

If you're a tax nerd, like me, you may be scratching your head. "Doesn't this guy know the current federal income tax bracket levels for married couples are twice those for singles for the first five brackets, which includes almost everyone?" That's true. But the last two brackets entail substantial marriage taxes and include some households. And there are other features of the federal income tax, like the Alternative Minimum Tax, that aren't marriage neutral. Moreover, under current law, the tax code reverts in 2028 to what it was prior to the 2017 Tax Cut and Jobs Act—a tax code that included far higher marriage taxes.*

There are also provisions in state income taxes and in the implicit IRMAA tax—the income-related monthly adjustment amount—that are unfavorable to clone marriage. IRMAA is a hefty income-related surcharge added to Part B premiums for married people on Medicare. Your IRMAA is calculated based on your modified adjusted gross income (MAGI) *from two years ago*. If taxing you this year based on your income from two years ago seems strange, that's because it is. IRMAA's treatment of high-income married people is also strange insofar as the provision taxes households with very high incomes for getting married.†

Our tax system's bizarre features pale in comparison to those of our myriad federal and state benefits programs. These programs include SNAP, Medicaid, Medicare, Obamacare subsidies, welfare benefits, housing support, childcare subsidies, and Social Security

---

* When you're married, you do have the option to file separately. But the tax disadvantages are substantial, with the tax bill much higher than that facing two partnered clones.

† If you're single and had a MAGI two years ago of $500,000 or more, you were charged close to $7,500 more in Part B premiums. If you're married and had a MAGI two years ago of $750,000, you and your spouse each paid the same annual premium as someone who is single and had more than half your total income.

benefits. Most of these programs' benefits are far from marriage neutral. In other words, were two clones to marry (particularly low-income clones), they'd lose some if not most of their benefits. For low-income Americans, assistance programs can produce 10 percent or larger marriage taxes. This said, the biggest benefits program—Social Security—actually provides extra benefits for getting married as well as for, after ten years, getting divorced. I'm referring here to the Social Security spousal, divorced spousal, survivor, and divorced survivor benefits discussed in chapter 3.*

Okay, there are economic upsides and fiscal downsides and upsides to marrying yourself. But what's the bottom line? Well, consider the case of childless New Mexico resident Peter, age thirty. Peter earns $50,000 a year and will retire at sixty-seven. He owns a $150,000 house with annual property taxes, homeowner's insurance, and maintenance totaling $1,500, $750, and $750 respectively. Peter's 3 percent, thirty-year mortgage equals 80 percent of his house's value. Apart from his house, Peter has just started contributing 3 percent of his pay to a 401(k), for which he'll receive an equal-sized employer match. His current regular assets are $16,666, or one-third of his annual earnings.

Let's now have Peter marry his clone, Peter. Since our two Peters can perfectly share one of their identical homes, marriage leaves each Peter's enjoyment of housing services unchanged. But in living together, the Peters now pay only one mortgage. They also now pay only one annual property tax, one homeowner's insurance bill, and one set of maintenance costs. Finally, by selling one of their two homes in order to live together, they free up that home's trapped equity. As for the home they occupy, let's assume they plan to leave

---

* These benefits aren't available to long-term partners if they live in the vast majority of states that don't recognize common-law marriage. Even those who live in states that recognize common-law marriage may not qualify for that categorization because their state has highly restrictive conditions, which they don't meet.

it to their two prospective children—Peter and Peter, who look like real chips off the old blocks.

With housing costs taken care of, what happens to their living standard associated with their discretionary spending—all the consumption they enjoy from buying goods and services? When single, each Peter's discretionary spending and living standard was $25,703. Married, their living standard jumps to $34,792. This latter figure takes into account that when one Peter spends money, the other Peter benefits to some extent because of sharing economies. In other words, it's each Peter's effective discretionary spending given that one Peter's discretionary spending is partly enjoyed by the other. That's a 35.4 percent difference between a single and a married Peter's living standard. Were the two Peters to partner rather than marry, the gain would be slightly higher at 35.8 percent. The difference reflects a relatively minor net tax on marriage.

Whether the Peters are married or partnered, we're talking about a lot of money. Just by sharing resources, each Peter's living standard rises by more than one-third. This is communism at its finest, assuming the Peters don't go to war over who left the dishes in the sink. The 35.4 percent figure also reflects the couple's ability to fully economize on housing as well as enjoy the other advantages of downsizing to one house.

Next, let's consider 3× Peter marrying 3× Peter, in which each Peter's economic variables are multiplied by three. The gain from marrying in this case is 34.7 percent. The gain from partnering is 37.4 percent. Thus, the net marriage tax is a bigger deal for 3× than for 1×.*

What about 2× Peter marrying 2× Peter? Now the gain is 34.3

---

* Part of the explanation for the higher net marriage tax is the Alternative Minimum Tax, which disproportionately affects higher-income households and is not neutral to clone marriage.

percent from marrying and 34.8 percent from partnering.* And the gain when 6× Peter marries 6× Peter? It's 36 percent from marrying and 41.7 percent from partnering. The differences represent a major net marriage tax, suggesting the rich might be better off partnering.

Here's the major take-home: marrying or partnering will, all else being equal, raise you and your mate's living standard *by more than one-third*. This is, surely, part of the reason why almost everyone has formally or informally tied the knot in the past. Sharing, provided you don't kill each other, really pays.

MARRYING UP AND MARRYING DOWN

What if 1/2× Peter marries 6× Peter and they live in 6×'s house? 1/2× enjoys a tremendous living-standard improvement. Compared with remaining single, 1/2×'s living standard rises by a factor of 5. His quality of housing rises by a factor of 12. Compared with marrying his 1/2× clone, his living standard rises by a factor of 3.7 with his housing quality still rising by a factor of 12.

What about 6× Peter? He takes a hit, with his living standard falling 22.2 percent compared to staying single, since he has to subsidize his poorer spouse. Compared to marrying himself, it falls 42.8 percent. Therefore, 6× might want to think twice about becoming enamored with a far less financially endowed version of himself.

Will 1/2× Peter have his Cinderella moment? And will 6× Peter be content to marry so far down, financially speaking? It's certainly possible! Granted, there is solid evidence of associative mating based on income—in other words, the rich marrying the rich. This also

---

* This calculation doesn't include the loss of benefits low-income households experience when getting married. Therefore the gain from marriage could well be several percentage points lower.

goes for education, as the highly educated tend to marry the highly educated. But love, as in compensating differentials, can conquer all. Moreover, the concern over marrying down financially may decline the richer one of the Peters becomes. Take a 50× Peter. He's arguably indifferent to the financial risks of hitching up with a 1/2× Peter or a 10× Peter. Yes, his living standard will be lower with 1/2x but it will still be so high that he may not notice.

This is why we observe "trophy" husbands and "trophy" wives— spouses who have below-average earnings but end up married to the superrich. Trophy spouses make up for their financial shortfalls with their other attributes. If you haven't already done so, watch the 1964 film version of the musical *My Fair Lady,* which won the Academy Award for Best Picture. Eliza Doolittle, a Cockney flower girl played by Audrey Hepburn, meets Professor Higgins, an illustrious, well-heeled professor of phonetics. Higgins wagers he can fix Eliza's thick accent, improve her vocabulary, and get her to mingle undetected in high society. Of course, Eliza wins Higgins's heart. However, Eliza is also courted by a socialite suitor—Freddy Eynsford Hill. The competition between Higgins and Hill is an important undertone of the story. It lets Eliza play the field and makes Higgins pay her market price. If Higgins wants to live long-term with what for him are a host of *"Je ne sais quoi,"* he needs to come to the table.

Some people look down on such "trophy" relationships. Money, they may say (correctly!), can't produce true happiness. Fair enough. But a billionaire may have the same capacity to provide emotional support, devotion, understanding, patience, ability to listen, and all the other characteristics of a successful spouse. We shouldn't condemn people who are rich simply because they are rich. Some of the most down-to-earth people in the world are "filthy" rich thanks to their own hard work and perseverance or, in lots of cases, the good fortune to have been born mouthing a silver spoon. This segment of the superrich spend their riches doing good, not eating caviar for breakfast, lunch, and dinner. But they also certainly enjoy what money can buy. As for Eliza, she's nobody's lunch meat. She knows Higgins has more to share than proper diction.

Even if both would-be Peter couples have similar earnings, it may be best for the lower earner to specialize in child-rearing and the high earner to specialize in working. The traditional split of having one spouse raise the kids while the other brings home the bacon may be financially optimal (though there's certainly no economic reason why that split should hew along traditional gender lines in a modern world). This is particularly the case when children are young, given the high costs of childcare. Indeed, for many US workers, childcare costs more than they can earn after taxes. Thus, if you're selling yourself as a full-time child rearer, what you could earn may make little difference to your marriage marketability. In this case, you may have just as good a chance of marrying rich as marrying poor.

The bottom line: If you're going shopping for a partner or a spouse, you might as well shop for someone who is earning a lot more than you. Yes, you're bringing less income to the table, but that may not be important in the other person's eyes. Your charm, erudition, Cockney accent, twinkle, compatibility, wit, talents, interests, and many other things may make you perfect for someone whom you absolutely adore—and not just because of their money.

GET A RING ON IT

Why get married if partnering produces the same or larger gains? Marriage has three advantages over partnering: protection against divorce for the lower-earning spouse, potentially substantial higher Social Security benefits for the lower-earning spouse, and huge risk mitigation for both spouses.

Protection against divorce comes in the form of alimony

payments, which I'll discuss in the next chapter. As for Social Security advantages to marriage? First, after just nine months, you're eligible to collect future widow(er) benefits. Plus, after just one year of marriage, you and your spouse are eligible to collect future spousal benefits. And if you stay married for ten years, you're eligible to collect divorced spousal and divorced widow(er) benefits. As we covered back in chapter 3, the way Social Security's benefits formulas work, the spousal benefit will be useful only to spouses who earn very little in absolute terms and also earn a lot less than their marital partner. The widow(er) benefit, on the other hand, can be of tremendous value to the lower-earning (or divorced) spouse, provided the higher-earning spouse (or ex-spouse) dies first.

Take seventy-eight-year-old pretend Bertha, living in Florida. She receives a $1,500 monthly Social Security check plus some help from her kids. Bertha's been dating pretend ninety-year-old Phil. Phil is a catch. He's in good shape, has a sharp mind, drives a Miata, roots for the Celtics, and, best yet, hauls in a much larger monthly Social Security benefit: $3,000. That's quite high for a ninety-year-old, but Phil waited till seventy to collect.

Bertha and Phil have been going steady for five years. They hang out in the pool when it's not crazy hot. Otherwise, it's cards, bingo, the book club, mahjong, and charades with several couples they've befriended. No way that Bertha wants to move in with Phil. Phil feels the same way. Both value their privacy. But Phil loves, loves, loves his Bertha, who cracks him up with her Jimmy Durante (look him up) impressions and sings his favorite Phil Ochs (check him out) songs.

Lately, Phil's been worrying about dying and leaving Bertha to fend for herself. Together, they've been living a comfortable life, sharing their $4,500 in combined monthly benefits. But how can Phil keep Bertha in the lifestyle to which she's become accustomed if he goes knock, knock, knocking on heaven's door? It's simple.

Phil just needs to slowly (*very* slowly) get down on one knee and ask Bertha for her hand in marriage. Phil also needs to stay alive for nine months. After that, he can die in peace, assured that Bertha will be financially set since she can collect his monthly $3,000 benefit as a widow benefit.*

Phil's been reluctant to propose because he wants to leave his kids his house and financial assets. Bertha wants to do the same with her assets. But arranging this is easy. Phil and Bertha simply need to draw up the appropriate prenup and wills. Also, Social Security only cares if you're married. It doesn't care where you live. Both Phil and Bertha can stay in their same homes.

The third financial advantage of formally marrying involves risk sharing. Set aside economies of shared living and consider again the Peter clones. How does marrying help them share risk? It doesn't if they continue to experience exactly identical lives. But say they start experiencing problems. When they do, they recall that "in sickness and in health" means they need to help each other out, financially and physically, as needed.

The risks the Peters face are the same ones we all face: unemployment, loss of a high-paying job, bad investment returns, unexpected out-of-pocket healthcare costs, uninsured property damage, age discrimination, and disability. Marriage insures against all these risks. If bad things happen to one Peter, the other Peter will come to the rescue, and vice versa. For example, if Peter becomes unemployed, the employed Peter will support them both. The two Peters can even share longevity risk by specifying each as beneficiaries in their wills. Then if one outlives the other, the survivor will have more resources to spend as he keeps on keeping on. This is also

---

* Social Security will describe this as Bertha receiving her own Social Security retirement benefit plus her excess survivor benefit, which equals Phil's retirement benefit less Bertha's retirement benefit.

a plan for un-trapping housing equity, as the survivor will get to spend the trapped equity of the decedent.

How much is all the free insurance the Peters receive via marriage worth? My estimate, from calculations I've made in a variety of research studies, is one-third of each Peter's lifetime earnings. In other words, were they to get the insurance but lose one-third of their future earnings, they'd be no worse off on balance.

Can't the Peters reap these insurance gains just as well by remaining partners? Maybe, but it's not guaranteed. If healthy Peter cares for sick Peter and sick Peter changes his will on his deathbed and assigns all his worldly possessions to yet another Peter, partner Peter may have a far harder time pressing his legal claim against the newcomer compared to doing so from the status as dead Peter's spouse.

RECAP

Rose Kennedy's dry Irish humor provides the twinkle to this chapter. Rose came from well-heeled stock. She married Joe Kennedy Sr., President Kennedy's father, for love. The marriage didn't come easy. Rose's dad, "Honey Fitz" Fitzgerald, was the mayor of Boston and didn't think much of the Kennedys. As Joe's fortunes improved and Rose lobbied, Honey Fitz relented. After a seven-year courtship, they married. Joe's fortune then went from good to tremendous. When Joe passed, Rose ended up, in today's terms, a billionaire. She had, indeed, got a little money along the way.

Unfortunately, setting your sights on a current or up-and-coming billionaire is quite a long shot—there just aren't enough to go around. Even hundred millionaires are few and far between. Millionaires, though, are a dime a dozen. There are twenty million in the country and many more in the making. Surely one is waiting for you. Or maybe you're a millionaire already, which means you can enter the marriage/partner market with a leg up.

But even if you marry someone who makes the same amount as you, shacking up can transform your material life. Let me recap this chapter's greatest hits:

- Whether nineteen or ninety-one, if you're single, you're in the marriage market.

- Being in the marriage market means selling your long-term companionship in exchange for someone else's. If you marry rich, you'll experience a meteoric rise in your living standard. If you marry poor, understand the living-standard price that entails.

- Today's Match.com is the ancient Babylonian bride auction, where we offer to merge our entire bundle of wares with someone else's. The transaction's not for an hour or a day or a year. It's till death or divorce do us part.

- Marrying up financially is a great goal. It doesn't make you a gold digger to search for more material well-being. Nor will it make you a saint to do the opposite. When you're searching for love, be on the lookout for money. And if someone admires you for your money, don't take offense. It may be your best feature.

- The bundle you're buying when you marry someone includes your spouse-to-be's assets, financial and real; earnings power, present and future; and liabilities, current and coming. These are key components to understand in choosing whom to fall in love with.

- Whether you formally marry or simply partner, shacking up long-term is money magic at its best. When you merge households, bingo: your living standard's at least a third higher.

- Marriage beats partnering long-term. It may mean somewhat higher net taxes, but it comes with an array of valuable implicit insurance arrangements, which the formality and legality of marriage help enforce. Marriage can also mean important extra Social Security benefits for the lower-earning spouse. And it can protect you, albeit to a highly imperfect and uncertain extent, if you're awarded alimony as part of what is an all too common part of marriage: divorce.

CHAPTER 7

Divorce Only If It Pays — Getting a Fair Split If You Split

Marriage is the triumph of imagination over intelligence.
Second marriage is the triumph of hope over experience.

— often attributed to Oscar Wilde

Can't live with 'em; can't live without 'em." This sums up Americans' relationship to marriage. Count from one to thirteen. By the time you reach thirteen another marriage made in heaven will end in hell (or at least fail). This rate of conjugal disunion translates into almost three hundred divorces per hour, more than six thousand divorces per day, close to fifty thousand divorces per week, and almost two and half million divorces per year.[1] Roughly half of US marriages end up on the rocks. And we don't get better with practice. The divorce rate for second marriages is 60 percent. For third marriages, it's 73 percent.

Given these astonishing figures, it's amazing that no one, at least at the outset, thinks it will happen to them. Ask any couple on their wedding day if they expect to get divorced. None will say yes. Economists call this "irrational expectation" — when people collectively believe something they know isn't collectively true. Irrational expectation abounds in all areas of life. Question freshmen about their expected college GPA. As a group, they expect to do better, on average, than the college norm. Ask stock investors the return they expect to earn. Their mean answer will exceed the historic average. Ask Americans if they're smarter than average. Two-thirds will say yes. Garrison Keillor captured this overoptimism perfectly at the start of each of his decades-long *A Prairie Home Companion* NPR radio shows. "Welcome to Lake Wobegon, where all the women are strong, all the men are good-looking, and all the children are above average."

My first money secret when it comes to divorce is to assume you won't do better than average. That's the hard truth.

Assume you'll get divorced.

Grim advice, especially coming from a huge fan of marriage. I just spent a chapter espousing the financial gains from marriage! But the divorce numbers don't lie. Marriage is risky business. When things are risky, we usually focus on the worst-case scenario and take measures to avoid or mitigate the problem. This is why we buy automobile, health, homeowner's, and life insurance. It's also why we supposedly drive defensively, eat healthy, inspect our home's wiring, and look both ways before crossing the street. In the case of marriage, the worst-case scenario is permanently parting ways. I'm going to discuss how to protect yourself to the extent possible against divorce. But let's begin with a more fundamental question. Is divorce really worth it?

DO YOU HATE THEM ENOUGH?

Many divorces are based on irreconcilable differences. Physical attraction is a biggie. A quarter of divorces are caused by infidelity, lack of intimacy, and objection to a spouse's physical appearance.

Another quarter are caused by money issues, addictions, and abuse. General lack of compatibility, including marrying too young or for the wrong reasons, accounts for the remaining half.

Clearly, you should jump ship yesterday if you're in any kind of abusive marriage. Verbal abuse, physical abuse, emotional abuse — all are totally unacceptable. Otherwise, be careful what you wish for. Divorce is one of the most destructive financial forces on the planet. If you're leaving your betrothed for a shiny object, make sure it's solid gold. And if you're leaving because you've had enough, realize that doing so may mean *not* having enough — not enough money to maintain your living standard. So before you call it quits, price your antipathy. Specifically, ask yourself how much of your current living standard you'd be willing to sacrifice to be rid of your beloved.

Suppose the answer is 30 percent, meaning you'd be willing to consume 30 percent less, measured in quantity or quality, of everything — housing, vacations, restaurant meals, entertainment, clothes, automobiles, healthcare, teeth cleanings, cigars, cars, mani-pedis, you name it. A 30 percent living-standard drop is a lot. Right, I get it. Your spouse is god-awful, and maybe it's worth it. But what if getting divorced will lower your living standard by 35 percent? Then sticking it out with God-awful beats splitting up. On the other hand, if getting divorced would mean only a 19 percent living-standard decline, the cost of your divorce will be lower than the 30 percent reduction you're willing to pay. In this case, go for it! In short, before you junk your marriage:

Do a careful cost-benefit divorce analysis.

Thinking systematically about the benefits and costs of divorce sounds impossible. How can anyone decide that breaking the holy bonds of matrimony is worth sacrificing precisely 30 percent of one's marital living standard? Why not draw the line at 22 percent or 39 percent?

Valuing the benefits from divorce is fundamentally no different from valuing a career you might pursue, a job you might take, a home you might buy, a car you might lease, or a coat you might purchase. You apply your preferences. Is that gorgeous red wool coat really worth the three hundred dollars they're charging? If you end up buying it, the answer is yes. If you don't, the answer is no. Your decision is based on your feelings about the coat, its price, and your resources, and you make the decision by incorporating your feelings and these other factors. Whether or not you're conscious of it, you compare your precise dollar benefit from owning the coat with its dollar price. And you come up with the coat's value to you by posing a simple question: *What's the most I'd pay for the coat?* When valuing divorce, that question turns into: *What's the most I'd pay to be out of this marriage?*

Clearly, regaining your freedom is far harder to value than a coat. That's particularly true if you have kids. Will they be adversely or positively affected? Psychologists report that kids of divorced parents do well if the parents stop fighting, if the kids have access to each parent, if each parent is happy postdivorce, and if each kid feels physically and financially secure. That's a lot of ifs. Still, most divorcing parents say their kids will be *fine*—they'll adjust, they're resilient, they'll be happier without the marital tension. This may be the case on average. But what counts is your own children's reaction, not the average. Could they get into trouble academically or socially? Will they experience anxiety, depression, alcoholism, or drug addiction? When it comes to divorce with children involved, their welfare, under good and bad scenarios, has to enter the equation as much as yours.

Let's say you've figured out that, all in all, the impact on the children included, you'll end your marriage if it doesn't cost more than 30 percent of your living standard. Now you need to measure that cost. Doing so requires thinking carefully about economies of shared living.

ECONOMIES OF SHARED LIVING MATTER BIG-TIME TO THE COST OF DIVORCE

Let's start with the best-case sharing scenario. You and your spouse, Doug, a.k.a. God-awful, can live as cheaply as one. In this case, every penny you collectively spend when married benefits both of you equally. If Doug buys a shirt, you get to wear it. If you buy a car, he gets to drive it. If you buy and eat an apple, Doug somehow gets to eat that same apple (maybe Doug is into regurgitation, which is why you want out).

How do you compute, and thereby compare, your living standard when divorced with your living standard when married? The math in this case is easy. Suppose you and Doug are able to jointly spend $100,000 a year, adjusted for inflation, on a sustainable basis. That means that each of your living standards while married is $100,000. Why? Because Doug's consumption is your consumption and your consumption is Doug's consumption. But once you divorce, the sharing stops. Suppose your resources when divorced, including anything you receive from Doug minus anything you give him, support $45,000 in annual spending. This means your sustainable living standard falls from $100,000 to $45,000 the minute you walk out the door. That's a whopping 55 percent drop. Let's assume that since you're willing to forgo at most 35 percent of your living standard to see the back of Doug and this divorce will cost you 55 percent, you stick it out with him.

But, of course, in the real world the two of you can't really live as cheaply as one. Doug is six foot five and you're five foot three. You can't share clothes. No matter what he says, you can't share apples.

You can't share cars, since you both drive to work. You can't share many other things. Say you and Doug can live as cheaply as only 1.5 people. In that case you need to divide the $100,000 by 1.5, which puts your individual marital living standard at $66,666—of the $100,000 you jointly make and spend, the economies of shared living produce the same living standard as earning $66,666 but as a single person. Now you have to compare $66,666 staying married with $45,000 being divorced and single. That spells a 32.5 percent decline. This is less than 35 percent, so it's "Sayonara, Doug!"

What's the right shared-living-standard factor for you? I'd use 1 for housing outlays, reflecting the assumption that housing can be fully shared. For all nonhousing spending, I think 1.6 is reasonable. So to calculate your living standard when married, you would add (a) your housing outlays to (b) your nonhousing spending divided by 1.6.*

Let's return to you and Doug and apply this little bit of math. Suppose one-third—$33,333—of your $100,000 marital spending is imputed rent. Add that to your nonhousing spending ($66,666) divided by 1.6, which would be $41,666. The result is $75,000. That's your current marital living standard. Your $45,000 living standard if you divorce is 40 percent smaller. Guess what? Based on this refined calculation, the divorce hit is too big for you to stomach. So it's sayonara to "Sayonara, Doug." You should stay married—indeed, go whole hog and have a marriage-vows renewal ceremony.

Here's the moral:

Factor in economies of shared living carefully in calculating the cost of divorce.

---

* If you rent, your housing outlays are your rent and utility bills. If you own, your housing outlays are your imputed rent (see chapter 5 for the method to calculate imputed rent) plus your utility bills.

Now for a caveat. If you get divorced, you have a one-in-four chance of remarrying. In this case, you could recoup your lost economies of shared living. But remember, you have only a 60 percent chance of staying remarried. That leaves you with only a 15 percent chance of remarrying for the long term. Remarriage is never for sure, so play it safe and plan to be single for the duration.

ALIMONY — WHAT'S FAIR?

The whole point of this chapter is to help you decide whether divorce is a smart financial choice. You're trying to ensure you aren't staying in a marriage you should quit and you aren't quitting a marriage you should maintain. You're getting richer by not buying something—whether that's a divorce or staying married—that costs more than it's worth.

But welcome to the divorce catch-22. You can't figure out if it pays until you know what alimony (money, apart from child support, that one ex-spouse pays to support the other as privately negotiated or judicially set in the divorce decree) you'll receive, and you can't know what alimony you'll receive unless you get divorced. Suppose you, Chloe, spent most of your early adulthood raising children and sustaining your marital home so your spouse, Harry, could pursue his education and career. Now, after twenty-five years of marriage, high-earning Harry has found a better option and wants to call it quits. How much alimony can you expect?

It depends on the state and even county in which you divorce. There are no federal laws governing alimony and child support, only state and local ones. Take a look at Maritallaws.com. As you can see, state laws generally say that alimony should take into account the length of your marriage, the income differences between you and your spouse, your standard of living while married, custody of your children, and child-support payments. But these laws provide only guidelines, not precise formulas for determining alimony. In the end, each state leaves it up to family court judges to decide whether alimony is justified and, if so, how much. This said, 95 percent or so of divorces settle out of court. This reflects the high legal costs and the perception that a judge will likely specify alimony based on state norms.

In general, alimony involves splitting assets and debts acquired during the marriage fifty-fifty. So if your soon-to-be ex has run up huge obligations, even without your knowledge, you can end up saddled with a mother lode of IOUs to repay. Another norm is that the alimony will last longer if you were married longer. Some states are far more generous to the recipient on this than others.

If you're the party receiving alimony, beware that if you remarry or move in with someone else, regardless of what they earn, your alimony may come to an abrupt end. Indeed, if you do remarry, you may be in for a double whammy: the end of alimony and the inability to collect a Social Security divorced spousal benefit.* Potentially worse, if you marry before age sixty and after you divorce your ex dies, you can't collect a Social Security divorced widow(er) benefit. These restrictions on divorced spousal and widow(er) Social Security benefits for those who remarry is part of Social Security's highly sexist benefit provisions, mentioned in chapter 3. Alimony may also end when your ex decides to retire, depending on contingencies to which you agree in your settlement or court-ordered changes in your divorce agreement. This needs to be codified in a secret:

Cohabiting can terminate alimony, remarrying can terminate both alimony and Social Security divorced spousal benefits, and

---

* Your rights to Social Security benefits lost due to remarriage are restored if you divorce your new spouse or if your new spouse dies.

remarrying before age sixty can preclude collecting Social Security divorced widow(er) benefits.

HOW MUCH ALIMONY CAN YOU EXPECT?

As for the amount of alimony you may receive, required payments differ dramatically by state. Let's start with Massachusetts, which enacted new divorce guidelines in 2011, based, in part, on the legendary Ginsburg formula, promulgated by Edward M. Ginsburg, a now retired justice of the Middlesex Probate and Family Court. The Massachusetts law provides for general term (periodic) alimony, rehabilitative alimony, reimbursement alimony, and transitional alimony.[2]

General term alimony is what we're most used to thinking about—regular payments from one spouse to the other for a period of time, if not indefinitely. Rehabilitative alimony is short-term and intended to help a spouse improve their earnings capacity. Reimbursement alimony compensates a spouse for special sacrifices, like having forgone a career to support the other spouse advancing theirs. Transitional alimony applies in short-term marriages to help a lower-earning spouse restore their premarital location and residence.

Let's consider what Massachusetts law suggests for Harry and Chloe, both age sixty, who have been married for twenty-five wonderful years. They have no children. Last week, Harry delivered a bombshell. He met a very shiny object and wants out. Harry makes $125,000, and Chloe $25,000. Assuming they will split their assets, Massachusetts guidelines would award Chloe alimony equal to 35 percent of the $100,000 difference in their earnings: $35,000.

Other states, like Texas, reference a one-third, one-third, one-third rule. They'd add up Harry's and Chloe's incomes, allocate one-third to taxes, one-third to Harry, and one-third to Chloe.

Consequently, Chloe's alimony would be one-third of $150,000 less Chloe's $25,000 in earnings, which would leave Chloe with $25,000 in alimony. That's 29 percent less than the Massachusetts number. The Ginsburg formula produces $41,667 in alimony in this case. The American Academy of Matrimonial Lawyers has its own formula, which would set Harry's alimony payment at $32,500. In Maricopa County, Arizona, they'd set alimony at $28,500. Santa Clara County, California, would set alimony at $30,000. Johnson County, Kansas, thinks $23,500 is the right number.

You're getting the point. Let's count it as a secret:

Want a fair alimony outcome? Choose your state/county of residency carefully.

Also, make that decision early. If Harry and Chloe have lived in Texas but Chloe wants to file for divorce in Massachusetts, she'll need to establish residency there, which will take a year. Even then, Harry, presumably still living in Texas, may have already filed or could still file for divorce in the Lone Star State. In this case, judges in each state will jointly decide where the divorce takes place. The state where the couple lived together longest will likely be chosen—but the key word is "likely"; a good divorce attorney may be able to finagle a different answer.

ILLUSTRATING HOW LONG ALIMONY WILL LAST

How long does alimony last? Let's go back to assuming Harry and Chloe live in Massachusetts. Under Massachusetts guidelines, alimony lasts for 50 percent of their married months if they were married for less than six years, 60 percent if they were married from six to ten years, 70 percent if ten to fifteen years, 80 percent if fifteen to twenty years, and permanently if they were married longer than twenty years—as is the case with our unhappy couple. Permanent, however, may not really be permanent but rather until Harry reaches Social Security's full retirement age. Therefore, every year you wait to divorce from a higher-earning spouse will limit your length of potential alimony receipt.

Since full retirement age is sixty-seven, Harry would need to pay alimony for twenty-seven years. Multiplying twenty-seven years by $35,000 per year gives us $875,000 in lifetime alimony under the Massachusetts guidelines. But for the Harry and Chloe who live in Texas, there's no alimony for marriages under five years, five years of alimony if the marriage lasts from ten to twenty years, seven years of alimony for twenty to thirty years, and ten years of alimony for more than thirty years. Since Harry and Chloe are just twenty-five years in, Harry would pay for only seven years. Seven times $25,000 is $175,000. Therefore, if the couple divorces in Texas, Chloe will likely receive, in total lifetime alimony, only one-fifth of what she'd receive in Massachusetts!

Imagine Harry and Chloe formally divorce nine years and three hundred sixty-four days after they marry, a day before they reach Social Security's ten-year marriage requirement needed to collect divorced and, potentially, survivor benefits on one's ex-spouse's income. This would leave Chloe with far lower lifetime Social Security benefits to add to her paltry Texas alimony payments.

The message here is:

Don't divorce too early or too late.

Unless your spouse wants to remarry, there's no legal imperative with regard to Social Security to get divorced. Chloe should try to delay divorce for the ten years needed to qualify for future Social Security divorcée benefits. Waiting to divorce will also likely raise the award and the alimony duration of the payment. On the other hand, Chloe may want to hurry the process in order to receive alimony for a longer period, since Harry will be sixty-seven in seven years.

Harry also has an incentive to wait ten years to get divorced. Anything that can help Chloe will reduce the pressure on Harry to support her down the road. On the other hand, Harry may want to get divorced as soon as possible to limit the alimony he'll need to pay.

On average, marriages that end in divorce do so after eight years. About 12 percent of divorces occur within five years. Roughly one-quarter of divorces occur within the first decade. Thus, almost one in four sets of divorcés may include a spouse who is forgoing long-term Social Security divorced spousal and, potentially, survivor benefits. Most likely, they don't realize such benefits are available.

DIVORCE LAWYERS CAN BE EXPENSIVE AND RISKY

If you decide to get divorced and then immediately lawyer up with your spouse doing the same, all of the lawyers involved will be rubbing their hands with glee. You've just given them a strong incentive to go to war. The longer they fight, the more they can charge. And after months or years, your enormous financial loss from divorcing will be dramatically compounded by astronomical legal bills. In the end, your slugfest may end in family court, where a judge has essentially unlimited power to decide what's a fair alimony settlement.

Judges can and do take sides. They, like everyone else, carry with them ingrained prejudices, including chauvinism, racism, religious bigotry, and political disposition. If you come before a judge, chances are the judge will learn, through the discovery process and direct questioning, everything there is to know about you and your spouse—your income, assets, spending habits, gambling, Botox treatments, cable plan, drinking habits, extramarital affairs, health statuses, parenting skills, job histories—with no regard to what you'd rather keep private.

If you've been playing golf at an expensive country club on weekends and ignoring your spouse and kids, the judge can decide you're a jerk (which you no doubt are) and make you pay more or award you less alimony. If you've spent what the judge views as excessive amounts on clothes, personal items, and spa visits compared to your spouse, you'll likely get dinged on an alimony decision. Some judges may simply not like your looks, your style, your attitude, or, indeed, your profession.

I attended a depressing divorce trial many years back involving two very close friends—an economist husband and an attorney wife. I wasn't there to take sides; one of the two ardently asked me to come to provide moral support. The trial took place after a year or so of divorce proceedings, involving separate and joint meetings, all brokered by top (high-priced) attorneys.

The judge put the husband on the stand, immediately asked about his work, found out he taught economics of law at Harvard Law School, and proceeded to go slightly nuts. He clearly didn't like economists, let alone economists who presumed they could teach law, let alone at Harvard. The judge proceeded to rake my economist friend over the coals, hitting him with all manner of questions that didn't pertain to the divorce dispute. When the judge issued his decision, he mostly sided with the wife. But even still, the decision was clearly within the range that the couple could have figured out from the get-go. Two years of legal fees gained neither party very much. Each had been persuaded by their counsel that they'd do far better than ended up being the case.

The lesson?

Avoid an expensive legal divorce war possibly ending in an arbitrary judge's verdict.

How can you get divorced without both you and your spouse retaining a lawyer? One answer is to work it out yourselves with the help of commercial software.* A second is to engage a divorce mediator, who can work with you and your spouse and handle all the paperwork. The mediator will be able to tell you how you'd likely fare if you have a legal dispute. This will provide a quick reality check on what each of you can reasonably demand of the other. But you need a baseline for determining what's a fair alimony settlement. This brings me to...

WHAT'S A FAIR ALIMONY AGREEMENT?

Believe it or not, the magistrate presiding over my friends' divorce was the legendary Judge Ginsburg mentioned earlier. Since I was thinking about developing a software tool to assist divorcing couples in reaching a fair settlement, I had learned about the Ginsburg alimony formula before my friends announced their split. That they landed in front of Ginsburg was a big surprise to me, but not to the wife's attorney, who seemed to have maneuvered things in that direction. I couldn't help but notice that Judge Ginsburg departed fairly far from the Ginsburg formula in his judgment. I was also surprised by the fact that the judge was unable to control his personal feelings.

I was intrigued by Judge Ginsburg's formula and the enormous range of guidelines for alimony that differ so greatly around the country. I also wondered how the judge had come up with his

---

* My company markets its divorce tool at Analyzemydivorcesettlement.com.

formula. Had he derived it mathematically? Or had he pulled it out of the seat of his pants? Was there a principled basis for the judge's formula or for any of the other state and county norms? How could ideas about treating two parties fairly differ by such extreme magnitudes just because they lived on one side or the other of a state line?

My curiosity got the best of me. I contacted the judge, told him I'd observed the trial and had some questions. We had a very interesting conversation over lunch. By the end, it was clear that the judge had derived his formula based on years of deciding cases and a general sense of what was right. But he had no guiding fairness principle he was following. And, at least to me, it was clear that his rule of thumb was too crude to achieve fairness in most cases.

I doubt Judge Ginsburg left our lunch with a better impression of economists. I suggested that the right way to set alimony was to equalize the postdivorce living standard of each spouse going forward, with adjustments for one spouse working longer or harder, each spouse's maximum remaining years of life, who had the primary responsibility of raising the kids, and other factors, particularly the treatment of the marital home.

The judge found my approach intriguing but assured me that his rule produced an approximation of the same outcome. I'm sure all the architects of all the state- and county-specific alimony guidelines feel the same way. They all think their solutions are fair for essentially everyone. But since their formulas and norms differ so markedly, they can't all be achieving fairness, however "fairness" is defined.

Moreover, the guidelines, formal and informal, have two big problems. First, the formulas and norms have no clear objective. Thus, there's no reason to think they're suggesting alimony settlements that are reasonable. Second, they omit basic factors. If you know what factors are being left out, you can put them on the table and, hopefully, end up with a better settlement.

In the end, if you and your spouse can come up with an arrangement you both feel is fair and the judge approves it as fair, you're done. Therefore, my advice is to try to work out a tentative divorce settlement on your own before you bring in third parties who may not have your best interests at heart. The deal should be tentative, because you'll want to check with a divorce professional, either a mediator or a lawyer, whom you can both consult, to confirm that you both fully understand what's being offered and accepted and that you aren't agreeing to something that no rational person in your shoes would.

What's a reasonable goal for alimony? It's not reproducing your current lifestyle. Given all the financial advantages of marriage, getting divorced means your married lifestyle is no longer affordable. If you've just been married two weeks, you should each pick up your marbles, take separate monthlong vacations in Alaska, establish residency there, and then get divorced. An even faster option is to divorce in Guam, a US territory. You can do this without ever setting foot there.[3]

Now, suppose you've been married for thirty years. By this point you've made all kinds of joint decisions and mutually beneficial investments. You've effectively become a financial partnership. This is the position of the nine states with community property laws. In a divorce, those nine states specify that all assets and liabilities obtained or incurred during the marriage are to be divided equally between the spouses. Other states stipulate that the couple's combined assets be divided up on an "equitable distribution" basis, meaning it's up for negotiation. What about differences in future labor earnings? This is the key factor in alimony decisions.

Does Chloe have an equal claim to Harry's future labor earnings? Let's suppose the answer is yes, perhaps because Chloe gave up a higher-paying career to keep their family financially afloat while Harry was in professional school. Or maybe Chloe stuck with a lower-paying safe job to let Harry gamble on a career with a higher payoff.

Harry could simply give Chloe half his labor earnings going forward. But is that fair? When divorced, Harry will have to pay much higher taxes. On the other hand, he'll receive a higher Social Security benefit, although that also helps lower-earning Chloe, who will be able to access divorced spousal and widow benefits, since given their age and the length of their marriage, they already meet the necessary conditions. This gets even more complicated if the spouses differ in age. Giving a younger spouse the same resources as a much older spouse may mean a remaining life of deprivation for the younger spouse and a remaining life of luxury for the older spouse. Why? Because the younger spouse has to spread their money over many more years.

MY ADVICE ON GETTING DIVORCED

Here's my suggestion—and it holds whether you've been married for thirty days or for thirty years: before anything else, agree on an equitable ratio of your living standards going forward. If you've been married for thirty years, you might both agree on a 1 to 1 ratio. In other words, each spouse would be able to afford the same living standard through their maximum age of life. If you've been married for thirty days, you might agree that your living-standard ratio should be precisely whatever it would've been had you never married. And if you've been married for twelve years, you might agree that a 1.5 to 1 ratio is appropriate, with the higher-earning and harder-working spouse having a 50 percent higher living standard than the lower-earning spouse.

Once you've made this basic fairness decision, calculate how much you and your spouse will be able to spend through your maximum ages of life *without* any alimony. Assume that all net worth is converted into cash (the house is sold, etc.) and that each spouse will receive half. Add to this the sum of your future net income (after taxes) plus the present value of Social Security and other income. Subtract any future off-the-top expenses assigned to each spouse, such as the children's college tuition (make sure to convert all future amounts into today's dollars before adding them).

The next step is to divide each of your lifetime net resources (your part of the combined assets, plus the sums of your future labor earnings and your other future income, minus your future taxes and any future expenses you'll have to cover) by your maximum remaining years of life.

This produces a number for each of you: your provisional living standard after the divorce. If the ratio of these provisional amounts doesn't correspond to the ratio you agreed was fair, try different amounts of annual alimony by subtracting from the payer's lifetime net resources and adding to the payee's lifetime net resources, until the ratio of the implied annual and sustainable living standards is equal to what you agreed to.

Once you've figured out the amount of alimony that generates a fair ratio of sustainable living standards, you'll want to tweak things. You'll want to decide what's fair in terms of how long each of you should be expected to work. Alternatively, you can agree that the spouse who is going to work longer at, perhaps, a high-stress, long-hours job should have a higher relative living standard. It may be that one spouse needs more cash in the short term to buy a home, whereas the other spouse will rent for a number of years. Or it may be that one spouse wants to contribute more to a retirement account but won't have the liquidity to do so. By providing the illiquid spouse more assets but less alimony, that spouse can be better off without a reduction in the other spouse's well-being. Also, any move that lowers one spouse's future taxes will permit both spouses to spend more over time via an alimony adjustment that gets the two spouses' living standards back to a target ratio.

The beauty of negotiating this way, *without lawyers and legal bills*, is that you start by figuring out what's fair before you get into the weeds of how you'll achieve that fair solution. Once you have a general handle on the fair amount of alimony, you'll immediately start working together to raise each of your living standards. Each improvement will leave you *both* better off.

Let me summarize with this secret for achieving a fair and amicable divorce settlement:

> **Agree on your relative living standards, then determine the alimony or division of other resources to achieve this result while making you both as well-off as possible.**

One more thing about designing your own divorce settlement: make sure you think through the contingencies. What if the payer dies, becomes disabled, or loses their job? Each of these outcomes jeopardizes future payments and receipts of alimony. One possibility is for the payer to obtain life insurance and disability insurance to protect the payee. The cost of doing so needs to be included in the payer's living-standard calculation as an off-the-top expense. The agreement should also become renegotiable in the case that alimony can't be paid for reasons outside the payer's control.

PRENUP YOUR POSTNUP

Prenuptial agreements are basically advanced divorce agreements, laying out what will happen if you split. Only about 10 percent of lovebirds enter into a prenup prior to saying "I do." My advice: if you're getting married, be part of that 10 percent. Specifying what will happen if you divorce may, ironically, keep you from doing so.

Imagine your wife-to-be, Nancy, wants you to support her through mortuary school, which costs $40,000. She also wants you to coinvest in a new $50,000 Cadillac XTS hearse. The hearse, she says, can double as a camper, as there's plenty of room to sleep in the back. Oh, and she wants you to go in on buying a $65,000 house trailer that can double as a funeral parlor. Her plan is to hitch the trailer to the hearse and make the funeral a moving event. When the service is over, the assembled will disembark at the grave site.

Since you'd have to borrow a ton to pull this off, you're naturally hesitant. What if your marriage ends after you've assisted with all the investments? You don't want to be saddled with Nancy's student loan, hearse loan, and trailer mortgage. This is where a prenup can help. You can specify that if you get divorced, Nancy will need to cover all of her career-related borrowing in excess of the sale value of the hearse, the trailer, and the leftover formaldehyde. You'll still be a signatory to the loans, but she can pay you off over time.

After much discussion, you and Nancy draw up and sign this unusual prenup. Good move. Unbeknownst to you, Nancy, always the optimizer, has a backup plan: running off with the scion of the McMurphy Funeral Home (whose masterstroke was a flashing neon sign that says READY WHEN YOU ARE!).

What else might you put in your prenup? You might want to specify the right to retain your 1951 Jaguar XK120, your precious hot pot, your treasured Xbox, your twelve-string Gibson SG, and your beloved Chihuahua, Gigi.

How about your savings or retirement accounts or particular real estate properties you own? Can you preserve them in a prenup? Absolutely. This is the main purpose of the agreement: keeping particular financial assets off the divorce dividing block, giving you the right to do with them as you please. This is especially useful for second or third marriages occurring later in life, when you have children from a prior marriage. In this case, you may want to preserve specific assets for your children if you don't live so long as to need to spend them. Here, again, sorting out these issues formally, whether in a prenup or via your wills, or both, can be valuable in making your kids feel financially comfortable with your new spouse and your spouse's kids feel financially comfortable with you.

That leads us to my final divorce secret:

Prenuptial agreements are a good idea. They protect you against divorce, help you avoid conflicts down the road, and set your children's minds at ease.

RECAP

Our heads are filled with romantic fantasies about marrying the perfect mate and living happily ever after. And if our marriage ends in divorce, we're often devastated. As the Neil Sedaka song goes, breakin' up is hard to do.

Breaking up *is* tough, but half of us do it anyway. Realizing this in advance will gird you financially and psychologically if and when your marriage hits the rocks. These takeaways may help:

- Marriages aren't built to last. They need constant minding. Don't take yours for granted or you may end up like almost half the country—divorced.
- Prenuptial agreements can protect you if you do divorce. But they can also help prevent divorce by enforcing mutual investment arrangements that strengthen and preserve your marriage.
- Divorce comes at a huge financial cost. Part of that is the cost of lawyers, which you can avoid via mediation or collaboration on your own divorce agreement. But mostly it's the loss of the tremendous economies of shared living associated with cohabitation.

- Divorce seems like it's all about feelings. But there are ways to translate feelings into dollars so the benefit from divorce can be compared with its financial cost.

- The first step in getting divorced is to decide if it's worth it. Ask yourself how much you'd pay, in terms of a reduced living standard, to escape your spouse. It may be a lot but still below, if not far below, the cost. In this case, stay where the grass isn't greener.

- To figure out the financial cost of divorce, you need to calculate your postdivorce living standard and compare it with your married living standard.

- Your postdivorce living standard may depend greatly on the alimony you pay or receive. The amounts and timeline involved vary greatly depending on the state in which you divorce. One state may be five times more generous with respect to alimony guidelines than another. So think carefully about the state in which you choose to live. It's where you'll likely divorce.

- The longer you're married, the longer you'll pay or receive alimony unless you're close to retirement age, in which case the opposite becomes true.

- If you divorce, do so after ten years. There may be sizable divorced spousal and divorced widow(er) benefits at stake. This doesn't require living together for the full ten years.

- Before lawyering up and going to divorce war, which may permanently scar you and your children, try to jointly decide on an equitable living-standard ratio independent of how you'll achieve it. Once you've got that down, the amount of alimony and other divisions of resources needed to achieve this result is easy to compute.

CHAPTER 8

Don't Borrow for College — It's Far Too Risky

Several years ago, I taught a course at Boston University on personal finance. I started out discussing consumption smoothing and other economics principles. Then I got into the weeds, laying out what people should do in practice. This included the message I've conveyed throughout this book — that paying off high-interest-rate personal debts, be they credit card balances, car loans, mortgages, or student loans, is the best investment going.

Since I was talking to college students, I focused on student debt.

"More than two-thirds of college students — and a higher percentage of minorities — take out student loans to help finance their educations. Collectively, they owe a whopping $1.6 trillion. Their parents owe upward of $100 billion on loans they have incurred on their children's behalf. Half of those who borrow for college have outstanding student loans twenty years after graduation. Plus, there are informal loans between students and their parents, which the students may feel morally, if not legally, obligated to repay."[1]

To make things concrete, I asked my fifty students if they had any student loans. About forty raised their hands. Next, I asked what interest rates their loans carried. Their answers ranged from high to very high to exorbitant. I asked everyone to raise their hands if they owed $10,000 or more. The same hands flew up.

"Okay, keep your hand up if you owe $30,000 or more." Most hands remained aloft. I moved to $60,000 plus. Now only a third of the hands stayed airborne. I kept going down this dark path until I reached $100,000 or more. One hand—Madeline's (not her real name)—remained raised, albeit at half-mast. The angle of her crooked arm shouted, *Please no!*

I should have stopped there. I'd already violated my students' privacy. But I asked Madeline if she minded telling the class how much she owed. She said $120,000.

Dumbstruck, I shifted to my most professional economics parlance. "Well, hmm, umm, gee, ouch, ugh, OMG, wow, that's, like, kind of a lot."

Then I tried to rationalize Madeline's situation. "I'm not surprised. Though it does provide lots of scholarships and grants, BU is one of the most expensive universities in the country based on its sticker price. Of course, you get to be taught by people like me." That last bit fell particularly flat.

Then it was back to Madeline. "Would you mind telling me your major?" Hoping it was in a lucrative field, like business.

"Art history."

"Ah, art history. Hmm, umm, gee, ouch, ugh, OMG, wow. Not the highest-paying field. And you're a senior and on the job market?"

"Yes."

At this point, I put both feet in it. "Any prospects?"

Awkward silence punctuated by deep sighs leading to Madeline's visage turning various shades of embarrassment, anger, and despair, culminating in uncontrollable sobbing. In between the flood of tears, Madeline relayed having sent off dozens of applications for a job in her field and receiving not a single offer. Most applications went unanswered.

This episode still haunts me. I apologized to Madeline profusely, in and after class. But the damage was done, and not just because she had broken down in front of the class. I realized that Madeline was in a world of financial hurt. The average salary in art history at the time was about $35,000. Madeline was averaging about 5 percent interest on her various loans. Paying them off over twenty years would require handing over $10,000 per year to her federal and private lenders. Yes, the repayment was moderate and would be watered down, over time, by inflation. Still, it would represent a major share of Madeline's after-tax art history career earnings. Short of moving in with her folks, marrying someone with deep pockets, or an act of divine intervention, Madeline had borrowed so much for a career in art history that she couldn't afford a career in art history.

This chapter covers several interconnected themes with the same conclusion I spoiled in the chapter's title: *Don't borrow for college!* The themes cover the following topics:

- the size, or rather the unknown size, of student debt;
- the unbelievably high college dropout rate, which dramatically magnifies the risk of borrowing;
- the different types of real student aid (grants, scholarships, and work study) and fake student aid (student loans);
- the awful cost of trying to default on your student debt;
- the astronomical sticker price of college;
- the potentially huge difference between the sticker price and the actual cost of college;
- the ways to lower the net cost of college by getting more education per dollar spent and paying fewer dollars per unit of education received;

- how to choose among colleges; and
- which loans are the least expensive and how to compare regular and income-based repayment plans.

I'll cover each of these topics, but there are more detailed treatments out there, including Ron Lieber's bestseller *The Price You Pay for College*. Lieber is the *New York Times'* leading personal finance columnist.

HOW MUCH STUDENT DEBT ARE COLLEGE STUDENTS INCURRING?

Madeline's borrowing is an extreme outlier. Or maybe it's not. Today's college students are graduating with, on average, close to $33,000 in *formal* student loans.[2] About 1 in 7 — more than 14 percent — *formally* owe more than $50,000.[3] These jumbo student loans account for more than half of total outstanding student debt. Older generations are, at the mean, $40,000 in *formal* college hock. This includes loans for postgraduate training as well as the accumulation of interest on loans that were unpaid or deferred in the past.

Many people are still paying off their student loans into their sixties. Even if they aren't paying their own college debts, they may be incurring or paying off loans under the federal Direct PLUS loan program, which includes Grad PLUS loans, for graduate and professional students, and Parent PLUS loans, made to parents and grandparents who aim to help their children and grandchildren attend college.* Parent PLUS loans have grown dramatically in recent

---

* Parents and grandparents can borrow, under their own names, to help finance their children's or grandchildren's higher educations. You'd think they would be a better credit risk than their children and grandchildren and get a better borrowing rate, but Parent PLUS loans charge a hefty origination fee and come with a far higher interest rate than standard federal student loans. There's also no limit on the amount one can borrow to cover tuition costs, so parents and grandparents are free to borrow far

years, now accounting for one in four federally sponsored student loans. Total outstanding Parent PLUS balances exceeded $100 billion as of 2020.[4]

The big question with these loans is whether the parent (or grandparent) or the child is the true borrower. Yes, parents are legally obligated to repay. Their names and signatures are on the loan documents. But the parents may be handing their children the monthly repayment bills to cover. In this case, Parent PLUS borrowing is simply additional borrowing by children, using their parents as middlemen. This question — *Who's actually on the hook to repay?* — is major for two reasons. First, parents can borrow up to the amount of the college's net price. If the net price is very high, parents may be borrowing huge amounts that they expect their children to handle — obligations of which their children may not be fully aware.

To make matters worse, the interest rate charged on Parent PLUS loans is almost twice the rate on direct, unsubsidized federal student loans. If repayment takes decades, every dollar of Parent PLUS borrowing will prove roughly equivalent, in repayment terms, to two dollars of direct student borrowing.

The concern about how much kids owe to their parents extends well beyond Parent PLUS loans. Parents may be "helping" their children attend their dream school by borrowing in other ways, including refinancing their homes, taking out second mortgages, or tapping into their retirement savings. Even if they have no expectation of payback, parents may implicitly be forcing their children to

---

beyond their remaining means. And if they die before paying up, Uncle Sam or the private student loan lender will be at the head of the line to recover the loan balance from their estate. This effectively means their kids or grandkids will be the ultimate payers. (Credit Summit, "Student Loan Debt Statistics — Updated for 2020," https://www.mycreditsummit.com/student-loan-debt-statistics/.)

repay. Unless the parents reduce their own lifestyles, they'll end up leaving their children less money—the money spent repaying their Parent PLUS loans—when they pass.

Since no one has collected data on the amount of student loans—as opposed to gifts—that children owe their parents, we simply don't know the true amount of debt today's young and middle-aged Americans are carrying. What we do know is that the $33,000 average *formal* debt of newly minted college grads doesn't include even a penny's worth of obligations to their parents or grandparents and may, therefore, significantly understate the true size of the grad's financial burden.

Data from American University in Washington, DC, illustrates this issue. Many parents of US college matriculants borrow under the Parent PLUS program. By graduation day, a good 15 percent have borrowed $60,000 or more on their child's behalf.* The children of these parents are quite likely graduating with $31,000 in Stafford loans (a type of federal loan made directly to students). That's the maximum amount one can borrow over four years under the program. Since the interest rate on Stafford loans is so much lower than that on Parent PLUS loans, parents would likely have their children borrow up to the Stafford-loan limit before borrowing at the higher rate. Therefore, if parents are explicitly or implicitly sticking their kids with the Parent PLUS loans, 15 percent of US students are graduating with more than $90,000 in debt!

So even if Madeline was the only member of my class who had incurred six figures of formal debt, I wouldn't be surprised if some of her classmates owed almost that much to a combination of the government and their families.

---

* This doesn't include deferred interest.

A REMARKABLY LARGE SHARE OF COLLEGE ENTRANTS NEVER GRADUATE

The concern over excessive borrowing to finance inherently unaffordable spending on college is dramatically heightened by the remarkably high probability that dollars spent on college are completely wasted.

Here's the most shocking college statistic around: six years out, 40 percent of those who started college have yet to graduate and likely never will.[5] Worse, most have surely borrowed for the privilege of calling it quits.

Each year some fifteen million high school grads head off to college, blissfully unaware that six million of them won't graduate but sure that they themselves will prevail. To mitigate uninformed or magical college thinking, the US Department of Education (DOE) should force colleges to include the following warning in their admissions letter:

WARNING—TWO-FIFTHS OF US COLLEGE MATRICULANTS NEVER GRADUATE! PAYING, LET ALONE BORROWING, LARGE SUMS TO ATTEND COLLEGE IS HIGHLY RISKY!

This warning might change behavior. Not many of us would borrow heavily to enter a game of high-stakes poker knowing our chance of leaving empty-handed is two in five. Well, I guess college dropouts aren't leaving completely empty-handed. On the way to folding their college hands, they can certainly learn marvelous things from marvelous teachers. But these days, those marvelous things can be learned from marvelous teachers online and for free.

The DOE doesn't provide this disclosure. But it does help you understand the dropout rate at schools you may be considering. Its website (Collegescorecard.ed.gov) covers more than 5,700 educational institutions, many of which are vocational. The list ranges from Toni & Guy Hairdressing Academy to Stanford University. Most institutions report their graduation and transfer rates, from which you can infer their dropout rates.

Though you might not expect it, colleges with high dropout rates aren't likely to be tougher academically. Take the University of Massachusetts, from which my wife, Bridget, took permanent leave after her freshman year. Its dropout rate is far higher than that of neighboring Amherst College. This doesn't reflect higher UMass academic standards. It reflects a different student body with different financial resources and educational interests. In Bridget's case, she was, in her own words, too young for college. After partying through freshman year, she headed to Colorado to be, again in her words, a ski bum. Three years later, she returned to Massachusetts and, after some job hopping, decided property management was her calling. She spent two years working during the day and earning a property management certificate at night.

Through the course of her career, Bridget managed several of the largest high-rise office buildings in Boston and worked for two of the country's top tech companies—earning, in the process, considerably more than the typical UMass grad (or, for that matter, Amherst grad). Her story, like CJ's in chapter 1, reminds us there are many paths to a successful career. It also provides an important college money lesson:

If you've started college, but it's clearly not for you, bail early!

If you aren't sure about college, don't make a huge investment. Start small, maybe at a community college or your state university. You can always transfer, as I'll address shortly. The most important college secret is:

Assess your chance of dropping out before deciding whether and where to matriculate.

GRADUATING COLLEGE IS THE EXCEPTION, NOT THE RULE

Our society puts far too much pressure on attending college. More than half of high school grads head off to college despite, to repeat, only a three in five chance of making it through. Those who don't get their degree may be embarrassed by that fact for the rest of their days. This is true even for those who end up being far more successful financially than most people who have a diploma hanging on their wall.

That's a pity. We are a highly productive economy with a highly productive workforce. But our workforce isn't productive by virtue of everyone having a college degree. Sixty-four percent of us never get a college degree.[6] In Switzerland, this share is even higher— 75 percent. Yet Swiss workers are far more productive, on average, than US workers.

In the recent past, a college degree was essentially a prerequisite for employment in cutting-edge companies. That's no longer the case. Take Apple. Half of its new hires haven't graduated college.[7] And there's certainly no college diploma needed for becoming fabulously successful. Recall that Apple's legendary founder, Steve Jobs, was a college dropout. So were Bill Gates and Mark Zuckerberg, who are among the richest people on the planet. The list of top companies whose founders didn't make it to college or get through college includes Twitter, Fitbit, WhatsApp, WordPress, Tumblr, Square, Stripe, Spotify, Oracle, Napster, Uber, Dropbox, Virgin, Dell, DIG, and IAC. Of course, these largely skew toward the tech sector, but the point is that a college degree is not the only means to success.

My purpose is not to dissuade you or your children from attending or finishing college. My purpose is to change the college conversation—to show it for what it is: an expensive and risky investment. It's an investment you or your children are free to decline or terminate as soon as you or they realize it doesn't, or no longer, makes sense.

WHETHER TO APPLY, WHERE TO APPLY, AND WHERE TO ATTEND

Risk aside, how do you decide whether to attend college and, if so, where to apply? And if you're accepted by more than one school, how do you know which to choose? As with all economic choices, you need to run the numbers, incorporating the compensating differentials. This is no different from choosing among careers or houses. It's simply a matter of considering the net benefit—the extra earnings less the costs plus the added bennies—from, say, borrowing to attend expensive Oberlin College versus not borrowing and attending cheaper community-based Santa Monica College.

In other words, does attending a low-cost, low-prestige, low-amenities school that doesn't necessitate borrowing beat attending a high-cost, high-prestige, high-amenities school that requires lots of borrowing, explicit and implicit? The answer depends on what the colleges actually cost and how much difference attending particular colleges will make to your lifetime earnings.

THE COST OF COLLEGE

There are more than fifty US colleges and universities now charging, before any student aid, more than $74,000 per year. This includes room, board, and fees. Four years at $74,000 is $296,000. If you borrow $74,000 each year at, say, a 5 percent rate, you'll graduate college with $335,000 of student debt. To put this in perspective, Americans earn, on average, about $53,000 per year (after tax, this is about $40,000). So it would take more than eight years of work for college grads earning the national average salary to pay for attending an elite school for four years. And that's if they plow every single after-tax dollar they earn into loan repayments—not realistic. If they use only one-fifth of their annual earnings on repayments, it will take more than forty years to become debt-free.

Yes, college grads earn more, on average, than non–college grads. A recent study by the Federal Reserve Bank of New York puts their average salary at $78,000—close to $30,000 higher than what non–college grads earn.[8] But the starting salary of college grads is closer to $50,000.[9] And the wage distribution is highly skewed, with the average pulled up by those earning very large amounts. The more typical median earnings of college grads, including mid- and advanced-career grads, is about $65,000. And about 16 percent of college grads earn less than $52,000; 10 percent earn less than $33,000.

Paying back, say, $20,000 or $30,000 over time is certainly possible for most college grads. But there are two big risks. The first is being among the one in five who borrow far more than the average. The second is not earning the high salary expected. Students, as a group, not only believe they will perform, on average, better in college than they actually do. They also believe they'll earn significantly more, on average, than ends up being the case.[10] Moreover, far more than three-fifths believe, starting out, that they'll graduate and do so within four years.

You're getting the picture. Absent significant financial aid in the form of grants, scholarships, and work-study jobs, college is incredibly expensive at many top-, middle-, and even low-ranked schools. Borrowing to pay for a superexpensive college greatly exacerbates the cost problem, since doing so will likely require borrowing mostly at high private rates. Hence, this chapter's main mantra:

Avoid borrowing for college if at all possible. It's too risky.

I don't say this lightly. I'm a college professor. I think higher education is of enormous individual and social value. But you can receive a fine college education without mortgaging your future and potentially dashing your career plans. It simply involves applying to less expensive, if generally less prestigious, institutions.

THE NET PRICE VERSUS THE STICKER PRICE OF COLLEGE

The saving grace, especially for students from low- and lower-middle-income households, is that the actual price of college — the net price — is far cheaper than it seems. This is because of scholarships and grants, offered by the government as well as the schools. Federal grants, called Pell Grants, and similar state grants (which differ by state and are often tied to state universities) are based on your calculated need.* College-provided grants are both needs based and merit based.

Depending on your parents' financial status, the difference between the sticker and net prices of college can be huge. Wellesley economist Phillip B. Levine is a leading expert on college financial aid. His book *Mismatch: The New Economics of Financial Aid and College Access* is, like Lieber's, a must read if you're heading to college. The book complements Phil's excellent, free website, Myintuition

---

* There are also Federal Supplemental Educational Opportunity Grants, Iraq and Afghanistan Service Grants, and Federal Teacher Education Assistance for College and Higher Education Grants.

.org, which lets you calculate the net price of attending more than seventy US colleges.

Consider Boston University. Its sticker price for academic year 2020/2021 is a jaw-dropping $77,662. That's broken down as $56,854 for tuition, $16,640 for a room and meal plan, and $4,168 for incidental charges. However, suppose your parents have a combined income of $50,000 and no assets. In this case, attending BU will cost, at most, $7,500! That's a 90 percent discount between the sticker price and the maximum net price. In general, coming from a low-income family is no fun. But when it comes to college aid, it's a wonder to behold. Yes, there's still the $7,500 (or less) per year to pay. But you can easily earn most of this working in the summer and during the school year. *There's no need to borrow even a penny!*

What if your parents have higher earnings and assets? Specifically, suppose they earn $100,000 annually and have $100,000 in the bank—money they've been saving to help you with college. Now Myintuition.org reports BU's maximum net price at $25,900. That's still miles below $77,662, but it's also far above $7,500. If you were to borrow this amount each year for four years, you'd leave college more than $100,000 in debt. Thus, student debt can be a major problem even for those coming from middle-income households.

If your parents earn $100,000 but have all of their savings parked in a 401(k) or some other retirement account, BU's maximum net price is $14,800. Assets held in retirement accounts aren't counted in determining a student's need.* Now, $14,800 is a lot more than $7,500, but it's also a lot less than $25,900.

---

* But, and there's always a but, "voluntary contributions from the taxpayer to these retirement plans during the base year (the prior tax year) are reported on the FAFSA and are counted as *untaxed income.* Employer matching contributions are not reported on the FAFSA. Untaxed income and benefits have a similar impact on aid eligibility as taxable income." See Mark Kantrowitz, "How Do Retirement Funds Affect Student Aid Eligibility?" FastWeb, October 6, 2009, https://www.fastweb.com/financial-aid/articles/how-do-retirement-funds-affect-student-aid-eligibility.

Suppose your family has a high income—$250,000 per year—owns a million-dollar house free and clear of any mortgage, and has $200,000 in the bank. Apart from merit-based aid BU may provide, you're now facing BU's full $78,000 sticker price.

If through Myintuition.org you calculate the net cost of attending even a handful of schools, you'll learn some surprising things. For example, if your family has $50,000 in earnings and no assets, BU is about $5,000 cheaper per year than UMass Amherst (even for in-state students, who pay less in tuition at UMass). BU ranks in prestige as 42nd, according to *U.S. News & World Report.* UMass Amherst ranks 66th. Yet the 70 percent more prestigious BU (assuming the *U.S. News* ranking captures prestige and only prestige, which we'll delve into shortly) is 40 percent cheaper than UMass Amherst.* This is a big money lesson:

Buy prestige and, potentially, a better education on the cheap via comparison shopping.

Again, what's cheap depends on your family's circumstances. If your parents have a high combined income and significant assets and you live outside Massachusetts, you'll have to pay UMass Amherst's $50,365 full sticker price. That's 35 percent cheaper than the relevant BU price. In this case, more prestige as well as a possibly better education comes at a higher price.

The big money lessons here?

Depending on your circumstances, a superexpensive school can be incredibly cheap. Understand different schools' net prices before applying, let alone attending!

---

* My measure of college prestige is 1 minus the *U.S. News* ranking divided by 100. In other words, BU's prestige is 0.42 or 0.58.

AVOIDING POTENTIALLY HUGE COLLEGE-AID TAXES

The examples just given suggest another big money secret: having more money reduces your child's calculated financial need and raises their net cost of college. You can calculate these implicit "college-aid taxes" on savings and income by using Myintuition.org to examine a specific school but with different income and asset inputs. In Boston University's case, there's a roughly 22 percent tax on assets outside retirement accounts and a 15 percent tax on earnings.

Let me clarify. If you have relatively low nonretirement assets and save an extra dollar, you'll lose about twenty-two cents of that dollar in the form of four years of reduced financial assistance for your child. And if you have a relatively low income and earn an extra dollar, you'll lose about fifteen cents of that dollar when your child's net college price is raised. Also bear in mind that although Myintuition.org focuses on current income, your child's financial need calculation actually considers your adjusted gross income two years before their application is submitted. The calculation is based on the FAFSA (Free Application for Federal Student Aid) form available at Studentaid.gov.

The message here is simple:

How you handle your finances can dramatically affect the net cost of college.

The following are some good money tricks to avoid college asset and earnings tests. Note, they only apply to people whose income and asset levels are low enough to matter to the student financial need calculation. I offer them with hesitation, as I think taking advantage of the student-aid system is unfair. But I also think hitting low- and middle-income households with these huge additional marginal taxes on saving and working is unfair. I'm also concerned that if parents with limited means are leaving their child to foot the net cost of college, they should do whatever they can to limit the burden. Even the feds realize they are imposing crazy extra taxes on what people should be doing: saving and working.[11] To help people avoid these implicit taxes, they've developed the FAFSA4caster tool (available at Studentaid.gov/h/apply-for-aid/fafsa). Hard to believe our government is effectively actively encouraging tax avoidance, but there you go.

If you're going to follow these steps, start doing so years before your children reach college age, and continue to follow them while your children are in college since student financial aid is recalculated annually.

Nine Ways to Minimize College-Aid Asset and Income Taxes

1. Contribute as much as possible to retirement accounts to limit the amount of your regular assets. If possible, arrange with your employer to receive more of your compensation as retirement contributions.

2. Use your regular assets to pay down your mortgage. FAFSA doesn't include home equity.*

3. Use regular assets to buy durables (maybe it's time for an electric Hummer?) and personal collectibles, including easily resellable jewelry, which aren't included in your child's financial need calculation.

4. Make your child's grandparents the account holders of 529 plans, education savings accounts, and other college saving plans, since these assets will otherwise lower your child's financial need.

---

* However, certain individual schools may incorporate home equity in computing a student's financial need.

5. Defer taking capital gains on regular assets, which will factor in the government's FAFSA income calculation.

6. Save within whole-life or universal-life insurance policies. The cash value in these policies is generally not included in student-aid calculations.

7. Defer withdrawals from retirement accounts, which will raise your FAFSA-measured income.

8. Keep assets out of your child's name. Your child's assets and income will limit their aid.

9. Defer getting married if this will lower your child's calculated aid by increasing your assets.

BEWARE THE STANDARD COLLEGE "AWARD" CON JOB

College acceptance comes with a financial award letter listing all your so-called financial aid. This includes federal and state student loans. But loans are not awards. Loans are not aid. Loans are not gifts. Loans are costs you will have to repay.

And what are the terms of the loans? What interest rates will you pay? The "award" letters don't say. The award letters also list Parent PLUS loans as awards without a peep about the rate being charged, the length of the loan, or the need for parents and their children to discuss in advance who will make repayment. They also don't explain that a work-study "award" is contingent on the student finding a job on campus. Nor do they necessarily explain whether any scholarship being offered by the college is just for the student's first year or whether it will renew annually contingent on satisfactory performance. The letters also don't indicate that federal and state grants are not guaranteed beyond the student's freshman year, and that if the parents' assets or income positions improve, those grants will be reduced or eliminated.

Who knows how many students and parents fall for the college award con. Most high school seniors don't know a thing about borrowing, debt, loans, interest rates, fees, or repayment periods. Their parents might not, either, or they might be hesitant to dissuade their kids from a prestigious, expensive school. These college award letters take advantage of all of this. As I write this, my blood is boiling. Imagine a real estate agent trying to persuade you to buy a house you can't afford by telling you the local bank will aid you by "awarding" you a mortgage based on terms the agent fails to disclose. The agent wouldn't last a day at their job.

It would be one thing if students could walk away from their "awards" if they weren't able to repay. With rare exceptions, that's not the case. Instead, they find themselves in a land of financial hurt.

WHAT HAPPENS IF YOU FAIL TO REPAY YOUR STUDENT LOANS?

To my lasting regret, I didn't stay in touch with Madeline. I don't know what job Madeline ultimately obtained nor how she handled her student debt. Hopefully, she didn't default. Doing so would likely have landed her in the modern-day equivalent of debtor's prison. Unlike other debts, which can be discharged via bankruptcy, student loans are the proverbial albatross wrapped tightly around your neck.[12] If you don't repay:

Your loans may be turned over to a collection agency, which can add 18 percent to the balance.

You'll be liable for collection costs, including court and attorney fees.

You can be sued for the entire amount of your loan and your wages may be garnished.

Your federal and state income tax refunds may be intercepted.

The government may withhold part of your Social Security benefits.

Your default will appear on your credit history for up to seven years *after* you've paid up.

You may not be able to get an auto loan, mortgage, or even credit cards.

You won't receive additional federal financial aid or most benefits.

You'll be ineligible for deferments and subsidized interest benefits.

You may not be able to renew a professional license or enlist in the armed forces.

I once visited a medieval debtor's prison near York, England. It consisted of an underground chamber with eight cells. It had no light, no air, no sanitation, and, according to the guide, it had served food unfit for rats. No doubt it killed its occupants, physically or mentally, in short order. It also taught others a lesson: *some forms of borrowing are just too dangerous.*

Mississippi still has a debtor's prison. Judges can lock you up and force you to work off your IOUs.[13] In the other forty-nine states, student debt means financial, not physical, misery. As the list indicated, your creditors, starting with Uncle Sam, will get their money by any means possible. In short, defaulting on your student loan, with rare exceptions, is not really an option. It just raises your outstanding balance, since interest and fees on unpaid obligations continue to accumulate.

Take the actual case of fifty-nine-year-old Chris.[14] Chris borrowed $79,000 to attend college and law school. Then he hit one bump in the road after another, often leaving him unable to make any loan repayments. In 2004, the feds started garnishing his wages. But the amounts they've been grabbing, for what is now close to two decades, have never sufficed to pay off any of the principal Chris owed. They haven't even covered outstanding interest due. This isn't surprising, given the very high average interest Chris is being charged, including interest on nasty loan-origination fees. And, of course, each month's underpayment of interest, including interest on unpaid fees, isn't forgiven. Quite the contrary. The underpayment is tacked onto Chris's balance. Today, after seventeen years of garnished wages, Chris's total outstanding student debt equals \$236,000—almost three times the amount he originally borrowed!

This is postbellum sharecropping in sheep's clothing. Under sharecropping, poor farmers (often Black farmers who were former slaves) were forced to borrow, at usurious interest rates, to buy seed and other supplies at inflated prices from the landlord's store. Once in debt, laws stated that they couldn't sell their farms or, effectively speaking, work for anyone else. This institution—slavery by another name—lasted through the 1930s.[15] In the case of student loans, the students borrowing for college are the sharecroppers, and the landlords are Uncle Sam and his higher-education compadres in this government-supervised financial crime.

That's strong language. How can an economist trained to respect free markets call a loan voluntarily made between two parties a crime? My answer is that high school students and often their parents don't have the information needed to engage in the transaction. In particular, I conjecture that well over half of students taking out college loans don't realize these loans can't be discharged via bankruptcy. Nor do they really understand what's involved in paying them back—something I'll help quantify next.

Given the financial dangers of student debt, it's time to ask whether schools with high net prices are worth it, let alone worth borrowing for.

YOU CAN'T EAT PRESTIGE

I've attended, taught at, or visited hundreds of colleges and universities in my day, both in the US and abroad. In the process, I've met thousands of students and faculty. I've also worked in the federal government, in the private sector, for foreign governments, for international agencies, and as a consultant to private companies. Here, too, I've met a small army of people, most of whom had a college degree.

What stands out from these acquaintances is the general irrelevance of educational pedigree to achievement. Where the person went to college or, indeed, whether they attended college just isn't a huge factor. Highly successful people work their tails off, learn on the job what's required to do their tasks, and do what my friend CJ did in his car-wash job way back in chapter 1: think for their bosses, solve their bosses' problems, and end up becoming the boss themselves. Because of these traits, they make it financially no matter the precise number or source of their educational medals. Elite schools gather successful people. They don't make them successful.

Yes, connections matter. Going to an exclusive school, attended by generally well-heeled and well-connected people, provides easier access to a high-paying first job. But if you aren't performing up to expectations, the Harvard sweater you wear to the office all summer long won't save your job. The slogan coined by Harvard's blue-collar, union workers in fighting over the years for higher pay and better working conditions sums up my point:

You can't eat prestige.

SITZFLEISCH

I learned firsthand that attending a prestigious school is no guarantor of success. Let me tell you about two members of my Harvard economics graduate school class. I'll call them George and Sam. When I and the other twenty-four students in my class started the program, George and Sam stuck out as far and away the most likely to succeed. Boy, were they smart. They were so smart that neither had bothered to graduate from high school. Even though they both dropped out in their senior years, they aced their SATs and were accepted at two of the nation's top colleges. As undergrads, they were so smart that neither bothered to attend classes or take exams. They just studied on their own—but only things they found interesting. This eventually led to their expulsions.

How did they manage to get accepted into Harvard's PhD program in economics? Pure genius. They somehow met each other and conceived their admissions plan. This involved identifying the faculty member—I'll call him Professor X—who was in charge of Harvard's graduate economics admissions. Next, they wrote a brilliant paper critiquing one of Professor X's recently written papers. George and Sam submitted their critique as part of their graduate school application. Professor X was floored. Imagine two kids who had failed both high school and college being able to find holes in his work. Bingo, they were in.

When the rest of us arrived at Harvard, we were quaking in our boots, suspecting the admissions office had made clerical mistakes when they accepted us. After we met George and Sam, our suspicions seemed confirmed. George and Sam looked like geniuses, talked like geniuses, knew a ton of highly advanced math, understood the university's computer hardware system inside and out, and seemingly outstripped everyone else in every way. Professor X exacerbated our insecurity. He not so subtly let us know that he'd discovered two Einsteins. Albert, after all, had had his own troubles getting through high school and college.

When it came time to take the first theory exam, we knew it was game over. George and Sam would leave us miles behind and

Harvard would fix its mistakes by sending us packing. All of us entered the exam room with our heads in our hands, except George and Sam, who were totally calm.

A few days later, though, something very strange happened. The professor posted the numerical grades. We all rushed to see how well George and Sam had done. But George and Sam weren't at the top of the grade list. They weren't near the top. They weren't in the middle. They weren't just below the middle. Instead, they were close to the bottom.

What happened? Very simple. George and Sam were still George and Sam. Admission to Harvard hadn't changed that. Neither George nor Sam had bothered to study. Neither had what the Germans call *Sitzfleisch,* which literally means "sitting flesh." It references the ability to sit in a chair for long hours studying, doing research, and writing. If you don't have enough padding down under, you won't get far in academia. George and Sam had too little padding.

George and Sam still somehow passed their classes and preliminary exams. But when it came to writing a thesis, their *Sitzfleisch* completely gave out. Our class geniuses couldn't be bothered to write a thesis. Consequently, they went a perfect three for three. They failed to graduate high school. They failed to graduate college. And they failed to graduate graduate school. For George and Sam, getting into Harvard wasn't even a ticket to getting out of Harvard, let alone a ticket to a successful academic career.*

George and Sam's story is, of course, unusual. Most people don't fail their way into Harvard. And most of those who attend Harvard do end up at the upper end of the wage distribution. But the reason they get in, stay in, and graduate isn't primarily effortless genius. And they don't end up well-off because they went to Harvard but

---

* The fact that George and Sam weren't cut out for academia doesn't mean they ended up impoverished. I lost track of their careers. They may well have succeeded far beyond most of us but in fields that don't require discipline and diligence.

because they know how to work. They are disproportionately hard workers. Their long-term career success is rarely a function of the institutional name on their college diploma. And what's true about Harvard grads is true of grads from all the nation's elite schools, and ones outside the upper echelon; nothing's different if you consider schools ranked below the top 50.

This isn't just my two cents. In a seminal 1999 study, economists Stacy Dale and Alan Krueger found that once you control for a high school student's GPA and other measures of their ability and work ethic, their future earnings don't depend on whether they attended an elite school.[16] This study reveals a huge money secret. It says that going to Harvard, Yale, Stanford, MIT, Columbia, Penn, Cornell, and so on isn't worth the high price of admission if you don't get significant (real) financial aid.

Let me record this as a money secret:

Paying, let alone borrowing, big bucks to attend an elite school is likely a huge waste of money.

Of course, I don't want to overstate the case. Recent research by economists Raj Chetty and John Friedman (along with others) suggests that attending particular elite schools might add value because they do a good job of training students in specific areas or because the schools are favored by recruiters.[17] For example, the University of Pennsylvania is a better place to go if you want to work on Wall Street than, say, Amherst College, because Wall Street recruits more heavily at Penn than at Amherst. So paying more for specific training or access to a job interview may be worth it in certain cases. But the bigger issue is whether the vast majority of students attending elite schools are paying a premium thinking that a fancy diploma is a ticket to life. It's more likely a ticket to penury if they're paying full price.

On the other hand, if your grandmother will go nuts if you don't satisfy her bragging rights, there are ways to attend elite schools on the cheap. We've already discussed the first: check the school's net price. It may be far lower than expected. The second is to get the best of both worlds—a cheap degree and an expensive education.

ATTEND AN ELITE SCHOOL AT A LOW COST

Consider Rutgers University in New Jersey. It's ranked 63rd among universities by *U.S. News,* but its sticker price is less than half that of many of the top 50 schools. Does its ranking *really* mean that Rutgers is the 63rd best place in the US to go to college? Is Boston University really 42nd best? Surely not. I could write an entire book about the defects of the *U.S. News* ranking system. The biggest problem is that *U.S. News* undervalues what should be of most concern in choosing a college: the quality of the faculty doing the teaching. That gets magnified by the fact that the same college may have very different quality levels between departments. If a school has a great department in your area of interest, that is far more important to you than its overall ranking.

My view? The best instruction is provided by the best researchers—faculty who publish in the top journals in their research fields. Why? Because being a top educator requires staying abreast of the latest research in your field, which top scholars are forced to do. You can't publish research without citing the literature. Nor can you publish something that's close to what's already been published. Thus, the old adage in academia—*Publish or perish*—has a corollary: *Read before you write.*

When I joined the economics department at Boston University in 1984, we were ranked 86th among economics departments across the country based on publication in top journals. That was an objective ranking; you could just open the past five or so years of top economics journals and count the number of articles written by BU faculty. The count placed us right where we were: nowhere.

When I came to BU, turning that situation around was a university priority. That required hiring top researchers and raising their standards in granting tenure. In 1985, I became chairman, and my colleagues and I got to work. Within fourteen years our department was ranked 7th based on the same criteria![18] Our department outranked those at Stanford, Yale, Northwestern, Berkeley, Brown, and other supposedly "better" places.

However, year after year, *U.S. News* took no notice whatsoever of the academic improvement of our economics department, let alone that of the overall university. But when the university built a splendid new gym, five-star dormitories, a gorgeous student center, and a state-of-the-art hockey rink, and made all manner of other cosmetic changes that had zero impact on the actual education being delivered, the ranking rose. Hence, some important college-shopping truth:

You can't trust college rankings.

This conclusion has profound implications for which colleges you consider, how much you end up paying for college, and, consequently, how much you go into debt. I hate to repeat myself, but the easiest and safest way to make money is not to lose it, particularly by overpaying for something that's actually second-rate. College is expensive. High school students often fall in love with a college because they like the tour guide or the sports teams or because it's located in a fun city or the dorms are fab. When I was department chair, I never once received a call or email from a high school applicant or parent saying they or their child might major in economics and asking about the research quality of our faculty.

This worries me. My sense is that millions of high school seniors and their parents are buying college educations blind. They may be doing so thinking that the more they spend, the higher the school's ranking, and the nicer the dorm rooms, the greater their chances of eventual financial reward. Yet, as the Dale-Krueger study shows, that's not the case. For all you know, Rutgers may be a far better university in your area of interest than most that are ranked in the top 20. If so, attending Rutgers may provide a far better education at potentially half the price. Other things being equal, this means leaving college with half the amount of student debt.

How can you sort out the quality of the education you're actually buying in choosing a college? I'd follow these steps: Think about ten fields in which you might major (there's no reason to narrow yourself too much, because an important part of college is being able to change your mind about your field of study). Then look online for the research or related rankings of the departments in those fields in each of the colleges you're considering.* Next, call up chairs of departments in schools you aren't considering and ask them which of the colleges you're considering are the best in their field. For example, if you're comparing political science at Wake Forest and Notre Dame, call up the political science chair at, say, the University of Michigan, and ask what they would advise.† I know this may seem unorthodox, but I want to encourage you to think outside the box, or at least the glossy admissions brochure. But the most important and easiest step in ascertaining academic quality is to check out the research records of the faculty of each department

---

* Be thorough. You may find different rankings based on different criteria. Repec.org appears to do the best research ranking of economics departments. BU ranks 11th among US economics departments and 15th worldwide. Rutgers ranks 38th among US economics departments and 68th worldwide.

† People into education are into education. Unless they're masquerading in their profession, they should be more than happy to spend a few minutes helping budding students with educational-path advice.

of interest at each school of interest. Their curricula vitae are easily found online.

If college rankings aren't necessarily connected to the education being provided and everyone is focused on the rankings, you can surely find an inexpensive school that provides first-rate education at a very affordable price. Thus, this money moral:

Find a superior college education on the cheap by forming your own rankings.

CREATE AN ELITE EDUCATION NO MATTER WHERE YOU GO

Doing your educational-quality due diligence is important even after you choose a college and major. In my department, as in most leading departments, we have lots of visitors and non-research faculty as well as top researchers teaching undergraduate courses. Suppose you've opted to major in economics. Furthermore, suppose you're paying upwards of $80,000 in tuition, room, and board. If you're paying this huge sum to get educated, you obviously want to make sure you get the best education your $320,000 can buy. Realize this is the price of a terrific house in most of the country. It's also the price of three Hummer EVs or a Rolls-Royce (the cheapo model) or eight years of work if you earn the average wage and figure in taxes.

So spend half the day it takes to identify your college's outstanding faculty, based on their research records, and take their courses. Don't rely on websites that offer teaching evaluations or even recommendations from fellow students, both of which may be completely misleading. Those who are most popular might be highly entertaining, but they're not necessarily the best in their field.

In this regard, let me convey an accidental conversation I had with a recent BU econ graduate. When we met and she learned I taught economics at BU, she beamed.

"I absolutely loved BU and majoring in economics."

I beamed back. "Did you take Professor Z's course? He's super."

"No, didn't take Z."

"What about Professor X? Surely, you took X's course?"

"No, sorry."

"And Professor Y? Did you have Y?"

"No, but I did take Professor W."

"Umm. Professor W isn't actually a professor. He's a grad student."

After further back-and-forth, I realized that this highly satisfied graduate had spent four years taking classes in BU's superb economics department without attending a single course given by one of our regular faculty (who teach their own sections of the courses), let alone one of our top research faculty. I don't know who paid for her education—Uncle Sam, BU, the State of Massachusetts, her parents, grandparents, rich aunt, or she herself, by borrowing. No matter how the bills were paid (or are still being paid), she didn't take full advantage of her education. We have great grad students, visitors, and faculty who specialize in teaching, but they aren't remotely as qualified to teach as the top research faculty. And what's true at BU is true at all universities.

That brings us to another secret:

Spend your education dollars carefully by studying with top research faculty.

GETTING EDUCATED AT ELITE SCHOOLS WITHOUT THE COST

When you're searching for the programs with the best faculty in your desired field of study, you'll certainly run into the fact that—though there are some hidden gems—many of the best faculties are indeed at expensive, elite schools.*

But given the wonders of the internet, you don't actually need to be a full-time, in-person student at those schools to take advantage of the learning from their top faculty. You can attend classes at more affordable schools and take free online classes at Harvard, MIT, Yale, Oxford, Berkeley, Stanford, and many other top-ranked institutions. Coursera is an online platform that offers almost four thousand courses, roughly a quarter of which are free. The rest can be accessed for about six hundred dollars per year. If you want to specialize and earn a certificate for taking a subset of courses in your area of interest, the price tag is far lower.

In 1962, President Kennedy gave Yale's commencement address and received an honorary doctorate. In accepting his diploma, the president famously said, "Now...I have the best of both worlds, a Harvard education and a Yale degree."[19] Kennedy had a marvelous, dry wit. The general view back then, at least among academics, was that a Yale education beat one from Harvard and that a Harvard degree beat one from Yale. With his simple sentence, Kennedy tweaked both institutions, and they knew it.

Today, Kennedy's playful words have a practical meaning. If you're a resident of Iowa, you can get a University of Iowa degree for less than $25,000 per year and an online Yale education. The extra costs to study online at Yale, with completion certificates

---

* Higher-ranked colleges and universities typically have better faculty, but they also have harder-working students with more accumulated knowledge, if not wisdom or street smarts. Academic nerds come in handy. Say you're an art history major but need to take Calculus I to satisfy a distributional requirement. In that case, it's great to have your roommate, Alfred E. Neuman, to explain L'Hôpital's rule. But the advantage of learning from peers has declined dramatically due to the internet. Now you'll find people to teach you from twelve time zones away. Google "L'Hôpital's rule" and you'll find Khan Academy, YouTube videos, a Wiki entry, and dozens of other ways to learn the rule online. This is true of most general topics across most fields of study.

including grades? Next to nothing. Then, in applying for jobs, you can state on your résumé that you graduated from Iowa but studied at Yale, attaching the certificates and grades as proof. This is worth codifying into a secret:

Get the best of both worlds — a cheap, debt-free degree and a superexpensive education.

This said, I've just reprieved Kennedy's irony. The University of Iowa trumps Yale in a number of programs, including the Iowa Writers' Workshop, which is far and away the most prestigious writing program in the country.

IS COLLEGE ABOUT EDUCATION OR SIGNALING?

Michael Spence received the Nobel Prize in Economics for his brilliant theory of signaling — the same one CJ discovered all on his lonesome. Spence's theory applies in a multitude of contexts. In the college arena, it runs, in extreme form, like this: A college education provides no direct value whatsoever to future employers. What matters is your getting into college, particularly a top college, and sticking it out. This shows employers that you're harder working, more creative, and a faster learner than others. Thus, getting into an elite college and succeeding there constitutes nailing an extended work interview with flying colors. If everyone was equally able to succeed in college, it would provide a poor signal to employers. But if those with higher on-the-job potential have an easier time in school, elite schools will emerge and their graduates will get top jobs.

Does this mean you need to pay a crazy sum to an expensive place to get their golden stamp of approval? Not these days. Again, taking online courses at a top school for a certificate and a grade is the answer. Suppose you attend Sitting Bull College in Fort Yates,

North Dakota. Doing so will cost $10,000 per year, which you can cover working part-time during the school year at the local McDonald's. Your dream, though, is to work for IBM on quantum computing. Okay, look up online courses on this subject. You'll find dozens given by top professors at top-ranked universities. Suppose you take ten courses on this subject at a cost of, say, $7,500, for a certificate and a grade. You can pay for this by working at Micky D's full-time in the summer. Bingo, you'll have a great dossier to send IBM when you apply for a job.

Let me summarize:

These days you can extract the signaling value of elite schools online and on the cheap.

THE TRANSFER GAME

One of the best ways to obtain an expensive education at low cost is to attend an inexpensive, low-prestige school for your first two years and then transfer to an expensive, elite school for your junior and senior years.

College hopping is ubiquitous. About 700,000 students—close to two out of five—transfer schools annually. A sizable 17 percent transfer more than once. Most, including large numbers attending community colleges, transfer from inexpensive schools to expensive schools. Indeed, one in four community college students transfer to regular colleges, with most getting their degrees from their new place of learning. In other words, if you spend two years at a less expensive school and then transfer into a more expensive one, you can end up with the more prestigious degree at a fraction of the price.

Want to attend Boston University and hang with me? The university receives more than 4,300 transfer applications each year and admits a surprisingly high 43 percent. That's almost twice its high school graduate acceptance rate, suggesting it's almost twice as easy to transfer to BU than to arrive as a freshman. Cornell gets 5,300 transfer requests and accepts 17 percent, while its freshman admission rate is only 10 percent. So, again, transferring may be the way across the threshold, while paying and borrowing tons less for college in the first, second, or third years before transferring. You can't always count on transferring into your dream school. Princeton is one of a number of elite destinations that accepts only a handful of transfer applicants each year. The reason is that almost everyone accepted as a first-year to Princeton stays all four years, leaving very few class slots to refill. Across all US colleges, though, the transfer acceptance rate appears to be similar to the standard admission rate.[20]

A big issue with transferring is what credits and how many credits your new school will give you based on courses you completed at your prior school.[21] If you have a transferring strategy in mind, spend time in advance talking to admissions offices at your transfer targets to understand their credit-conversion policy and when it's best to apply. Also, be aware that your transcript will likely report different GPAs—one from each school you attend.

To sum this up:

Consider playing the transfer game to nab a cheap degree from an expensive place.

DROWNING IN STUDENT DEBT

Thus far I've focused on the potential dangers of getting in over your head in student debt. If you think this warning doesn't apply to you, please think again. In 2019, 12 percent of student loans were in default and another 14 percent were in deferral or forbearance.[22] In other words, at least one in five of the forty-five million Americans with student debt weren't able to repay what they owed. This troubling stat—a 20 percent chance of not being able to cover your obligation in normal economic times, let alone bad economic times—should make anyone think twice about borrowing for college.

Beyond issuing a warning about student debt, I want to expand on available actual as well as pretend student aid, to consider the potential for receiving debt forgiveness, and to discuss the best way to handle paying off what may end up being multiple loans. By "best way," I'm referring to which loans to pay off first and which to try to extend and whether to opt for income-dependent loans.

STUDENT FINANCIAL AID — THE NITTY-GRITTY

As you now know, there's good aid and bad aid. The good aid doesn't need to be repaid. It comes in the form of outright grants (also called scholarships) provided by a number of sources: the federal government, your state government, the college to which you apply, or a private charity or organization. Grants and scholarships can be based on financial need or merit. The federal government provides Pell Grants of up to $6,345 annually (as of 2021) to college applicants from low- to moderate-income households. If you're in fairly dire need, there's an additional Federal Supplemental Educational Opportunity Grant (FSEOG) that will provide up to $4,000 annually.

Some states also have student grant programs. California's Cal Grant is an example. The grant is calculated based on your need and your California high school GPA. But it's available only if you apply to a college that's part of the University of California system, the California State University system, or the California Community College system. In addition, virtually all states have special targeted college scholarships for which you can apply.

A good place to start your search for state scholarships is the National Association of Student Financial Aid Administrators, or NASFAA (Nasfaa.org/State_Financial_Aid_Programs). I looked up the best college scholarships in Arkansas. I didn't find a Cal Grant–type program, but I did discover scholarships targeted to kids who were into horses, choral singing, tech, cars, pest control, wastewater, nursing, and nature's conservation, or were children of law enforcement officers or disabled or deceased Arkansas vets.

Colleges have their own criteria for awarding needs- and merit-based scholarships. If you're a top student or athlete or stand out in some other way, colleges will likely bid for you. Let them. Once they've sent you your acceptance and award letters, you can appeal for more aid. Tell them about your special circumstances, let them know what other schools are offering, and see if they can dig deeper to get you. Search on the web for guidance on expressing your case in an appealing manner.

Needs-based aid is calculated by subtracting your family's expected family contribution (EFC) from the sticker price. The EFC formula, which Myintuition.org calculates, is, as we've discussed, based on your family's income, non–retirement-account assets, number of siblings in school or heading to school, etc.

Say the sticker price is $75,000 per year and your EFC is $45,000 per year. Then your need is set at $30,000. The school will try to fill this need with federal and state grants, a work-study job, and the needs- and merit-based scholarship it can afford. If the unfilled need isn't met, well, you're stuck paying the difference on top of your $45,000 EFC. That's your net cost.

Though these grants don't generally need to be repaid, certain circumstances can change that. Suppose you party on down, sleep through classes, drink to excess, and do vast quantities of recreational drugs. Well, chances are, you'll end up dropping out or being tossed out. In this case, Uncle Sam, and potentially other grantors, will ask for their money back. If you don't have the money to return, your Pell Grant will be turned into a loan, forcing you to pay back the grant with interest.

BAD AND REALLY BAD "AID" — STUDENT LOANS

Nine out of ten student loans are made by Uncle Sam under a number of federal programs. The rest are private loans. If you must take on loans, you should avail yourself of federal loans first. They come with fairly low fixed interest rates, options to repay as a share of your income, loan forgiveness if you work in particular jobs, loan-postponement options, and, in some cases, lower rates for faster repayment.

Federal loans currently being issued include Direct (also called Stafford) loans, Direct PLUS loans, and Direct Consolidation loans. Direct loans are made to undergraduates and graduates as well as professional students. Undergraduates with financial need can receive Direct loan subsidies, which may delay interest charges until six months after they graduate and during any deferment periods they may be granted down the road. Direct PLUS loans are made to graduate and professional students (Grad PLUS) and, as stated previously, to the parents or grandparents of undergraduates (Parent PLUS). Direct Consolidation loans let a student consolidate all their federal loans into one IOU with one monthly payment.

The maximum amount you can cumulatively borrow for college via a Direct federal loan in 2021 is $31,000 for most applicants. It's $57,500 if you're not financially dependent on your parents. It's $138,500 if you're getting a graduate or professional degree. Clearly, if you're attending a college that's charging a net price of $75,000 per year, $31,000 is just one-tenth of the four-year total cost.

The interest rate on federal loans is 2.75 percent for undergraduate students, 4.3 percent for graduate and professional students, and

5.3 percent for Parent PLUS loans. These are all fixed rates. However, fixed-rate private student loan interest rates range from roughly 3.5 to a crazy-high 14.5 percent. Variable student loan interest rates can range from 1 to 12 percent. If your credit rating (FICO score) is low, you'll face a higher private borrowing rate. The same is true if your parents cosign your loan and their FICO score is low.

HOW BAD IS REALLY BAD "AID"?

Even a 2.75 percent borrowing rate is high compared to what you can earn investing in, say, twenty-year Treasury bonds (1.5 percent as I write this). But paying 4.3 or 5.3 percent or even higher? Now we're talking *really* harmful aid.

Let me make this concrete. Suppose you're Jessie and you've just graduated from high school. You're aiming to get a degree in education and expect to earn $50,000 annually after inflation and taxes. If you retire at sixty-two, you'll have earned $2 million over your career. Spread over the eighty-two years you may live (your maximum age of life is one hundred and you're now eighteen), that's roughly $24,000 you get to spend each year, ignoring the cost of college, taxes, Medicare B premiums, and future Social Security benefits.

Your parents have a lot of money. As a consequence, you're facing a net college cost of $25,000 per year in today's dollars since you don't qualify for needs-based grants. Fortunately, your parents promised to pay the full freight. At least until today.

Today you totaled their brand-new S-Class Mercedes, which they failed to insure for collision. Their reaction? "The car cost more than your college, which is now on you. See you in four years." Your chosen school offers sympathy but no additional support. So you're on your way to borrowing $100,000. If you could borrow at the prevailing zero long-term inflation–adjusted interest rate—essentially for free—it would cost you $100,000 to get back $2 million.

Sounds like an excellent investment, right? Not so fast, since you need to consider the alternatives. What if you find a career you like as much as teaching that offers the same lifetime salary without requiring you to go to college? Your uncle offers to take you into his guitar shop and train you to be a luthier, which would fit the bill and will never be automated. If you'd enjoy that occupation as much as teaching, you'd be tossing away $100,000 by going into teaching.

Still, you're intrigued by teaching and simply love the college that loves you, even if not enough to cut you a break. At a zero borrowing rate, your lifetime spending budget is $1.9 million—the $2 million less the $100,000. Now your annual sustainable spending is down to $23,000. Not a huge decrease but probably enough to feel it somewhere along the line.

This, though, is the best-case scenario. You can't borrow for free. More likely, your average borrowing rate, given you'll need to take out private loans, will be 7 percent before inflation and 5.5 percent after inflation. If you arrange to pay off the loan over twenty years, this will cost you another $62,000 in lifetime spending, raising the cost of college by 62 percent. This $62,000 cost is equivalent to 2.7 years' worth of spending. It drops your annual sustainable spending to roughly $22,400. In other words, you're facing a 7 percent spending cut every year for the rest of your potential eighty-two years. That's almost six years' worth of spending! A life in the guitar-repair trade is starting to look better.

But the bad aid story gets worse. I'm assuming you would net $50,000 annually while teaching. But teaching salaries start low and rise with tenure. Thus, $50,000 net is reasonable as an average over a teaching career, but your initial net pay will be closer to $35,000. Your annual student loan payments will average around $8,000.

Thus, you'll have little money to save in your early years. This will make it tough to accumulate a down payment for a home or much of a reserve fund or to pay for out-of-pocket health expenses. Certainly there are ways to hack this, some of which we've already covered in previous chapters. You can live with friends, use public transportation and Zipcars, forgo travel, forget Milk Duds at the movies, actually forget movies, forget restaurants, etc. But most likely you'll forgo saving, and if you lose your job, that will mean missing student loan payments with the potentially dire consequences you've digested. This bleak scenario isn't the typical outcome. Most students are able to pay off their student loans eventually. But it shows why roughly one-fifth of people with loans aren't paying back or paying back in full.

What if you repay in ten, not twenty, years? This cuts your lifetime repayment to $130,000 but worsens your short-term cash flow. Now you have to fork over $13,000 for the first ten years, compared with $8,000 with a twenty-year repayment. And with a thirty-year repayment? Then the loan averages around $6,500 per year at a cost of $195,000 in lifetime spending. This translates into a 10 percent lower annual and lifetime living standard compared to being a luthier.

FIXED VERSUS INCOME-DRIVEN REPAYMENT PLANS

Studentaid.gov lays out different ways of paying off your federal loans. The Standard Repayment Plan is available for all loan types and entails paying a fixed monthly amount for a number of years up to ten (for consolidated loans, the term ranges from ten to thirty years). The Graduated Repayment Plan is the same as the standard plan except the monthly payment starts lower and rises over time.

There are three income-driven plans. The first is the Revised Pay as You Earn Plan, or REPAYE Plan, which charges 10 percent of your discretionary income, defined as your adjusted gross income less 150 percent of the poverty level for your family size and state. If you haven't repaid after twenty years (twenty-five years for loans taken out for graduate or professional school), the remaining principal plus interest is forgiven. Grad PLUS, Parent PLUS, Direct Consolidated, and loans under discontinued programs aren't eligible for repayment under this plan.

Being able to quit student loan repayments after twenty or twenty-five years provides insurance against having earnings that are low relative to the amount you borrowed. So does the fact that your repayment falls as your earnings fall. For example, when you're unemployed, your repayment is reduced. On the other hand, if you do well, you can easily end up repaying far more than what you originally borrowed, since 10 percent of a high income level can be, well, a big number. How can this happen? It's no different from the balance on your credit card. If you don't pay the interest due, the balance will grow, making the cumulative payback much larger than the original amount you rang up on your card.

Furthermore, if you get married, you'll need to pay 10 percent based not just on your own earnings but your spouse's as well! You may want to include this tidbit in your marriage proposal. "Will you please marry me together with my student loan?"

Another drawback: Say you pay your income-driven student loan for twenty or twenty-five years. Finally it's over, right? Not quite. The IRS will tally up all your unpaid principal plus interest—its "forgiveness"—and add it to your taxable income. This can produce a huge increase in your taxes. If you can't pay the taxes all at once, not to worry. The IRS will let you pay the extra taxes with interest over time—in other words, you're back to paying off a loan (albeit a smaller one).

The second income-driven plan is the Income-Based Repayment Plan, which requires having high student loan debt relative to your income. The repayment is either 10 or 15 percent of your current income, depending on how much money you make. However, your annual repayment will never exceed what you would've paid under a ten-year standard repayment plan.

This last sentence needs parsing. Say your standard-plan repayment was $12,000 a year for ten years. Under the Income-Based Repayment Plan, if your earnings are above $120,000, your annual repayment will still max out at $12,000 each year, but you'll need to keep paying for potentially many more than ten years. This, again, is due to interest that accrues while making less than the standard payments in the years after graduation when your income is low.

The point of forgiveness is either twenty or twenty-five years out depending on when you received your first loan. Again, forgiven amounts are taxable. As for getting married, now your spouse's income is included in the income subject to the 10 or 15 percent hit but only if you file a joint return. Otherwise, you can file as married but filing separately and have the pleasure of paying higher taxes. Now your pitch: "Please marry me and we'll be as one except for tax purposes."

Lastly, the Income-Contingent Repayment Plan charges you the lesser of a standard twelve-year fixed repayment plan payment (adjusted for your income) or 20 percent of your discretionary income. If your parents consolidate their Parent PLUS loans, they can also use this method of repayment. Like the Income-Based Repayment Plan, there's a ceiling on your annual repayment. But in this case, it's a sliding ceiling—one that's lower when your income is lower. But the cost of this added insurance is very high, namely 5 to 10 percent more of your income.

CAN YOU GAME REPAYMENT?

If your income is low, it may seem like you can't lose by going for an income-driven plan. As long as your income is low, you get to repay less than would have otherwise been the case. Then if your income rises, it seems reasonable that you'd be able to switch to the Standard Repayment Plan and pay what you'd otherwise have paid had you started with that plan.

Wrong! Uncle Sam is full of nasties. If you start on an income-driven plan and then switch back to the Standard Repayment Plan, you'll find that your balance is higher.

What? How?

If you pay less than the ten-year Standard Repayment Plan required, Uncle Sam will accumulate, with interest, the underpayment and add it to your balance.

There is one clear way to pay less under an income-driven plan. That's by making larger retirement-account contributions. This will lower your adjusted gross income and, therefore, your requisite payment.

FORGIVENESS PROGRAMS AND DISCHARGES

The federal government has two Direct loan forgiveness programs. The Public Service Loan Forgiveness program lets you off the hook after making ten years of payments, provided you work for a qualified employer, which includes federal, state, local, or tribal governments as well as nonprofits. For those ten years, your payments must be based on one of the income-driven plans just described. Once you reach year ten, the amount forgiven is not taxable. The Teacher Loan Forgiveness Plan forgives up to $17,500 of Direct loans and some grandfathered loans provided you teach in a low-income elementary or secondary school or with an educational service agency.

Total and permanent disability or death will also lead to full discharge of your student debt. Probably not a route anyone would choose. Another possible but long-shot path to student loan discharge is to declare bankruptcy under Chapter 7 or Chapter 13. But here your lender gets to argue in court that you can repay all or some of what you owe. So it's a wild card, and whatever discharge you receive will be predicated on showing that you are permanently unable to maintain a minimal living standard—in other words that repaying your student loans will, effectively, lead to your death.

SHOULD YOU CONSOLIDATE YOUR FEDERAL STUDENT LOANS?

You can consolidate your federal loans once you graduate, leave school, or enroll less than half-time. Consolidating one or more of twenty different federal loans, including seemingly private loans owned by the Department of Education, incurs no cost, can simplify repayment, and lowers your monthly payments by extending the term. It also will give you access to the income-driven repayment plans. But it may land you with a longer-term repayment schedule—something that the earlier example showed is costly. You may also lose credit for months of payments you made in the past under the Public Service Loan Forgiveness program. The interest rate on your consolidated loan is a weighted average of the rates on the loans being consolidated.

Two calculators can help you compare federal loan repayment options. One is at Studentaid.gov/loan-simulator. The other is the VIN Foundation's Student Loan Repayment Simulator at Vin.com /studentdebtcenter/default.aspx?pid=14352&id=7578014. The latter calculator is focused on veterinary students, but it works fine for any student.

OPTIMAL REPAYMENT STRATEGIES

Interest rates on student loans are moderate, high, or extremely high. If you have the ability to pay a fee in order to refinance your loans at a lower rate, consider the option, but do so carefully. Private lenders are just as likely to try to con you into paying more as they are to help you pay less. The best way to see what's being offered is to make as close to an apples-to-apples comparison as possible. If you have a twelve-year loan with monthly payments of $1,000, ask the lender to tell you what you'd pay in total each month with their loan in which the fee is paid off on a monthly basis as well. If the monthly payment they'd charge you based on this calculus is lower, go for the loan.

Your main focus should be on paying off high-interest-rate loans first and, if possible, extending the payment of low-interest-rate loans. One way to do this is to consolidate your low-rate federal Direct loans into a fixed-term Standard Repayment Plan with a long maturity and use the reduction in the monthly payment on those loans to accelerate the payoff of your high-interest-rate loans, be they private or federal.

As for income-related repayment plans, they strike me as questionable. If you're sure your income is going to be quite low for the next twenty to twenty-five years, then you'll likely pay less with any of the income-driven repayment plans. But if you make more money, you could well end up paying more. Insurance is about paying something for sure to reduce downside risk. Here the government is asking you to pay something that's unsure to protect you against the downside. Looked at closely, none of the three income-related plans appear to have a real ceiling on the maximum that may have to be paid. And the repayment that would arise on average under each plan is highly dependent on the variability of the debtor's future earnings. Therefore, it would take a very careful analysis to assess for any given person the economic gains versus costs of these repayment schemes. My general rule is to stay away from complex financial arrangements that are hard to assess. Thus, my money secrets here are:

Extend the maturity of low-rate loans to accelerate paying off high-rate loans. And stick with standard fixed-rate repayment plans unless you're absolutely sure you'll have very low earnings.

RECAP

There's a lot here to summarize, but here goes:

- After mortgages, student loans, totaling more than $1.6 trillion, are our nation's largest form of debt. Two out of three college students borrow. A growing number of parents are borrowing large sums to help finance their children's educations.
- Most loans are federal, with low-interest rates for undergrads and higher interest rates for graduate students, professional students, and parents. The amount undergrads can borrow from the feds is small. This forces a segment to borrow at exorbitant rates from private lenders or have their parents borrow at high rates.
- Parents are increasingly borrowing under the Parent PLUS federal loan program on their children's behalf. The key question is who is the real payer? If children are expected to repay their parents, the amount of debt students — including graduate and professional students — are accumulating is far higher than reported. Parents who intend for their children to repay or share in the repayment of their "contributions" need to discuss their actions with their children in advance since their children are often financially naive. This disclosure also applies to parents who intend to bequeath less to their kids because of their Parent PLUS loan repayment.
- Going to college is financially risky and borrowing to take the gamble greatly exacerbates the risk. Some 40 percent of

college students don't graduate because they lack *Sitzfleisch* or run out of money. Many who drop out do so having borrowed tens of thousands of dollars to attend classes they could have frequented for free online. Those who do graduate leave college laden with, on average, $33,000 of formal debt. One in seven graduate with more than $50,000 in formal debt.

■ Some borrowing is too risky and expensive. Borrowing money with a 40 percent chance of getting nothing in return is extreme high-stakes poker. Even if you get your degree, you may have borrowed so much as to rule out the career that brought you to college.

■ The way to attend college and not go into excessive debt is to get educated on the cheap. If you're from a low- or middle-income family, colleges with crazy-high sticker prices may end up being cheap because the net price they would charge you is very low. You need to comparison shop to understand each school's net price. Parents need to take steps early to limit at least the specific assets, if not the income, that will raise their children's net college prices given what enters the government's needs-based formula. And applicants need to form their own research-based rankings of the departments of interest in the schools to which they apply. National rankings by *U.S. News* and similar organizations are popularity polls. They aren't serious comparisons of research excellence, which, in the end, is the basis of outstanding teaching.

■ A college education is arguably mostly about signaling your ability to work hard, to focus, to persevere. But these days, you can go to an inexpensive school and signal these qualities by simultaneously taking inexpensive online courses from elite institutions for a certificate and a formal grade. You can also transfer from an inexpensive, less prestigious college to an expensive, more prestigious one. A strikingly large share of undergraduates college hop, some more than once.

- There is good financial aid (basically grants and scholarships) and bad aid (namely loans that must be repaid). Colleges lump both types of aid into one figure called financial aid. Don't let that fool you. A loan is a burden, not a form of help. Failure to repay loans can lead to draconian consequences, including the amount owed growing over time and your wages and even Social Security benefits being garnished.

- The interest rates on student loans all exceed what you can earn by investing, and some exceed it by a mile. The longer you take to repay them, the higher their cost. But paying off large loans quickly will likely leave you strapped for cash. This bolsters the argument for getting well educated inexpensively and *not borrowing*.

- There are standard, graduated, and income-driven student loans. If your future income is definitely going to be very low and you've borrowed a ton, the income-driven loans, which set repayments as a share of income and provide forgiveness after twenty or twenty-five years, may be best. But bear in mind, early repayment is the safest option, as the interest on student loans is out the wazoo. Personally, given the uncertainty surrounding repayment of income-driven loans, I'd stay miles away.

- Optimize your student loan repayment by lengthening the maturity of low-rate loans and using the freed-up funds to accelerate repayment of high-rate loans.

CHAPTER 9

Invest Like an Economist — Control Your Living-Standard Trajectories

Our country has hundreds of thousands of financial advisors with a dizzying array of titles.* What unites them is their willingness, for a fee, to tell us precisely how to invest. Funny, then, that they don't provide the same advice. Some will tell you to hold index funds. Some will push life-cycle funds. Some emphasize international stocks. Some are goldbugs. Some insist that Bitcoin is your future. Others focus on commodities or foreign bonds, exotic-sounding currencies or private equity. Then there are clean energy, health, EV, tech, and other sector experts — the hotter the sector the better. And don't forget chartists, who base their advice on patterns of return and trade volume. Nor can we leave out technical analysts, value investors, devotees of utilities, dividend-stock aficionados, and...

With so many people recommending so many different investment

---

* The list includes certified financial planner, certified financial analyst, stockbroker, chartered financial consultant, registered investment advisor, chartered investment counselor, financial risk manager, certified mutual fund counselor, retirement manager advisor, master in financial planning, and certified fund specialist.

strategies, one thing's for sure: they can't all be giving the right advice. Indeed, most "experts" are wrong most of the time. But not to worry—they'll charge you either way. Studies of mutual fund managers are particularly telling. This year's overperformers are, for whatever reason, next year's underperformers.

Yes, there are great investors who can beat the market on a long-term basis. But they are few and far between. They also charge a pretty penny for their asset management. And their success can ebb. Take the legendary Warren Buffett—the Oracle of Omaha and one of the world's premier investors. In 2019, his investments underperformed the S&P 500—the stock price index covering the 500 largest US companies—by a colossal 37 percent! Of course, no one's counting Warren out. But he'd be the first to repeat the industry mantra:

Past performance is no guarantee of future results.

This chapter will convey economics-based investment advice. I'm not going to give you any hot insider tips, telling you to "invest in plastics" or some other next big thing. Rather, I want to create a framework for achieving a higher living standard over time with less living-standard risk. As always, there will be lots of tricks. The first is particularly easy to do. It's simply to avoid taking conventional investment advice. As I'll explain, that advice is predicated on your making four major economic mistakes. Indeed, conventional investment advice is like using a map of Los Angeles to drive in New York City. You're bound to end up in the East River. I'll start by keeping you on dry land, then I'll shift to economics-based guidance.

When it comes to investing, economics isn't focused on how much wealth you'll accumulate or how well your investments will perform. It's all about your bottom line—your living standard over time. Your future living-standard path is, of course, uncertain. Yet where the path generally lies and its dispersion — the average level and variability of your living standard in each future year — is largely under your control. If you adopt a riskier career, overspend, underinsure, retire too early, borrow to invest in risky assets, fail to diversify, vacation in Vegas, etc., you'll greatly exacerbate your downside living-standard risk. That said, such behavior could also raise your upside risk. However, even if risky behavior actually raises your living standard's expected or average level, it will still leave you popping Xanax. That's a warning that investment averages, including the average chance of staying solvent, shouldn't be your sole or even primary focus.

To understand economics-based investment advice, I want you to picture a very important graph — a graph of all your different possible living-standard paths. In this graph, your living standard (LS) is on the vertical axis, and the year, starting with the current year, is on the horizontal axis. All your potential living-standard trajectories fan out from your current living standard — this year's spending per household member.

The following figure shows five sample trajectories, on average: very high, high, in the middle, low, and very low. These are based on five hundred Monte Carlo simulations of an upper-income, middle-class household.

Although all of your possible LS paths start at the same place, they immediately begin to bounce around in different directions in response to random events you might experience over time. These events include the different paths of asset returns you will experience. The fact that your living standard adjusts annually to what you experience makes perfect economic sense. Consumption smoothing implies such adjustments. In particular, when you earn high returns on your investments, you should share this gain between the present and the future. This entails spending some of

Percentile Trajectory Values

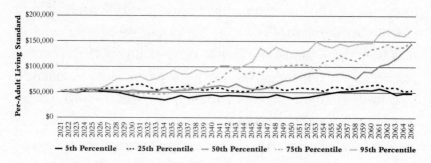

the gain now and saving the rest for later. Equivalently, when you earn low returns you should spend less now, while planning to do the same in the future.*

Given this ongoing adjustment to your spending, your LS paths look like wiggly snakes wandering in different directions, frequently crossing over one another. Most of your LS snakes will hang out in the middle of your graph—at the typical level of your living standard. Some will wiggle their way north or south for a number of years and then reverse course, only to continue to go up and down over and over. Others will steadily trend one way or another.†
As the figure indicates, the chart of your trajectories forms the general shape of a cone, both increasing and decreasing from your current living standard. And, as indicated, the tails of all the snakes are tied together (along with all the other, unpictured snakes' tails) in the current year—all LS trajectories start at the same value.

Personally, I hate snakes. So I'm grossing myself out and probably you, too, with this mental exercise. Sorry. But I need you to visualize your living-standard paths to deliver the payoff:

---

* Not adjusting—that is, placing your spending, at least in retirement, on autopilot— means that if you earn an unexpectedly low return on your investments this year, you'll load this year's loss onto your living standard in future years. The only way for this not to happen is if this year's negative return shock is systematically offset by a positive return shock next year or in some other future year. Unfortunately, nothing guarantees that the loss you suffer today on an investment, including an investment in the entire stock market, will be made up by gains down the road.

† Even if you end up on a really great trajectory, one that has a very high average living standard, there will be years of bad, even awful, returns. Every trajectory will cross others, meaning that even if you spend more, on average, along any given path there will be years when you'll spend less. An example here is a trajectory that generates lots of bad returns initially but after, say, fifteen years does phenomenally. That trajectory will likely cross one that has lots of great returns early on but becomes a dud repeatedly thereafter. Doing well or poorly over extended periods early generates a "sequence of return risk." It affects where your living standard can ultimately land. It's no different from where you finish in a footrace. It you get off to a slow start, you'll have a tough time fully recovering. But if your start is quick, your chances are better of beating the pack.

**Your financial moves affect your LS paths and LS cone. Thus, you
have the power to improve your LS cone.**

Your LS cone has three key features: height, upward tilt, and spread. Improving your LS cone means raising it, tilting it upward, and narrowing it. Doing so leaves you with a higher average living standard with less living-standard risk. Generating a better LS cone involves combining all of the financial alchemy we've already discussed with proper spending, investing, diversification, and debt-immunization decisions.

Allow me one last snake reference: raising, tilting, and narrowing your ninety-fifth best and worst trajectories is analogous to tying all your snake tails at a higher point on the vertical axis and luring them with some mice to head more north while staying closer together. (Okay, that one might have crossed the line.)

In discussing how to picture and improve your LS cone, I'm going to draw, in large part, on classic research by two Nobel laureates—Robert C. Merton and Paul Samuelson—as well as Boston University's brilliant professor of finance Zvi Bodie. Their work and that of a small army of other economists specializing in traditional finance as well as the relatively new subfield of behavioral finance (mentioned in the preface) has, over the years, culminated in a set of financial prescriptions that differ fundamentally from conventional advice. Each of these prescriptions represents a money magic trick you'll want to learn in order to produce a better-looking LS cone.

The best of these tricks is the one I'm reserving for last. It's a simple way to set a living-standard floor while still investing in risky securities whose performance can raise your living standard above that floor. That way you'll have a lower limit to your living standard, and instead of your risky investments potentially lowering your future living standard, you'll face the possibility of higher future living standards. That's why I call this strategy "upside investing." It entails no chance your living standard will fall below your floor. This strategy—setting a living-standard floor and experiencing only the risk of your living standard permanently rising above the floor—may be just right for you.

But enough of LS cones and floors for the moment. Let me start with what I urge you to stop: relying on conventional investment advice.

CONVENTIONAL INVESTMENT ADVICE AT ITS MOST BASIC AND TROUBLING

Standard investment advice begins with four questions: How large are your current assets? How much are you saving for retirement? How much do you want to spend in retirement? How are you currently investing?

Given these inputs, it's easy to run Monte Carlo simulations to determine the probability that "your" plan will succeed—in other words, that you don't run out of money. Monte Carlo is, as you probably know, a town on the French Riviera noted for its casino. (Check out the Bond classic *Casino Royale*.) Like gambling, investing involves a major element of chance. Monte Carlo simulations look at the results from repeating a given random process. The simplest example is throwing a fair die again and again. Each number will come up, on average, one-sixth of the time, with this frequency getting closer and closer to one-sixth the more times you throw the die.

Conventional Monte Carlo simulations calculate the share of the time your financial plan stays above water during your whole life. If the probability of this plan succeeding is small—if too many of the simulations lead to your running out of money before you run out of breath—your advisor will shake their head and say: "Sorry, this dog don't hunt. Not to worry, though. If you invest in our higher-yielding vehicles, your plan's success rises above 95 percent. Yes, these investment products come with higher fees and more risk, but they'll make it possible to meet your goals."

Many a client of many a financial advisor falls for this pitch. And virtually all advisors making it believe it's entirely appropriate. After all, this method of portfolio risk analysis is taught in all of the financial industry's myriad advisor certification programs. Unfortunately, it bears no connection to the analysis economics recommends. Worse, it simulates your making four major economic mistakes:

1. continuing to save what is surely the wrong amount;
2. putting this surely incorrect preretirement saving on autopilot;
3. setting a retirement-spending target that's not anchored to what you can realistically afford; and
4. putting this retirement-spending target on autopilot.

A plethora of studies suggest that most people don't save enough for retirement to ensure a steady living standard through their entire life. Yet conventional analysis takes your current saving level as appropriate, even when it's more likely than not far too low. Encouraging you to put this surely incorrect preretirement saving on autopilot—putting x amount into savings every year—is equally troubling. It means that in each year before retirement, when your income or fixed outlays (think tuition payment for your kids) rise or fall, which they'll surely do, your spending, and thus your living standard, will need to give, meaning your spending will need to rise and fall since you're effectively being told not to adjust your saving.* This is consumption disruption, not consumption smoothing.

---

* How so? Because income less fixed expenses (call this y) is either spent to support your living standard (call this c) or saved (call this s). Hence, $y = c + s$. If from one year (or month, week, day) to the next y goes up or down and s stays fixed, c will have to go

As for setting a retirement-spending level, the sky appears to be the limit. Personally, were a financial planner to ask me, "How much do you want to spend in retirement?" (they might phrase it as "What's your number? Your target? Your goal?"), I'd answer, "One billion dollars a day." The advisor would likely respond, "Sorry, that's unaffordable. Let's go another route. Let's plan for you to spend 80 percent of your preretirement income annually. That's the industry's standard replacement rate."

I could go on for pages about the problems with the replacement-rate calculation. But I'll spare you the rant and say simply that this rate is far too high for most households. It generally leads to high Monte Carlo failure rates, particularly for households that are investing cautiously. This, of course, supports your supposed need to invest in riskier, more expensive, but potentially higher-yielding ways. Sure, the chance of your plan's success rises dramatically. But so does the chance of your losing your shirt and your pants. Of course, the elevated downside risk of huge losses from investing in higher-yield securities isn't so much fun to discuss. Therefore, when your plan is presented, the downside will likely be buried deep in the bowels of your thick financial report.

Let me reiterate the major problem with conventional investment advice: it recommends overly risky and expensive investments.

Another big problem with this approach involves leaving money on the table when your plan succeeds. Suppose you make a killing in the market. But if you're spending per your plan, your spending

---

up or down by precisely the same amount. For example, let's say your pipes break and you need to spend $10,000 out of your annual after-tax income of $50,000 to fix the problem. Your consumption will take a hit of $10,000. Maybe you have $80,000 in assets (in a checking, savings, or brokerage account). Economics and common sense would say to use those assets to pay the $10,000. But doing so means reducing your saving by $10,000 since saving references the increase in net assets from year to year. Tapping your holdings would lower your net assets and thus this year's saving, which, according to conventional planning is a no-no.

will stay fixed. Thus, you'll die with a ton of unspent money. Is this really financial success? Yes, your kids will inherit more. But you may be childless, or you may have set aside funds for them already, or they may be doing just fine financially. The old adage applies: *You can't take it with you.*

FEES MATTER! (BUT DON'T RUN OFF AND FIRE YOUR ADVISOR!)

Of course, accumulating wealth to no end does help someone: an advisor who charges a percentage of assets under management. Be aware of what you're paying financial professionals. Here's an example. Suppose you're sixty, you're retired, you live in South Dakota, and you have just one resource: a brokerage account worth $3 million. You're counting on earning 2 percent above inflation on your investments. After covering taxes, you'll be able to spend close to $100,000 every year through age one hundred. But what happens if you have to pay 100 basis points (1 percentage point) to your advisor per every dollar invested? The answer's not pretty. Your sustainable living standard drops by 13 percent to $87,000! The decline would likely be even bigger since most advisors underperform the market. The moral to this story? Paying a "small" percent-of-assets fee for bad investment advice can be superexpensive.

Despite all of my gripes with common investment advice, my concern with conventional planning is not an indictment of its practitioners. Conventional financial planners aren't out to gouge you. They're out to help you. The fact that the industry provides them with no economics training and gives them tools designed to sell expensive products isn't their fault. In many cases, financial advisors are prohibited by their companies from using any but the "approved" tools. Moreover, many planners providing conventional financial advice understand the shortcomings of their methods and make their ultimate recommendations based on experience and professional judgment, not simply what a particular piece of software recommends.

In other words, I'm not encouraging you to run off and fire your financial advisor! Even a hefty annual investment fee may be well worth paying if your advisor truly has specialized investing acumen or is keeping you from making major blunders. Also, your advisor may be encouraging you to save more, finding ways to lower your taxes, guiding you to higher Social Security benefits, and performing other money magic. My point is that what may sound like a small fee, like 1 percent of assets, can be very large as a share of your sustainable spending. If you think you're overpaying, ask for a lower fee or try to buy the advisor's advice by the hour. Better yet, insist your advisor do economics-based planning for you.

While I'm scrutinizing conventional financial planners' motives, it's only fair that I subject myself to the same scrutiny. I'm not a disinterested critic. Recall, my company produces economics-based planning software, indeed the only such software that exists. So if you ask your advisor to plan based on standard economics, they will probably buy this book, our software, or both. However, to help convince you that I'm not just another huckster trying to sell my own brand of snake oil, let me provide two independent pieces of evidence about how the economics profession views conventional financial planning. One, I've yet to find a single PhD economist who endorses it. Two, I've never heard of a top PhD program in economics or finance that includes conventional personal finance in its curriculum.

If you told your advisor this, they would likely reply, "I've never heard of a conventional financial planning certificate-degree program that includes economics-based planning in its curriculum, either." Fair enough. Either we economists have it wrong, rendering a century of research on saving, insurance, and portfolio choice pointless, and the Nobel committee has awarded a slew of prizes in economics by mistake, or the financial planning industry needs to fundamentally rethink what it's teaching and doing.

ECONOMICS' BIG POINT ABOUT RISKY INVESTING — IT WIDENS YOUR LS CONE

Let me return to economics-based investment advice. I want to start by making clear how risky investing affects your living-standard risk, thus widening your LS cone. To get my drift, forget for a moment all the uncertainties you face except one: the annual return on your investments. To make things even simpler, assume you always invest 100 percent of your savings in stocks. The stock market is really risky, constantly going up and down. Consequently, those trajectories are going to bounce around from year to year as you adjust your spending in response to doing well or poorly in the market. Your LS paths will spread out over time because the stock market largely follows what's known as a "random walk."

The classic reference here is *A Random Walk Down Wall Street,* by Princeton University economist Burton Malkiel. The book is in its twelfth edition and has sold more than 1.5 million copies. It's a great read about the history and workings of the financial system. But its popularity also underscores an important lesson that all investors in the stock market need to learn:

> When it comes to stocks, what goes up won't necessarily come down, and what goes down won't necessarily go up.

A random walk describes a variable, which, over time, is as likely to rise as it is to fall. This means that if the variable declines this year, it's as likely to decline again next year as it is to change course and increase. If a variable follows such a process, you can see how its possible positions will fan out over time.

Now think of a given security, say, a share of Tesla stock. Theoretically speaking, the price of Tesla should evolve as a random walk, just like any other asset.* This implies that real (inflation-adjusted) asset prices are just as likely to fall as to rise. This is true for next year, for the year after, and indeed for all future years. Thus, stock prices in the long run won't, on average, be higher or lower than they are today. Stated differently, if any given stock falls this year, there is no reason it will recover in the future. Indeed, the chance of a further decline is just as great as the chance of recovery.

Your first reaction may be, "Gee, the value of the stock market generally rises over time. So how can this make sense?" The stock market does generally rise, but that's because companies typically reinvest much or most of their returns. Reinvested returns (profits) are called "retained earnings." By analogy, suppose you own a house that you rent out. Say you use your rental income to upgrade the building—repointing the brick, painting the trim, fixing the foundation, replacing the roof, etc. Your home's value will rise due to the money you've poured into it, not because real house prices per square foot have risen. They may rise. But they may also fall. After one controls for reinvestment in the asset, house prices, like stock prices, are, theoretically speaking, random walks.

Here's the important theoretical and, indeed, empirical punch line from this brief finance lesson:

---

* If asset markets are efficient, the current price of an asset should reflect all available information. In other words, only new information—new news, which can be good or bad—should move an asset's price. New information is, by definition, unexpected—random. The random arrival of new news is the source of the stock market's random walk.

Stocks aren't safer in the long run. The more you invest in them and other risky assets, the more your LS cone will spread out over time.

Please read this several times over, because it cuts against the grain of conventional financial advice. Most investors, financial advisors, and financial companies appear convinced that stock losses incurred in the present will be recouped in the future.*

Professor Bodie at Boston University has convincingly debunked the notion that the longer you hold stocks, the safer they become. As Bodie points out, buying insurance against losses in the stock market costs more the longer the time period of the protection being purchased. In other words, insuring against the market being, say, a third below its current value is more expensive, indeed a lot more expensive, if you're insuring against that outcome twenty years from now than, say, five years from now. The reason is that over twenty years, the market's near-random walk will have had more time to reach any given low price than over five years.† To be clear, the high positive historic average real return on stocks means the

---

* Indeed, many financial planners recommend buying and holding different investments to be cashed out at different future dates based on the belief that particular securities are safe over specific periods of time. Under this so-called bucketing approach to investing, people should put assets that are supposedly safe in the short run in one bucket, assets that are supposedly safe in the medium term in a second bucket, and assets that are supposedly safe in the long term (stocks) in a third bucket. The idea, then, is to spend down each bucket after it's had time to deliver its guaranteed payoff.

† Moreover, were stocks actually safer the longer you held them, people would dump securities, like thirty-year TIPS (Treasury inflation-protected securities), which are the safest long-term real investment. That would raise the average return on a TIPS (its coupon would stay fixed, but its price would fall, making the ratio rise) and lower the average return on stocks (its average return wouldn't change, but its price would rise, making the ratio fall). But people haven't dumped long-term TIPS for stocks. In fact, the difference between the average returns of these securities—the "equity premium"—is bigger today than ever! What's the upshot from all this? Simple. Don't kid yourself that stocks are a surefire way to save for retirement. Their excitingly high average return naturally leads us to include stocks in our portfolios. But what share of our

odds that your stocks will fare well rise the longer you hold them. But the size of the potential loss if they don't do well also rises. *And we care more about downside than upside risk!* This is why stocks are riskier the longer you hold them.

WHY YOUR LS CONE FANS OUT

The fact that, as voluminous finance research shows, asset prices follow or come close to following random walks means that if you've done well (or poorly), you'll want to spread that joy (or pain) over all future periods.* The reason is that tomorrow's returns won't, on average, punish you for today's gains; nor will they reward you for today's losses. Thus, because they can be expected to be permanent, your living standard should respond to the returns you receive in the market *as you receive them.* So here's economics spending advice when you're investing at risk:

> If you do well, spend somewhat more. If you do poorly, spend somewhat less.

But how much more or less should you spend? This depends on how much more you worry about the downside versus how much you yearn for the upside. The greater your downside concern—the more "risk averse" you are—the more cautious you are toward spending in general, meaning you'll want to increase your spending less in response to good news and decrease your spending more in response to bad news.

---

assets we invest in stocks, or, for that matter, any excellent but risky investment, requires understanding our cone of living-standard trajectories.

* My "come close" caveat reflects findings that stock prices do exhibit some "regression to the mean"—some tendency to come back up if they've dropped and to drop if they've gone up. But the degree of mean regression is too small to make stocks a safer, let alone a much safer, long-run than short-run asset.

Regardless of how cautiously or aggressively you adjust your spending to investment-return news, your adjustments will obviously be determined by the sign and size of the random returns you earn. Thus, changes in your living standard arising from unexpected investment returns will, themselves, evolve like a random walk. This is why your LS cone spreads out over time. Indeed:

If you're investing at risk, your LS cone will, in part, reflect a random walk.

KNOW YOUR CONE

Due to the nature of their resources, some people naturally have rather narrow LS cones and others quite wide ones. Take Jack and Bill, both seventy years old. Jack has $10,000 of assets and otherwise lives on a big monthly Social Security check. Bill has $1 million in assets and no Social Security. If Jack and Bill invest their assets solely in different maturities of TIPS, inflation-indexed US Treasury bonds, and hold them through maturity, neither will face any investment uncertainty. Let's assume that, in this case, both have the same lifetime spending. Now suppose both invest all their assets in stocks. Both of their cones will spread out from essentially a straight line. But Bill's cone will spread out dramatically whereas Jack's will barely budge.

The reason is that Jack's living standard is almost entirely dependent on his safe Social Security benefits. Whether his $10,000 falls to $1,000 or soars to $50,000 won't matter much to the amount he has to spend and will spend over time. For Bill, it's an entirely different story. If stocks drop by 86 percent (as they did in the first three-plus years of the Great Depression), or if they drop by even just 50 percent (as they did between 2000 and 2002), or if they drop by 53 percent (as they did in the Great Recession), or if they drop by

34 percent (as they did at the start of COVID), Bill's immediate and likely future affordable LS will fall dramatically as well. On the other hand, if the market skyrockets (as it did for years after 2009), Bill will experience a tremendous increase in his living standard.

RAISING YOUR LS CONE

As the Jack and Bill example shows, your LS cone is only partly under your control. But to the extent you can control it, you want to raise it, tilt it upward, and narrow it. I've spent most of the book telling you how to raise your living standard safely. I mean "safely" in the truest sense, meaning it won't come back to bite you regardless of anything, including whether or not your investments do well.

Let me illustrate. Imagine you're Bill, and you persuade your superrich aunt Helen (who's on her deathbed and fully juiced on morphine) that you're not the complete sod she thought you were and that she should set you up with a TIPS trust fund that pays you $100,000 a year real through your maximum age of life. Presto, your cone will shift up. However, its tilt and spread won't change. Your LS will simply be higher in each future year.* Planning to retire later will also shift up most of your cone's trajectories, apart from those in which you unexpectedly get fired or become disabled. So will investing in securities with lower loads or with the assistance of planners who charge lower fees. And so will prepaying your mortgage, doing properly timed Roth conversions, and optimizing Social Security. Let me summarize:

Making safe LS moves raises your LS cone.

---

*To be more accurate, taxes will change, so the trajectories forming the cone may not simply shift up uniformly by the same percentage across trajectories or for a given trajectory across years. Also, safe increases in resources may alleviate cash constraints, which will differentially affect particular trajectories.

TILTING YOUR LS CONE UPWARD

How do you tilt your cone upward, so that even the worst trajectories will be less dire? The answer is to spend more cautiously over time, regardless of how your investments turn out. Spending cautiously means you'll bring more assets into each future period than would otherwise be the case. And this, in turn, will mean lower potential living-standard downsides as you age.

This is a big deal. Depending on your circumstances, spending cautiously can be as important as investing cautiously in limiting your long-term LS downsides. Indeed, spending more cautiously provides you with the leeway to invest more aggressively. To restate:

Spending cautiously over time leaves you better prepared for bad returns down the road and tilts your LS cone upward.

NARROWING YOUR LS CONE

There are two key financial moves to consider here: diversifying your asset holdings and choosing the share of your assets to invest in risky securities.

Asset diversification—spreading your dollars across multiple kinds of investments—narrows your cone. The earliest Nobel Prizes in Economic Sciences were awarded for work showing that diversification could raise average returns for a given level of risk as well as reduce risk for a given average return.

To see the power of diversification in stark relief, suppose you can invest in assets A and B. Each has an equal chance of quadrupling or dropping to zero. Also assume that they can't both succeed at once—when A quadruples, B goes poof, and vice versa. If you invest all your money in A, each dollar invested will either become four dollars or zero dollars. Same if you invest everything in B. No matter which you pick, on average, you'll end up earning two dollars per dollar invested. But an average doesn't do us much good in this scenario because you face massive return risk—a 50 percent chance of losing your wad. What if you, instead, invest half of your assets in A and half in B? Now you'll receive two dollars per dollar invested *for sure*. In other words, you diversified your investments, which lowered your risk *to zero* without lowering your average return!

In this example, assets A and B are perfectly negatively correlated. When one does well, the other does equally poorly. As we just saw, when combined in the same proportion, the A and B portfolio can generate a perfectly safe asset. Pause a moment to digest this. Investing in either A or B is extremely risky. Investing equally in both A and B is perfectly safe!

Now let's suppose that A and B are uncorrelated but otherwise have the same return properties. If you invest fifty-fifty in both A and B, you'll earn, on average, the same return but reduce your return's risk—its "standard deviation" (the average variation around the mean return)—by 30 percent. This is still a huge reduction in risk. In short:

A small amount of diversification can go a long way.

If you could invest in a hundred assets with the same return characteristics as A and B, you could cut your risk by 90 percent. Unfortunately, we don't have perfectly negatively correlated or lots of uncorrelated assets. Even so, there are still ways to achieve major risk reduction these days, at essentially no cost, through the magic of diversification.

DIVERSIFYING IS INCREDIBLY CHEAP AND EASY

So now you understand that pouring all of your money into Tesla stock isn't the smartest idea. Since Tesla's stock price is a random walk, Tesla is just as likely to crater next year as it is to gain value. So you decide to broaden your portfolio to focus on not just Tesla but clean energy companies as a whole. Does that count as diversification? Buying one company's stock is far riskier than buying a little of a lot of companies' stock. But still, having all of your assets in one sector remains a risk. For example, if someone invents an incredibly cheap way to sequester massive quantities of carbon, all your clean energy stocks, including electric car stocks, will tank in unison and you'll be kicking yourself for not holding coal mines. Plus, if you've decided a particular sector will do well and you're actually correct, other investors have surely reached the same view. Hence, the price of the hot sector will already have been bid up in response to this expectation, leaving smaller margins for potential gains. Only news that's unexpected—that *nobody's* anticipated—will move the price. Such new news, positive or negative, arrives at random, and once again we're back to a random walk. This is true whether we're talking about an individual stock, a collection of sector-specific stocks, or the entire stock market. The only way you're going to make a killing or even a higher than generally expected return on a publicly traded security is if you know something someone else doesn't. The hallmark of an efficient financial market is that all available information is immediately used and reflected in asset prices.

What if you could easily buy a little of every stock on the stock market and hope the market goes up as a whole? Well, I've got good news for you: you can! In fact, economists recommend that to the extent you hold stocks, you simply hold an index fund of the entire stock market. You can currently buy ETFs (exchange-traded funds) encompassing the entire stock market on an indexed (weighted-average) basis at an incredibly low cost—3 basis points, or three-hundredths of 1 percent of the amount invested. Thus, if you're investing $50,000 in an ETF of the overall market, the transaction will cost a whopping $15. The entire stock market is, itself, a security class. A total stock market index fund includes all of the roughly 3,500 publicly listed stocks in proportion to their share of the total valuation of the market. So unless you *legally* possess and can *legally* trade on specialized knowledge, economists recommend against trying to pick winners and losers. This oldie but goodie secret is worth repeating:

Economics says if you're buying stocks, hold the market on a value-weighted basis, not individual sectors, let alone individual stocks.

Economics actually goes further. It says to hold the entire financial market, not just the stock market, on a market-weighted basis. The entire financial market includes private and government bonds, REITs (real estate investment trusts), commodities, gold and other precious metals, Bitcoin and other electronic currencies, foreign currencies, foreign stocks, and foreign private and US government bonds.

Clearly, it's not practical to buy claims to each and every global security. The transaction costs would wipe you out.* But there are ways to cheaply invest abroad, albeit indirectly. For example, you can invest in US companies that do lots of business and hold lots of assets overseas. More than 40 percent of US Fortune 500 company sales constitute purchases by foreigners. This isn't Parisians buying Ford F-150s in the US and shipping them to France. It's Ford selling

---

* This is not the case with buying individual US stocks, which can be done.

cars, mostly built outside the US, in France and other foreign markets. The point?

Diversify internationally by investing relatively heavily in US companies that are, themselves, investing relatively heavily abroad.

DELEVERAGING TO REDUCE LS RISK

Remember in chapter 5 when I urged you to pay off your mortgage? I pointed out that owing a mortgage while simultaneously owning risky assets is, essentially, borrowing to gamble. To apply our new vocabulary, it widens your LS cone, producing greater upside as well as downside LS risk. As Zvi Bodie points out in his terrific book *Risk Less and Prosper,* any fixed obligation, such as paying your child's future college expense, is a debt closely analogous to a mortgage. If you don't pay off or otherwise immunize these obligations, you're effectively borrowing to gamble with all the attendant downside-risk implications.

To make this crystal clear, suppose you have two fixed obligations worth $300,000 each. One is paying $3,000 a month on your mortgage for the next ten years. The other is paying $3,000 a month for your daughter's private school for the next ten years. To simplify things, assume there's no inflation or tuition-price changes. If your commitment to sending your daughter to her school is just as strong as your commitment to living in your house, one obligation is no different from the other. If you have the cash up front, you could buy ten-year US Treasury bonds to cover (immunize) both obligations. Indeed, in the case of your mortgage, you could immunize it by simply paying it off immediately. Having done so, the risk of being forced to cut your living standard to cover one or both of these commitments would go away. Your LS cone would narrow.

In contrast, if you took the money that you'd otherwise use for the immunization and invested it in the stock market, you'd, in effect, be borrowing to invest at risk. The moral here is clear.

> Paying off or immunizing debts narrows your LS cone. Debts include fixed spending obligations whether to yourself or to third parties.

INVESTING IN SAFE VERSUS RISKY ASSETS — THE FIXED LIFETIME PORTFOLIO BENCHMARK

In addition to spending cautiously, diversifying, and deleveraging, altering your mix of safe and risky assets is the other major way to influence the spread of your LS cone.

As we saw in the Jack and Bill example, the composition of your total resources, positive and negative, help determine your LS cone. This fact makes deciding how to invest the asset component of your remaining lifetime resources tricky.

To get a handle on this, let's consider the findings of Merton and Samuelson, which I mentioned earlier. They considered the case in which resources consist of just fungible (tradable) assets. Here's what they showed:

> The smaller your tolerance for risk, the more safely you should invest and the more conservatively you should spend.

That's a fairly intuitive conclusion, which we already touched on. Their second conclusion, however, is quite astonishing:

> As you age, your mix of safe and risky resources should stay the same. Aging does not mean you should switch from riskier to safer investments.

This Merton-Samuelson portfolio law—to keep your portfolio composition the same over time—hinges on several reasonable assumptions with one exception: that all your resources, like your future wages, can be immediately sold and turned into cash ready to be invested. But the law also holds important money secrets even when, for example, you can't sell off your future labor earnings and optimally invest the proceeds.

In addition to the assumption that all resources are fungible, the Merton-Samuelson investment law is predicated on three other key assumptions: One, households have standard preferences about spending over time and not, for example, habit formation preferences (discussed next). Two, financial markets function perfectly—in particular, there are no transaction or tax costs of buying or selling securities. Three, the distributions of asset returns don't change over time. In other words, particular assets don't become riskier or start yielding a higher return on average.

Like the fungibility condition, none of these assumptions is fully met in the real world. Still, the Merton-Samuelson portfolio law can take you a long way in deciding how to invest. Indeed, I'm going to use it to deliver three financial shockers.

Shocker 1: The rich should invest in bonds and the poor in stocks.

If you're used to conventional financial planning recommendations, this advice may sound bizarre, but it's predicated on the same idea we saw in the Jack and Bill example earlier, plus it's upheld by the Merton-Samuelson-based dictum. It's easy to understand if you'll indulge me in a final clone example. It stars Rich Emma and Poor Emma, age sixty-five. Both receive $25,000 annually in Social Security benefits, but Rich Emma has $10 million in assets and Poor Emma just $1,000. Assume the two can invest in stocks or safe bonds, nothing else.

Here's the trick question: Which clone should invest a larger share of her assets in stocks?

It's Poor Emma. Indeed, she should put 100 percent of her money in stocks.

The reason? Poor Emma has essentially nothing to lose. If her $1,000 goes bye-bye, this will make little difference to her sustainable living standard. Her assets represent just one-thousandth of her total life resources. Moreover, Poor Emma's already effectively investing, albeit involuntarily, everything she has in safe bonds. Apart from their names and differences in taxation, Social Security benefits are no different from a fixed stream of TIPS coupons. So Poor Emma's already loaded, actually overloaded, with safe assets. The best she can do to balance her resource portfolio—to get as close as possible to the Merton-Samuelson optimum—is to invest her entire $1,000 in fungible assets in stocks.

For Rich Emma, investing all $10 million in stocks would be nuts. If stocks go poof, Rich Emma's living standard will follow right behind them. Think of the clones' LS cones. Because Poor Emma has so few assets relative to the living standard securely supported by Social Security, her cone's angle is almost zero. Investing her $1,000 in stocks will increase the angle by next to nada. But if Rich Emma puts all her assets in stocks, she'll widen her cone dramatically. Therefore, she needs to be a much more cautious investor. In her case, she might follow the Merton-Samuelson prescription by allocating, say, half but certainly not 100 percent of her assets in stocks.

The lesson here?

All else being equal, invest relatively less in stocks the richer you are.

I doubt many super-wealthy people get this advice from their investment advisors. The industry view is the exact opposite: the wealthier you are, the more you should invest at risk. Indeed, private wealth managers—the self-branded, gilded name for advisors to the rich—will tell you their clients don't need money to consume. They just want to maximize the estates they'll leave their kids, and the way to do this is to invest for the long term in high-yield securities. This is misguided. The reason parents leave money to their children is, presumably, to improve their children's (and further generations') living standards. So gambling with their children's inheritance—in particular, by pretending stocks are safer in the long run—is gambling with their children's welfare. And make no mistake: higher yield always comes with higher risk—plus, in the case of private wealth managers, higher fees.

Shocker 2: The young should invest a lot in stocks, but not because stocks are safe in the long run.

This principle is front and center in life-cycle funds, which invest your money primarily in stocks when you're young and then move you increasingly into bonds as you approach retirement. Makes sense. The young have very few assets. Their main resource is their current and future labor earnings—their human wealth. For most of us, our earnings are not closely correlated with the stock market. Therefore, when we're young, our current and future labor earnings are generally closer to bonds—indeed, TIPS, since earnings generally grow with inflation and then some—than they are to stocks.

Moshe Milevsky, a brilliant professor of finance at York University in Canada, wrote a lovely book with the seemingly strange title *Are You a Stock or a Bond?* The book expands on a terrific finance paper by Bodie, Merton, and Samuelson (Bill Samuelson this time, Paul's son). Milevsky's point is that if you're young and your earnings don't move with the stock market, investing heavily in stocks is what's required to move you closer to your desired, all-resources-are-fungible, Merton-Samuelson, age-invariant portfolio choice.

Milevsky also considers the rarer alternative: that your earnings are highly dependent on the stock market. An example here is working for a yacht company. If the market tanks, the rich, who disproportionately own stocks, will likely cut back on buying yachts. In this scenario, your boss may cut back on you. In this case, Milevsky would say you're a stock, not a bond. Therefore, to get as close as possible to the Merton-Samuelson optimum, you should allocate your assets to bonds, as you effectively are already heavily invested in stocks.

Let me memorialize this:

If you're a young bond, invest primarily in stocks. If you're a young stock, do the opposite.

Note that this advice may seem at odds with many of the examples I've just presented in which households of all ages were investing in long-term TIPS. But the points made were about safe ways to raise your living standard, setting to the side the issue of risky investment.

Suppose you're neither a stock nor a bond but a Bitcoin. In other words, your labor earnings vary tremendously, but the variation is not correlated with the stock market. Maybe you're like my friend Harris, who writes screenplays for a living. From one year to the next Harris has no clue whether anyone will buy his latest work for a small fortune or reject it after skimming the first paragraph. If he could churn out a screenplay a month, Harris could play the odds. But he spends a year working on each opus. So, yes, he's a Bitcoin.

Should Harris invest more or less in the market than someone with dependable earnings? The answer is less — far less. Though he can't count on the stock market tanking when his earnings drop (so he's not a stock), the market could certainly drop independently right when a project he hoped would be lucrative went belly-up. Harris can't afford to take that risk. Yet he's been kicking himself for years for not making the same killing in the markets as his friends.

Harris is now sixty. He likes to give himself a hard time. But he actually played it smart. Not only did he avoid the market, he also saved like crazy. The consequence is he's in a highly secure financial position. Indeed, he can enjoy a higher LS through the rest of his days than he experienced while working. The takeaway here is simple:

> **Don't double down on risk. If your earnings are volatile, the market is not your thing.**

Shocker 3: Retirees should invest more heavily in stocks the older they get.

Here's another financial shocker brought to you by Merton and Samuelson's work. Standard advice says the elderly should move out of stocks the older they get. However, this ignores the fact that many, if not most, of the elderly spend down their assets as they age. Their asset spend-down reflects the prior-discussed point that if you're not highly risk averse, it's worth gambling on dying before your maximum age of life. The gamble involves choosing an LS age-based profile that declines gradually starting at an age, like eighty, when your ability to travel, hit the gym, go skiing, and engage in other expensive activities declines. Setting this LS age-based pattern entails spending more earlier in life, with the knowledge that the longer you live the less you'll be spending. As you age, your assets will get smaller. But your bond-like Social Security benefits will remain fixed. Thus, trying to maintain a constant ratio of risky to safe assets, as Merton and Samuelson advise, entails holding an ever-larger share of your ever-shrinking assets in stocks.

Let's restate:

As the elderly run down their financial assets, they should invest more of what's left in stocks.

SELL YOUR EMPLOYER SHORT

For most US workers, their human capital represents their largest economic resource. However, the longer you stay with a company, the more you accumulate job-specific human capital. These are skills that aren't easily transferable to another company. (A close-to-home example is making COVID vaccine under a nondisclosure agreement.) Thus, your company's risk of doing poorly and going under becomes your risk. You become a stock—not a general stock but rather your company's stock.

Ideally, you'd like to buy insurance that pays off if your company tanks. But there's no market in such policies. Why not? If enough employees bought such insurance, they might collectively shirk work in order to bring their companies down and reap an insurance payoff. Insurers, realizing this in advance, wouldn't supply the policy.

There are, however, ways to sell your company short if it's listed on the stock market. The safe way to do this is to purchase special financial securities called put options that pay off if your company's stock drops below a certain value. Unfortunately, such options are expensive to buy and you'd need to keep buying them each year that your company was still hiring you. So this, too, isn't, as we economists would put it, in the feasible set.

There are two things, though, that are feasible. If you've been vested with your company's stock as part of your compensation package, sell it. Otherwise, when the company fails, not only will you lose your job but also your company stock will become worthless. The second move entails investing in your company's competitors' stock (or the stock of any company that would benefit from your company's demise). This may sound disloyal, but it's just hedging your bets and protecting your living standard. It's like buying B when you own A, where A and B are the previously described, perfectly negatively correlated securities. To put this succinctly:

> **No matter how much you love your company, sell it short if possible.**

TIME THE MARKET FOR RISK, IF NOT RETURN

As indicated, one of the Merton-Samuelson assumptions is that return distributions, including the volatility of the stock market, called the VIX (volatility index), stay fixed over time. This is basically true, but over short periods—like during the Great Recession and the onset of COVID—the VIX shot way up. This changes the standard directive against trying to time the market, which implies you know something the market doesn't. Here's the upshot:

> **Time the stock market for risk. When market volatility rises, reduce your holdings of stocks and other risky assets.**

Again, this practice isn't a means to beat the market; it's a means to keep you safe. If your investment options have, as a group, become far riskier, reallocate to safety.

UPSIDE INVESTING

So far we've been discussing how standard *homo economicus* should manage their finances. But as the Romans used to say, *De gustibus non est disputandum* — essentially, "There's no arguing over taste." People like what they like. Some people, it turns out, are incredibly wedded to their current lifestyle. Such households have "habit preferences." Sure, they'd like to consume more than they did in the past, but they truly hate having to reduce their living standard. They're happy to see their living standard rise but can't handle its decline.*

How can you invest in anything risky if you live in mortal fear of seeing your living standard drop? The answer is actually remarkably simple. You invest in risky assets, which I'll proxy here as simply the stock market. And you do so just like most people gamble at a casino.

Let me regale you for a moment about casinos and economists. The first time the American Economic Association held its annual convention in Las Vegas was the last time. My fellow nerds and I did just what the Las Vegas convention bookers expect convention attendees to do. We got off the plane, checked in at our hotels, and headed straight to the casinos. But unlike your average Vegas-goers, we didn't go to gamble. We went for the free drinks and to do some casual research — namely, to see for ourselves that a cross-section of Americans like to hang out in a noisy, garish space with stale air, playing variations (craps, slots, blackjack, etc.) of the big game: See How Fast You Can Lose Your Money.

Unlike the stock market, casino gambling has a negative, not a

---

* Mathematically, their current happiness, which economists call their "utility function," depends not just on their current living-standard level (spending/consumption per household member) but on their past levels as well. There are different formulations of these preferences. Past levels could, for example, be summarized as an average.

high positive, expected return. In human speak, it's gambling at less than even odds. Thus, the longer you play, the better your chances of losing all your chips.

Virtually all of us stood for hours observing, dumbfounded at what we saw. A couple of us dropped a few bucks in the slots. But there was a lot of peer pressure not to participate in the big game. Since the big game violated economic rationality, no one wanted to show their colleagues they were, economically speaking, nuts. That would stick to them like a scarlet letter for the rest of their academic careers.

During the days, we had our meetings in various hotel conference rooms. At night, we headed straight back for the free drinks and to observe, firsthand, what economic theory says can't happen. Consequently, Las Vegas informed the American Economic Association to *never come back*.

It took a while, but I eventually realized that we haughty economists were missing something big. Most of the people gambling were doing so with a fixed amount of money they were willing to lose. Indeed, many, if not most, had left their credit cards back in their hotel rooms and had entered the casino with only cash. That's what my ex-wife and I did when we stopped in Vegas on a trip to the national parks in Utah. There were no economists around to observe my violation of the rationality oath, so we enjoyed the experience of losing (unfortunately within a half hour) the hundred dollars each we'd put in our pockets.

In leaving behind our credit cards, we set a floor to our living standard. We could lose two hundred dollars, but our vacation and future LS were otherwise fully secure. Upside investing is an essentially identical way to gamble in the stock market (*but at much better than fair odds*) while establishing a floor to your living standard.

The idea is very simple. Figure out how much you have currently invested in the market, figure out how much more and when you'll add to your investments, and then make the extreme assumption that *every* cent invested will be lost. On this basis, make a lifetime consumption-smoothing plan that entails investing, to maturity, solely in TIPS or I-bonds (which you'll learn more about next). Since these investments are perfectly safe in real terms, you can arrange a living-standard path that's guaranteed. You'll have established a floor to your living standard.

Next, set a date when you'll start withdrawing *all* your money from your stock investments, assuming there's something still there. Also set the duration of your withdrawals. Suppose, for example, that you set the age of first withdrawal at sixty and the age of last withdrawal at seventy-five. Then when you hit sixty, withdraw one-fifteenth of the total and use some of these withdrawals to raise your age-sixty spending. Invest the rest in TIPS, spending a portion of the principal and real return in each future year. In other words, you're increasing your age-sixty spending only to the degree that you can increase your spending in all future years by exactly the same amount. When you reach sixty-one, withdraw one-fourteenth of the remaining balance, and again raise your sustainable spending, investing all remaining funds in TIPS. Proceeding in this manner will leave you with only upside living-standard risk relative to your safe standard-of-living floor. The only possible outcome is that you'll spend more in each future year between age sixty and seventy-five. After age seventy-five, your living standard will stay fixed at its age-seventy-five level. That's why I call this "upside investing."

Think of the investment in stocks as the cash my wife and I took to the casino. Our strategy was not to spend a penny of any winnings, if we made any, until we had left the building—that is, until it was no longer at risk of being lost via subsequent gambling.

To summarize:

Upside investing allows you to invest in the stock market while maintaining a living-standard floor.

If you're going to engage in upside investing, which I strongly recommend for most people, you'll need to understand TIPS and their better-looking cousin, I-bonds.

I-BONDS

As explained previously, TIPS (Treasury inflation-protected securities) are bonds of different maturities issued by the US Treasury with inflation protection. Each year the bonds' coupon payments and promised terminal principal payments are adjusted for the prior year's inflation. The nominal interest component is taxable. But unless taxes are dramatically raised or Uncle Sam defaults on his official debt, TIPS are a perfectly safe, real investment. In other words, you'll get back exactly what you were promised in terms of today's dollars.

If you do invest in TIPS, holding them to maturity is the way to go. The price of TIPS rises and falls continuously as with other marketable securities. When the price rises, the yield on TIPS (the coupon they pay divided by the price) falls. But the product of the new price and the new yield stays fixed. This is why simply holding TIPS and ignoring their price fluctuations ensures you of a fixed real payoff.* An analogy is your home. Its stream of housing services is the same regardless of whether its price rises or falls. As an owner, you're better off if the price of your home rises. But as a renter, *to*

---

*Unlike TIPS held to maturity, conventional bonds, particularly mid-term and long-term conventional bonds, are risky. As I write, the market is pricing in thirty years of roughly 1.5 percent inflation. But if it's wrong by just 1 percentage point—if inflation over the next thirty years is 2.5, not 1.5, percent—a dollar received in thirty years will be worth roughly one-fifth less in real terms than the market now projects. Conventional bonds pay a stream of dollars—a nominal stream, not a stream of dollars adjusted for inflation. If inflation is higher than projected, the entire payout path from each and every private and government bond will lose purchasing power. A sustained rise in inflation is a very big risk with conventional bonds—a reason their prices can fall overnight and by a lot.

yourself of your own house, you're worse off because you're implicitly paying higher rent—the imputed rent goes up. These two effects cancel each other out, which is why if you just sit in your home, the house-price change doesn't matter.

I-Bonds (formally, series I savings bonds) are the better-looking cousin of TIPS. They were introduced in 1998, and you can buy them directly from the US Treasury. Rather than have the market determine the yield, the Treasury sets it. I-bonds pay off only when you sell them—they are "zero-coupon" bonds. The sale price is adjusted for the inflation that has ensued since you bought the bond and for the interest rate set at the time of purchase. The bonds mature in thirty years but can be sold at any time. Since Uncle Sam, not the market, is setting the interest rate, I-bond yields can be dramatically higher than those of TIPS. And they have great tax advantages. The interest on I-bonds isn't taxable until they're sold, the interest is exempt from state and local taxes, and the interest is federal-tax exempt if you use the sale of I-bonds to pay for higher education! Each family member can buy I-bonds worth from $25 to $10,000 each year. So if yours is a family of five, you can buy up to $50,000 in I-bonds annually!

Here's the key point:

I-Bonds and TIPS are terrific assets to have regardless of your investment strategy. They're also ideal for establishing your living-standard floor if you're pursuing upside investing.

RECAP

- Conventional investment advice is dangerous to your financial health. Its recommendations are based on the assumption that households will make four major financial mistakes— mistakes that the planning encourages.

- Economics-based investment advice is focused on the cone of your living-standard trajectories. Your cone is wider and includes more downside risk if you invest or spend more aggressively.

- Using this book's tricks for raising your living standard safely will raise your LS cone.

- Economics-based investing advice entails adjusting your spending annually in light of your annual returns. The need for this adjustment reflects the random-walk nature of security returns.

- The fact that stock prices follow a random walk means they are riskier, not safer, in the long run.

- You can control the height of your LS cone by following this book's tricks. By spending more cautiously, you can rotate the cone up. By diversifying you can have the same living standard, on average, but with less risk. This will narrow your cone.

- Full diversification entails holding all risky assets in proportion to their share of the global market, thereby reducing the spread of your LS cone.

- Investing more in safer assets, like TIPS and I-bonds, serves to reduce your living-standard risk, meaning it reduces the angle — the spread — of your LS cone.

- You should set a global lifetime portfolio balance assuming all your resources are fully fungible. Then adjust your asset allocation over time in light of your inability to directly diversify your full resources. This adjustment entails, generally speaking, the young holding disproportionately more stocks, the rich holding disproportionately fewer stocks, and the elderly holding an ever-larger share of stocks in their portfolios as they age.

- Determine if you're a stock or a bond and invest appropriately, including indirectly selling your employer's stock short.

- If you're a creature of habit and can't tolerate having your living standard decline, engage in upside investing, which is modeled on the way responsible people go to the casino. Set a living-standard floor that you can sustain via investing in TIPS and I-bonds. Invest resources not used to establish your floor in the stock market. But don't spend out of your stocks until you have sold any winnings and used the winnings to establish a higher living-standard floor. Any winnings not spent when sold should be invested in TIPS and I-bonds.

CHAPTER 10

Making Your Own Money Magic — My Top Fifty Secrets

Making your own money magic is simple. Just perform the tricks I've laid out for you and yours. Clearly, certain tricks are designed for particular situations, like being eligible to take Social Security. Therefore, keep *Money Magic* handy and review its spells as you take life's challenging financial journey or notice that your favorite niece, Nancy, is about to get stuck with a double scoop of horse flesh. For sure, the spells won't just stick in your brain. They don't stick in mine and I'm consulting them most days. And many will change over time as Uncle Sam "reforms" our taxes and benefits and as new and better financial products come on board. So look out for revised versions of what I hope you'll come to view as a financial bible or, at least, a financial almanac. Also, hang out at Kotlikoff.net, where you'll find columns covering my latest and greatest tricks of the financial trade.

An age-old teaching adage is *Tell them what you're going to tell them, tell them, and tell them what you've told them.* Telling you what I told you is a tough lift. Let me instead convey my top fifty money magic secrets in no particular order. Their disarray underscores perhaps the most important money secret of all: everywhere you look, there are ways to safely make a lot more money, become far happier with a given amount of money, and become financially more secure.

1. Invest with someone you know—yourself—by paying off your debts.
2. Use retirement-account contributions, conversions, and withdrawals to cut your lifetime taxes. And make sure to contribute enough to get your employer's match!
3. Almost everyone should wait till age seventy to take Social Security retirement benefits.
4. Don't borrow for college. It's far too expensive, it's far too risky, it can haunt you for life, and it can keep you from pursuing your dream career.
5. Choose careers and jobs that everyone but you hates.
6. Mortgages are tax and financial losers. Pay them off as fast as possible.
7. Your living standard is your bottom line. Simulate its potential paths based on alternative investment and spending strategies to see where these strategies can land you.
8. Marry for money. You're worth it. And yes, money *can* buy you love. (Okay, fall in love, too!)
9. Price your lifestyle decisions to get the most joy for your money.
10. The richer you are, the less you should invest in stocks.
11. When it comes to holding risky assets, diversify across the gamut of securities that you can buy at low transaction costs.
12. Your perfect home may be far cheaper several time zones away. Or it may be a state away that has no state income tax, no state estate tax, and no state inheritance tax.

13. Holding a mortgage or retaining other fixed spending obligations while investing at risk is borrowing to gamble.

14. A sure way to beat the market is to buy I-bonds.

15. Stocks are riskier the longer you hold them. Avoid bucket strategies, which dangerously pretend otherwise.

16. If you're a stock, buy bonds. If you're a bond, buy stocks.

17. Credibly signal your loyalty to your company, strive to make it succeed, but protect yourself by selling it short financially.

18. Retiring early is, for many, financial suicide. You can end up retired longer than you worked.

19. Longevity is an emotional dream and an economic nightmare.

20. You can get the best of both worlds: an elite education at a dirt-cheap price.

21. Conventional financial planning is dangerous to your financial health. It bears no relation to economic theory and recommends patently absurd financial behaviors.

22. You can't count on dying on time. Plan to live to your maximum, not your expected, age of life. Deal with longevity risk by spending at a higher level at younger ages, not by assuming you'll die for sure before you might.

23. Free "trapped" equity by downsizing, renting, cohabiting, or establishing a leaseback with your children. Reverse mortgages are expensive and risky. Best stay clear.

24. If you're widowed and in your early sixties, starting survivor and retirement Social Security benefits simultaneously can cost you a fortune.

25. Divorce war has no victors. Agree to a fair living-standard ratio with your spouse and then jointly optimize the settlement.

26. HSAs and other merit-goods savings vehicles are the best tax loophole going.

27. Tap your retirement-account money to delay taking Social Security retirement benefits.

28. Aggressive spending can be as risky as aggressive investing in producing downside living-standard risk.

29. Avoid income-driven federal student loans unless you're absolutely sure you'll always be a low earner.

30. Inflation represents a potentially enormous financial risk. It will reduce the real purchasing power of any nominal future receipt, be it wages, annuities, interest payments, etc. The US is dead broke and both borrowing and printing money out the wazoo to pay its bills. This makes, in my view, medium- and long-term nominal bonds, including Treasuries, extremely risky. Therefore, in forming portfolios to build LS cones, I recommend including TIPS, not conventional bonds.

31. Fixed-rate mortgages have one great feature: they hedge against inflation since you repay in watered-down dollars.

32. Conventional investment advice is, to be nice, of dubious value. It's predicated on your making four major economic mistakes: saving the wrong amount when young, putting your preretirement saving on autopilot, spending the wrong amount when old, and never adjusting to market conditions.

33. Career shop, job shop, and house shop till you drop. Understand your options at all times.

34. In retirement, hold an increasing share of your investments in stocks and other risky assets with each passing year.

35. Did you take your Social Security retirement benefit early? Suspend it at full retirement age and grow it till age seventy at 8 percent per year (albeit, not compounded).

36. All lifestyle decisions—switching careers, moving homes, getting married, having children, getting divorced—come at a price. Measure these prices in terms of your sustainable living standard.

37. You can be any age and still raise your Social Security benefits if you earn enough. Anyone age sixty or over earning above the taxable earnings ceiling is in this boat. So are those with very short or spotty (lots of small values) covered-earnings records.

38. Social Security has thirteen use-them-or-lose-them benefits. Make sure you get what's yours.

39. The biggest 401(k)/IRA/Roth tax benefit isn't deferring taxes but shifting taxes to low-bracket years.

40. Economies of shared living are enormous. Move in with Mom if it comes to it. She's likely a better cook.

41. Are you losing Social Security benefits by earning too much? No worries—you'll almost surely get them back. The earnings test is a diabolical policy. It convinces people who take benefits early that they face massive taxes on working, which generally is completely untrue.

42. If you're very worried about downside risk, play the stock market like a casino. Set a floor to your living standard and spend only out of stocks that have been converted to safe assets.

43. Social Security's Program Operations Manual System has hundreds of thousands of rules, which its staff routinely get wrong, in part or in full. Talk to multiple offices and do your own research.

44. If your parents are borrowing for your college, discuss who will repay. And consider whether they're blowing your inheritance or sacrificing their welfare by "helping" you attend an unaffordable college.

45. Consider working for yourself. It comes with maximum job security.

46. Withdrawing from a Roth or even a regular IRA to pay off a mortgage can pay off big-time.

47. There's a major tax break to homeownership. It has nothing to do with having a mortgage.

48. In deciding whether to rent versus own, don't ignore the value of trapped equity. Leaving your house to your kids or keeping it as a financial security blanket to buy into a nice Medicaid facility is not a housing cost.

49. When you get married, count on getting divorced. It's as likely as not. Protect yourself and the love of your life with a prenup.

50. Raise, tilt, and narrow your living-standard cone by following this book's safe moneymaking secrets, spending cautiously over time, and investing less aggressively by limiting and diversifying your holdings of risky assets. Unlike upside investing, this entails absorbing downside living-standard risk. But the reward may be worth the risk.

If, like me, you're always short on time, you surely headed straight to this closing chapter to get these fifty bottom lines. What you found is a list of hard-nosed, emotionally unintelligent, counterintuitive, puzzling, cryptic, and seemingly crazy financial directives.

Who tells a ninety-year-old to buy stocks?

Stocks are riskier the longer you hold them? Come on!

I should plan to live to one hundred when my parents died in their eighties?

"Jointly optimize your divorce?" Really? Why should I help that SOB?

"Living-standard cone?" Here's the evidence! This guy's a conehead.

What you've actually discovered is a sample of economics advice, fully explained earlier, that's based on my profession's century-long study of personal finance. My people aren't trained to pull punches—to bend what economics says to fit popular misconceptions, to conform to conventional advice, to justify standard behavior, or to deliver its messages with sweeteners. We're hard-nosed, but not hard-hearted, conscientious fiduciaries trained to provide real financial cures, not fake elixirs that will undermine the public's personal financial health.

And truth be told, it's high time for economics-based financial medicine. We Americans are financially quite sick. As a group, we undersave, underinsure, under-diversify, pay for bad investment advice, rely on dying early, retire too soon, take Social Security at the first chance, free far too little trapped equity, borrow to invest in stocks, convince ourselves that stocks are safe long-term, live house poor, marry assuming we'll never divorce, divorce assuming we'll maintain our living standards, borrow to attend colleges we don't finish, pretend love is all there is, ignore our housing and job markets, get duped by conventional financial planning, underutilize and mismanage our retirement accounts, buy highly complex financial products carefully designed to con us out of our money, and routinely make lifestyle decisions without knowing their true living-standard prices. And far too often we disassociate. We treat our personal finances as someone else's problem—namely our future selves who can damn well take care of themselves!

This book is designed not simply to avoid these financial mistakes but to make financial planning immensely fun and rewarding. To get rolling, start with the following six financial checkups.

A SAVING CHECKUP

Please ask yourself the following foundational question: *Am I smoothing my consumption?* Or to put it differently: *Am I saving enough to maintain my living standard?*

To check, calculate, on a *highly* conservative basis, your disposable lifetime resources.* Next, divide this amount by your household's remaining years of life.† This, roughly speaking, is what you should spend this year on a discretionary basis. Now compare this recommended discretionary spending with your actual discretionary spending. If you're over the line, well, cut back to ensure a stable living standard. In other words, you need to save more. If you're spending less, you get to spend more and save less.

Where's the money magic? Clearly, if you get to spend more, that's very cool. That's found money—money you wouldn't otherwise have felt free to safely spend. And if you have to spend less? Well, it's better to learn that immediately and get on the right track. Please do this consumption-smoothing exercise every three or so months. This will ensure you adjust your spending on a timely basis to changes in projected earnings, in the value of your assets, and in your off-the-top expenses.

A CAREER/JOB CHECKUP

You should do this checkup routinely as well. It entails considering alternative careers or jobs within your current career. Say you're like Nancy, happily working as a mortician. Ask yourself this basic question: *Do I still really enjoy my quiet, composed clients?* If the answer's no, check out the BLS's occupational website. If the answer's yes,

---

* That's the sum of your future labor earnings, your future Social Security benefits, your current net worth (assets less liabilities) less the sum of your off-the-top expenses (all the things for which you absolutely have to pay—your taxes, housing expenses, alimony payments, out-of-pocket healthcare expenses, etc.). As always, put annual amounts in today's dollars before adding them up. If you and your spouse/partner have eighty years max to live and the kids will spend fifteen more years at home, your household's remaining years of life is ninety-five.

† You may want to measure a year of child spending as 0.7 year, not 1 year, if you feel your kids are cheaper to support. You may also want to reduce the weight on years beyond some pretty old age if you feel you'll be spending less beyond a certain age.

study the mortician market. Maybe the funeral home in the neighboring county or state could use your services.

If you want to jump career ship, there's always time to do so. Yes, this may require retraining. But as Bob Dylan sang, "Tomorrow is a long time." A nurse I know (Mary) started law school at thirty-nine, practiced malpractice law for eight years, had a blast suing doctors, but decided she was doing more good as a nurse. Since she'd been nursing part-time to make ends meet, she simply switched back to full-time. Mary's happy she got her law degree, thrilled she nailed bad docs, but glad to be back doing what she realized she loves the most. Mary's was a complicated path to Mecca with the journey beating the destination.

How about you? The chance you've miraculously landed at what is for you the best career/job on the planet is small. Do the career/job checkup, including sending out your résumé, setting up informational meetings, networking, engaging a headhunter, etc. Do this checkup every three months. Something better will likely turn up or you'll confirm, like Mary, that you've got the best gig going.

AN INSURANCE CHECKUP

You are surely on top of your home, auto, liability (umbrella), and health insurance. Life insurance? That's a tougher thing to figure. Most spouses/parents have far too little or far too much. This means if they kick the bucket, their survivors will face either a major decline or a major rise in their living standard. The calculus for adequate life insurance is pretty simple. Assume you'll die right after reading this book. Add up the disposable lifetime resources of your surviving spouse/partner. Divide by the number of years they could live plus the years your children will require support. This is the maximum survivor years. Compare this per-person discretionary spending level with the level they'd enjoy were you and your spouse/partner to live to the max. The living-standard difference, multiplied by the maximum survivor years, is your required life insurance. Compare it with what you hold and buy more or less as needed.* As with your saving checkup, there are two payoffs from this life insurance checkup—both good. Either you have too much life insurance and may want to cut back, leaving you more fun money, or you have too little and, once you address the shortfall, you'll sleep more soundly.

MARRIAGE AND DIVORCE CHECKUPS

You now know the drill to compute your living standard per person. You can do this for each suitor if you're still in the market for a permanent mate. And if divorce is crossing your mind, you can compare your per-person living standard as a divorcé versus staying married. Clearly, where you'll be if you divorce will depend on the settlement you reach. Therefore, you'll want to make *highly* conservative assumptions about how that settlement will go down.

Of course, you're not going to marry or divorce solely for money, but as with every financial and lifestyle decision, marrying and divorcing come down to a cost-benefit analysis. *Do I really love Joe enough to forgo Jordan's bid—a new car every three years and the McMansion I've dreamed of? Do I really detest Kathy enough to see my living standard drop 32 percent?* Figure out precisely how much of your living standard you'd sacrifice to marry Joe versus Jordan versus nobody or, as the case may be, to ditch Kathy. If, for example, life with Kathy is distressing you to the tune of 24 percent of your living

---

* Incidentally, you may discover another financial shocker: that the more kids you have the less overall life insurance you need. The reason is that more kids means a lower living standard per person when you and your spouse/partner are alive. This, in turn, means the insurance needed to maintain your spouse's/partner's living standard is lower.

standard, but both of your living standards, in the settlement you envision, would drop only 14 percent and you have no kids to consider and you know Kathy would give up 80 percent of her living standard to be rid of you, well, it's time to call it quits.

HOUSING, RETIREMENT AGE, AND OTHER MAJOR CHECKUPS

These checkups are no different. Do the benefits of moving to a particular home exceed the living-standard cost? Is retiring three years early worth a 10 percent lower living standard for the rest of your days? How big a dent will that Tesla put in your living standard? (The answer is arguably a bulge, not a dent. Teslas can run up to 500,000 miles on the original battery pack. Indeed, it may be the last car you buy.) Doing lifetime budgeting may uncover things you want that are actually cheap, on a lifetime basis, even though the initial outlay is very large.

AN INVESTMENT CHECKUP

Calculating your living-standard cone will require more work. I'm footnoting the details.* But with not much effort you can generate a

---

* First, collect data on the historic returns of the portfolios (collection of assets) in which you'll be investing. Suppose, for example, you expect to hold a 50-50 ratio of stocks and short-term US Treasury bonds between your current age, fifty, and age sixty-five, when you plan to retire and then switch to a 20-80 ratio of stocks to Treasury bills. (This, btw, ignores economics advice to gradually raise your portfolio's share of stocks as you age.) For each year in the past in which you have returns on both securities, write down what these two portfolios—50-50 and 20-80—would have yielded. This will leave you with two columns of numbers: historic annual returns on the 50-50 portfolio and historic annual returns on the 20-80 portfolio. Next, start at your current age, fifty, and determine, based on a conservative (I recommend zero) real return assumption, what you'll spend this year—namely, your disposable lifetime resources divided by the number of remaining person years. Next, pick at random one of the years of returns from your 50-50 investment portfolio-return history. This draw slew of LS cones. The basic idea is to figure out how much you'll spend this year per person based on a highly conservative estimate of your average real investment return through time. Then take a draw on your portfolio's performance, advance your economic position to next year, and repeat. Proceeding in this manner through your maximum age-of-life planning horizon gives you one LS trajectory. Then return to your current age and make another and then another and... You'll soon see the shape of your cone, particularly the issue of most concern: the downside risk. Repeat the entire exercise but with a riskier (safer) portfolio and less or more aggressive spending behavior. If you feel you're taking on too much risk—there is too much downside to your cone—plan to hold portfolios through time with less risky assets and to spend less aggressively. (A zero real return assumption in determining spending is very conservative.) Keep this up until you're comfortable with your LS cone.

With upside investing, the process is similar, except you proceed to age *x* as if everything you've invested and will invest in risky assets (for example, stocks) is lost entirely. Invest your other assets in TIPS and I-bonds. Then calculate your sustainable spending per family member (disposable lifetime resources divided by your household's maximum number of person years). Spend that amount

---

will determine your age-fifty asset income. Add this age-fifty asset income to your age-fifty labor income and subtract all your spending (discretionary and nondiscretionary, where nondiscretionary includes housing costs, required spending on things like alimony, and taxes [including Medicare Part B premiums]) for a net of benefits you'll receive. The result is your saving, which you'll add to your age-fifty assets to determine your net worth at age fifty-one. Next, repeat all these steps for ages fifty-one through sixty-five, picking again at random, at each age, one of the historic returns a 50-50 portfolio would have generated. At sixty-five and thereafter, start drawing at random from the historic returns of a 20-80 investment portfolio. Once you've simulated up to age one hundred, you've produced one LS trajectory. If you start back at age fifty and redo everything based on another random selection of annual returns, you'll make another trajectory. As you make more and more trajectories, you'll fill out your LS cone.

annually until age *x*, after which you start to gradually convert your stocks to TIPS or I-bonds.* Each time you make some of your stock holdings safe, you have the wherewithal to permanently and safely raise your living standard. This produces nothing but upside risk to your living standard.

In doing this exercise, you'll see that the less you invest in stocks (my stand-in for your bundle of risky assets), the higher will be your LS floor, but the lower will be your upside, and vice versa. Thus, you can quickly decide whether more upside is worth the sacrifice in terms of your living-standard floor. In my experience, most middle-class households will find that putting one-third to half of their assets in the stock market gives them plenty of upside and that maintaining a higher living-standard floor is far more important.

ECONOMICS-BASED PLANNING SOFTWARE CAN HELP

If all of these calculations feel too intimidating to work out on your own, I get it—understanding the theory behind the calculations is important, but making these calculations can feel like work when my goal is to make financial planning a pure joy. So let me draw back the screen and reveal MaxiFi Premium—the premium version of my company's software tool, available at Maxifiplanner.com, which does all this book's analyses for you within seconds. (If you

---

* This permits you to safely and permanently raise your spending-per-family-member living standard. If, for instance, you intend to withdraw all your stocks between sixty-seven and seventy-seven, start back at age fifty, draw a trajectory of stock-market returns from fifty through seventy-seven, and figure out what the withdrawals would be at sixty-seven, sixty-eight...through seventy-seven. At sixty-seven you'll sell off one-tenth of your stocks. At sixty-eight you'll sell off one-ninth...and at seventy-seven you'll sell off what's left. You'll quickly produce an upside cone—a cone with a flat floor and living-standard trajectories that rise between sixty-seven and seventy-seven and are flat thereafter. In other words, you'll get a cone exhibiting only upside LS risk relative to your floor.

prefer to work with an advisor, they can run MaxiFi PRO for you.) It can, for example, compare your lifetime discretionary spending from jobs A and B, from retiring early, from marrying Joe rather than Debbie, from moving to your dream home in Hong Kong to...* As for investment analysis, that's also a breeze. And there are big bonuses compared to making your own calcs. The program deals fully with inflation, handles cash-flow constraints, adjusts for economies of shared living, and handles present-value calculations when the safe real return isn't zero and you can't simply add together future amounts. The software also calculates all your current and future federal and state taxes, Medicare Part B premiums, and all the Social Security benefits for which you may be eligible. Finally, MaxiFi lets you consider future increases in inflation, future tax hikes, future Social Security benefit cuts, and higher growth rates in Medicare Part B premiums. In short, MaxiFi is your money magic wand waiting for the flick of your wrist.

BEWARE — MAKING MONEY MAGIC IS ADDICTIVE

Most people view examining their finances as akin to having a root canal—a necessary torture to be put off until the absolute last minute. But making money magic is not your father's financial planning. It's fun and exciting to find safe ways to raise your living standard. It's fun and exciting to discover what different lifestyle moves would cost you and which ones would pay off. It's fun and exciting to see your LS cone in full relief and learn what a higher average LS means in terms of additional LS risk. It's fun and exciting to trade off a higher living-standard floor against a lower upside living-standard potential. All these things are fun and exciting

---

* Our tool at Analyzemydivorcesettlement.com can figure out a fair and cooperative way to divorce poor Kathy if it comes to it. And using the two tools can help you compare your living standard when married with that when divorced.

because, at long last, they put you in full control of your financial welfare. And when you have the means to control your welfare, you have the means to improve it.

I know the fun and excitement of economics-based financial planning from twenty-eight years of experience. I founded Economic Security Planning, Inc. in 1993. It took about seven years to develop an initial version of our current software. Since then, we've helped tens of thousands of customers make their own money magic. I've talked and emailed and met with many of them. What I've learned in these exchanges is positively alarming: performing money magic can be highly addictive. Some people simply can't stop. They tweak their financial plans not yearly, not monthly, not weekly, but daily. So let me end with this warning: once you start making your own money magic, you'll find it very hard to do anything else. It's truly a blast.

Acknowledgments

Money Magic had a long gestation and a quick delivery. My superb but tough agent, Alice Martell, rejected one prospectus after another until I finally saw her light. The quick delivery is thanks to my fabulous editor: Marisa Vigilante. Like all her colleagues at Little, Brown Spark, Marisa wields a magic wand and presto! The book, with its to-die-for cover, was done. Well, I take the presto back. In truth, Marisa was quick and I was slow. I'm a compulsive rewriter. Ten is the number of tortures I inflict on a typical sentence. Now, if you're married and are rewriting everything ten times, you'd better have a patient, supportive, encouraging, and fun spouse. My wife, Bridget Jourgensen, is all of those things. Most important, she's my balancing stick. If my writing got too arcane, too academic, too goofy, or too "funny," it was whack, whack, whack, and whack! But all the whacks were dead-on and delivered with a big smile and a raft of encouragement. I deeply thank Bridget, Marisa, and Alice, and all my other *Money Magic* teammates, particularly academic and company colleagues. I'm also incredibly grateful to Boston University for its decades-long support of my research, including my research on personal finance. But my biggest thanks go to you, my reader. I'm honored that you're reading this book, and if it delivers real financial help, I will be thrilled. For in the end, I wrote this book for just one person: you.

Notes

Preface

1. ValueWalk, "A Brief History of the 1929 Stock Market Crash," Business Insider, April 8, 2018, https://www.businessinsider.com/the-stock-market-crash-of-1929 -what-you-need-to-know-2018-4?op=1.

Chapter 1: *My Daughter the Plumber—The Path to a Dollar-ful Career*

1. Stacy Curtin, "Forget Harvard and a 4-Year Degree, You Can Make More as a Plumber in the Long Run, Says Prof. Kotlikoff," Yahoo! Finance, March 18, 2011, https://finance.yahoo.com/blogs/daily-ticker/forget-harvard-4-degree-more -plumber-long-run-20110318-063704-224.html.
2. Mutaz Musa, "Opinion: Rise of the Robot Radiologist," *The Scientist,* June 25, 2018, https://www.the-scientist.com/news-opinion/opinion--rise-of-the-robot -radiologists-64356.
3. Gina Belli, "How Many Jobs Are Found Through Networking, Really?" Payscale, April 6, 2017, https://www.payscale.com/career-news/2017/04/many-jobs -found-networking.
4. Ball State Center for Business and Economic Research, "How Vulnerable Are American Communities to Automation, Trade, & Urbanization?" *Vulnerability Study,* CBER Data Center, June 19, 2017, https://projects.cberdata.org/123/how -vulnerable-are-american-communities-to-automation-trade-urbanization.
5. Andrew Soergel, "Study: 1 in 4 U.S. Jobs at Risk of Offshoring," *U.S. News & World Report,* July 17, 2017, https://www.usnews.com/news/economy/articles /2017-07-17/study-1-in-4-us-jobs-at-risk-of-offshoring.
6. Economic Innovation Group, *The New Map of Economic Growth and Recovery* (Washington, DC: EIG, May 2016), 9, https://eig.org/wp-content/uploads/2016 /05/recoverygrowthreport.pdf.

Chapter 2: *Hang In or Hang Out?—Divining the Right Time to Retire*

1. PK, "Average Retirement Age in the United States," DQYDJ.com, June 3, 2018, https://dqydj.com/average-retirement-age-in-the-united-states

/#:~:text=The%20average%20retirement%20age%20in,ages%20of%2057%20and%2066.

2. America's Health Rankings Analysis of U.S. Census Bureau, American Community Survey, 2019, "Public Health Impact: Able-Bodied," United Health Foundation, https://www.americashealthrankings.org/explore/senior/measure/able_bodied_sr/state/ALL.

3. Bob Pisani, "Baby Boomers Face Retirement Crisis—Little Savings, High Health Costs, and Unrealistic Expectations," CNBC, April 9, 2019, https://www.cnbc.com/2019/04/09/baby-boomers-face-retirement-crisis-little-savings-high-health-costs-and-unrealistic-expectations.html.

4. Pisani, "Baby Boomers Face Retirement Crisis."

5. Dhara Singh, "'Alarming Number': Boomers Struggle to Save Enough for Retirement, Survey Finds," Yahoo! Money, June 22, 2020, https://money.yahoo.com/boomers-struggle-to-save-enough-for-retirement-survey-finds-205447433.html.

6. Center on Budget and Policy Priorities, "Policy Basics: Top Ten Facts About Social Security," last modified August 13, 2020, https://www.cbpp.org/research/social-security/policy-basics-top-ten-facts-about-social-security#:~:text=Social%20Security%20benefits%20are%20much,aged%20widow%20received%20slightly%20less.

7. Center for Retirement Research at Boston College, "National Retirement Risk Index," https://crr.bc.edu/special-projects/national-retirement-risk-index/.

8. Katia Iervasi, "The Odds of Dying in the US by Age, Gender, and More," Finder, last modified December 28, 2020, https://www.finder.com/life-insurance/odds-of-dying.

9. Steve Vernon, "Living Too Long Is a Risk!" CBS News, July 24, 2013, https://www.cbsnews.com/news/living-too-long-is-a-risk/.

Chapter 3: *Social Security—Ten Secrets to Maximizing Your Lifetime Benefits*

1. Social Security Administration, "Unfunded OASDI Obligations Through the Infinite Horizon and the 75-Year Projection Period, Based on Intermediate Assumptions," in *The 2020 OASDI Trustees Report* (Washington, DC: SSA, 2020), table VI.F1., https://www.ssa.gov/oact/tr/2020/VI_F_infinite.html#1000194.

2. Office of Audit Report Summary, *Higher Benefits for Dually Entitled Widow(er)s Had They Delayed Applying for Retirement Benefits (A-09-18-50559)* (Washington, DC: Social Security Administration Office of the Inspector General, February 2018), https://oig.ssa.gov/sites/default/files/audit/full/pdf/A-09-18-50559.pdf.

Chapter 4: *Give Yourself a Tax Cut—Top Tax-Saving, Retirement-Account Moves*

1. Investment Company Institute, *Investment Company Fact Book,* 60th ed. (Reston, VA: ICI, 2020), https://www.ici.org/pdf/2020_factbook.pdf.

2. US Bureau of Labor Statistics, "51 Percent of Private Industry Workers Had Access to Only Defined Contribution Retirement Plans," *TED: The Economics Daily,* October 2, 2018, https://www.bls.gov/opub/ted/2018/51-percent-of-private-indus

try-workers-had-access-to-only-defined-contribution-retirement-plans-march
-2018.htm.

3. Internal Revenue Service, "2020 IRA Contribution and Deduction Limits Effect of Modified AGI on Deductible Contributions If You ARE Covered by a Retirement Plan at Work," last modified November 2, 2020, https://www.irs.gov /retirement-plans/plan-participant-employee/2020-ira-contribution-and -deduction-limits-effect-of-modified-agi-on-deductible-contributions-if-you -are-covered-by-a-retirement-plan-at-work.

Chapter 5: *Get House Rich — Shack Up with Mom and Other Smart Housing Moves*

1. Richard Fry, Jeffrey S. Passel, and D'vera Cohn, "A Majority of Young Adults in the U.S. Live with Their Parents for the First Time Since the Great Depression," Pew Research Center, September 4, 2020, https://www.pewresearch.org/fact -tank/2020/09/04/a-majority-of-young-adults-in-the-u-s-live-with-their-par ents-for-the-first-time-since-the-great-depression/.

2. Evan Webeck, "Coronavirus: Share of Young Adults Living with Parents Higher Now Than Great Depression, Pew Poll Finds," *Mercury News,* September 9, 2020, https://www.mercurynews.com/2020/09/09/coronavirus-share-of-young -adults-living-with-parents-higher-now-than-great-depression-pew-poll-finds/.

3. Jacob Ausubel, "Older People Are More Likely to Live Alone in the U.S. Than Elsewhere in the World," Pew Research Center, March 10, 2020, https://www .pewresearch.org/fact-tank/2020/03/10/older-people-are-more-likely-to-live -alone-in-the-u-s-than-elsewhere-in-the-world/.

4. Office of Single Family Housing, "Home Equity Conversion Mortgage: Homeowner," Federal Housing Administration, September 2019, https://www.hud .gov/sites/dfiles/SFH/documents/hecm_09-23-19.pdf.

Chapter 6: *Marry for Money — The Oldest Financial Trick in the Book*

1. Doug Wead, *The Raising of a President* (New York: Atria, 2005), 228.

2. "Dowry," Wikipedia, last modified May 18, 2021, https://en.wikipedia.org/wiki /Dowry#:~:text=While%20bride%20price%20or%20bride,family%2C%20 ostensibly%20for%20the%20bride.

Chapter 7: *Divorce Only If It Pays — Getting a Fair Split If You Split*

1. Wilkinson & Finkbeiner, "Divorce Statistics: Over 115 Studies, Facts, and Rates for 2020," https://www.wf-lawyers.com/divorce-statistics-and-facts/#:~:text=Every %2013%20seconds%2C%20there%20is,and%202%2C419%2C196%20 divorces%20per%20year.

2. Stevenson & Lynch and Kelsey & Trask, "The Divorce Spousal Support Calculator: An Alimony Formula Resource," last modified November 17, 2011, https:// www.skylarklaw.com/Docs/SpousalSupport.pdf.

3. "Resources," LegalZoom.com, https://www.legalzoom.com/articles/what-is-the -fastest-way-to-get-unhitched.

Chapter 8: *Don't Borrow for College—It's Far Too Risky*

1. Marty Johnson, "Inequality of Student Loan Debt Underscores Possible Biden Policy Shift," *The Hill,* November 28, 2020, https://thehill.com/policy/finance /527646-inequality-of-student-loan-debt-underscores-possible-biden-policy -shift.

2. Zack Friedman, "Student Loan Debt Statistics in 2020: A Record $1.6 Trillion," *Forbes,* February 3, 2020, https://www.forbes.com/sites/zackfriedman/2020/02 /03/student-loan-debt-statistics/?sh=76a0d49f281f.

3. Kaitlin Mulhere, "A Shocking Number of Americans Now Owe at Least $50,000 in Student Debt—and Many Aren't Paying It Down," *Money,* February 22, 2018, https://money.com/50000-dollars-student-debt-default/.

4. Kevin Carey, "A Parent Trap? New Data Offers More Dire View of College Debt," *New York Times,* December 24, 2020, https://www.nytimes.com/2020 /12/24/upshot/student-debt-burdens-parents-too.html?referringSource=article Share.

5. Lynn O'Shaughnessy, "Federal Government Publishes More Complete Gradua- tion Rate Data," College Insider, Cappex, https://www.cappex.com/articles /blog/government-publishes-graduation-rate-data#:~:text=The%20official%20 four%2Dyear%20graduation,a%20degree%20in%20six%20years and https://edu cationdata.org/number-of-college-graduates.

6. United States Census Bureau, "U.S. Census Bureau Releases New Educational Attainment Data," news release, March 30, 2020, https://www.census.gov/news room/press-releases/2020/educational-attainment.html.

7. Allana Akhtar and Andy Kiersz, "College Grads Still Earn More Than Workers with No University Degree. This Map Shows the States with the Widest Salary Gaps," Business Insider, July 15, 2019, https://www.businessinsider.com/how -much-more-college-graduates-earn-than-non-graduates-in-every-state-2019-5.

8. Jaison R. Abel and Richard Deitz, "Despite Rising Costs, College Is Still a Good Investment," *Liberty Street Economics,* New York Fed, June 2019, https://liberty streeteconomics.newyorkfed.org/2019/06/despite-rising-costs-college-is-still-a -good-investment.html.

9. Abigail Johnson Hass, "College Grads Expect to Earn $60,000 in Their First Job—Here's How Much They Actually Make," CNBC Make It, February 17, 2019, https://www.cnbc.com/2019/02/15/college-grads-expect-to-earn-60000 -in-their-first-job----few-do.html.

10. Nathan Allen, "College Students Overestimate Their Future Salaries," Poets and Quants for Undergrads, June 20, 2019, https://poetsandquantsforundergrads.com /2019/06/20/college-students-overestimate-their-future-salaries/#:~:text =According%20to%20the%20survey%20of,is%20%2447%2C000%2C%20 the%20study%20says.

11. Elaine Rubin, "FAFSA Financial Information: Reducing the Impact of Assets and Income on Your FAFSA," Edvisors.com, October 1, 2020, https://www.edvisors .com/fafsa/guide/student-parent-financial-information/#reducing-the-impact -of-assets-and-income-on-your-fafsa.

12. "Default on Student Loans," Finaid.org, https://finaid.org/loans/default/#:~:text
=If%20you%20do%20not%20make,loans%20will%20be%20in%20
default.&text=You%20can%20be%20sued%20for,Your%20wages%20may%20
be%20garnished.

13. Anna Wolfe and Michelle Liu, MississippiToday/Marshall Project, "Modern Day
Debtors Prison? Mississippi Makes People Work to Pay Off Debt," *Clarion Ledger,*
January 9, 2020, https://www.clarionledger.com/in-depth/news/local/2020/01
/09/debtors-prison-miss-still-sends-people-jail-unpaid-debt/2742853001/.

14. Matt Taibbi, "Student Loan Horror Stories: Borrowed: $79,000. Paid: $190,000.
Now Owes? $236,000," TK News by Matt Taibbi, December 3, 2020, https://
taibbi.substack.com/p/student-loan-horror-stories-borrowed.

15. "*Slavery by Another Name*: Sharecropping," PBS.org, https://www.tpt.org/slavery-by
-another-name/video/slavery-another-name-sharecropping-slavery/.

16. Stacy Berg Dale and Alan B. Krueger, "Estimating the Payoff to Attending a More
Selective College: An Application of Selection on Observables and Unobserv-
ables," *Quarterly Journal of Economics* 117, no. 4 (2002): 1491–527, found at National
Bureau of Economic Research, https://www.nber.org/papers/w7322.

17. Raj Chetty, John N. Friedman, Emmanuel Saez, Nicholas Turner, and Danny
Yagan, "Income Segregation and Intergenerational Mobility Across Colleges in
the United States," *Quarterly Journal of Economics* 135, no. 3 (2020): 1567–633.

18. Richard Dusansky and Clayton J. Vernon, "Rankings of U.S. Economics Departments," *Journal of Economic Perspectives* 12, no. 1 (1998): 157–70, https://pubs.aeaweb
.org/doi/pdfplus/10.1257/jep.12.1.157.

19. John F. Kennedy, "Commencement Address at Yale University, June 11, 1962,"
John F. Kennedy Presidential Library and Museum, https://www.jfklibrary.org
/archives/other-resources/john-f-kennedy-speeches/yale-university-19620611.

20. Jordan Friedman and Josh Moody, "Transferring Colleges: 10 Frequently Asked
Questions," *U.S. News & World Report,* February 1, 2019, https://www.usnews
.com/education/best-colleges/articles/2017-09-22/transferring-colleges-10
-frequently-asked-questions.

21. David K. Moldoff, "How Does College Transfer & Course Credit Assessment
Process Work?" CollegeTransfer.net, https://www.collegetransfer.net/AskCT/How
-does-the-course-credit-transfer-process-work#:~:text=Generally%2C%20
60%20credits%20from%20a,institution)%20to%20earn%20a%20degree.

22. Maurie Backman, "Student Loan Debt Statistics for 2019," The Motley Fool, February 5, 2020, https://www.fool.com/student-loans/student-loan-debt-statistics/.

Index

investing and, 241–44, 243n*, 243n†,
250–53, 260–61, 277
marriage and, 161–64, 168
raising, by moving states, 20
during retirement, 246
shared, 174–76
smoothing, 49, 103, 104
sustainable, 13, 17, 50, 279
living-standard (LS) cones, 244, 273
calculating, 286–87, 286n
height of, controlling the, 274
improving, 244, 255–57, 260–61, 274,
279, 281
risky investing and, 250–52, 253–55,
261–67, 287
safe investing and, 261–67
loans. *See* mortgages; student debt;
student loans
long-term care facilities, 131, 136, 153
long-term care insurance, 136
long-term care plans, 131, 136
low earners
delayed retirement and, 51, 67–68
retirement accounts and, 101
LS (living-standard) cones. *See* living-
standard (LS) cones

macro economy, study of, 3–4
MAGI (modified adjusted gross income),
91, 92, 93, 96–97, 111, 159, 159n†
Malkiel, Burton, 250
Marcos, Imelda, 9
Maritallaws.com, 176
marriage, 155–69
advantages of, 164–67, 168–69
average number of years of, ending in
divorce, 181
common-law, 160n
housing costs and, 158, 160–61
living standard and, 161–64, 168
in minimizing college-aid asset and
income taxes, 208
for money, 155, 167, 168
prenuptial agreements prior to,
188–90, 281
remarriage, 176
tax, 158, 159, 161n, 169
trend away from, 158–59
Marshall, Alfred, 10

Massachusetts, alimony/divorce
guidelines in, 178, 179–80
MaxiFi Planner, 8, 288
MaxiFi Premium, 288–89
Maximize My Social Security,
61n†, 76n
maximum age of life, 45–46, 47–49, 53,
278
Medicaid, 131–32, 159, 281
Medicare
eligibility for, 18
HSA contribution deductibility and
enrollment in, 108–9
Part A, 109
Part B IRMAA (income-related
monthly adjusted amount)
premium, 96, 97, 97n, 159
Part B premiums, 51, 96, 97, 106, 111
merit-goods accounts, 84, 85, 108–10,
112, 278
Merton, Robert C., 4, 244, 261–62,
263
Merton-Samuelson portfolio law,
261–62, 263, 265, 268
micro economy, definition of, 4
Midas, King, 9
Milevsky, Moshe, 264–65
millionaires, number of, in the United
States, 167
Mismatch (Levine), 203
Mississippi, debtor's prison in, 210
modified adjusted gross income (MAGI),
91, 92, 93, 96–97, 111, 159, 159n†
Modigliani, Franco, 4
Moeller, Phil, 61n*
Monte Carlo simulations, 241, 245–46,
247
mortgages
avoiding, 123–25, 153, 277, 278
cashing in retirement accounts to pay
off, 20, 125–28, 153, 280
interest rates, 120–23, 125–26
living standard and, 255, 260
in minimizing college-aid asset and
income taxes, 207
reverse. *See* reverse mortgages (RMs)
morticians, 34, 117, 283–84
My Fair Lady, 163
Myintuition.org, 203–4, 205, 206, 226

About the Author

Laurence Kotlikoff is a professor of economics at Boston University, fellow of the American Academy of Arts and Sciences, fellow of the Econometric Society, research associate of the National Bureau of Economic Research, president of Economic Security Planning, Inc., and director of the Fiscal Analysis Center. Professor Kotlikoff has written nineteen books and hundreds of professional articles and op-eds. He is a *New York Times* bestselling author and a frequent television and radio guest. His columns have appeared in the *New York Times,* the *Wall Street Journal,* the *Financial Times,* the *Boston Globe, Bloomberg, Forbes,* Yahoo.com, *Fortune,* and other major publications. In 2014, *The Economist* named him one of the world's twenty-five most influential economists.